P9-AOT-573

MULTIDIMENSIONAL MARKETING

MULTIDIMENSIONAL MARKETING:
Managerial · Societal · Philosophical

W. Thomas Anderson, Jr.
The University of Texas at Austin
Catherine Carlisle Bentley
The University of Texas at Austin
Louis K. Sharpe, IV
The University of Utah

Austin Press
Educational Division of
Lone Star Publishers, Inc.
P. O. Box 9774
Austin, Texas 78766

Library of Congress Card Number: 75-13358
ISBN: 0–914-872-06-0

Cover design by Bob Grigsby

Printed in the United States of America

Onward through the fog.

. . . Oat Willie

Preface

Multidimensional Marketing was written in response to a number of errors of omission or commission by marketing practitioners and analysts.

- It has become increasingly evident that the *marketing concept*, the idea that the sole goal of the business firm is consumer satisfaction, is glaringly deficient as a rationale for marketing decision making in the context of ever tightening environmental constraints and fundamental alterations in the priorities, purposes, and structure of American society. Business legitimacy is contingent upon far more than consumer satisfaction.
- Conventional functional or managerial approaches to the study of marketing only serve to perpetuate the myth of the marketing concept, at the expense of environmental conservation and the interests of society-at-large. Marketing management is far more than a process of identifying and satisfying consumer wants and needs.
- While much lip service has been paid to the necessity of "broadening the marketing concept" to encompass noneconomic applications of conventional marketing techniques, very little tangible headway has been made toward reconciling the marketing concept with the need for energy and environmental conservation and the long-term interests of society-at-large.
- While the "systems" perspective has long been thought to provide the key to organizing and coordinating marketing operations and reconciling the marketing concept with environmental constraints and social priorities and needs, precious little progress has been realized toward integrating systems thinking into the marketing process.
- The role of marketing in perpetuating social values has been virtually ignored, leading to severe dysfunctional consequences for society, the environment, and the social system. Marketing performs a vital role in the achievement of social as well as enterprise objectives.
- Marketing practitioners and analysts have long operated under the influence of myths which have magnified the dysfunctional consequences of marketing activity. The need for a radical revision in the philosophy underlying marketing decision making has become increasingly evident, but has initiated little to replace it.

Multidimensional Marketing assumes a systems perspective of the marketing process, reformulating marketing responsibility in light of the *formative* and *adaptive* relationship between the firm and its environment. Legitimacy for the firm is established through an intricate process of simultaneous anticipation and adaptation to demands emanating from a constellation of environmental forces, of which consumers constitute but one.

Implicit in the notion of the firm as a system is an understanding not only of the managerial process through which the firm (1) anticipates and adapts to the kaleidoscope of demands and constraints imposed by environmental forces, including consumers, and (2) gauges the impact of marketing activity upon society, the environment, and the economic system. Equally essential is an understanding of the role of the firm and marketing activity in society and the philosophy which guides marketing decision making. For only by analyzing the foundation, structure, and operation of American society can one fully comprehend the vital role of the economic system, the business firm, and marketing in perpetuating cultural values and attaining socially sanctioned goals. Only by examining the philosophical foundations of American society and the economic system can one decipher how continued adherence to conventional barometers of social and economic progress can only result in increasingly severe social and economic malfunctions and magnifying challenges to the continued legitimacy of the firm and the economic system.

The societal and philosophical perspectives have been virtually ignored by marketing practitioner and marketing analyst alike. *Multidimensional Marketing* presents a balanced retrospective and prospective analysis of marketing encompassing three essential perspectives: marketing as a *managerial process*, as a *societal role*, and as a *managerial philosophy*.

We are intellectually indebted to Dr. Donald A. Taylor, Professor of Marketing, Michigan State University, whose concepts form the foundation of the interpretation of marketing presented in this text.

TABLE OF CONTENTS

page

PREFACE vii

LIST OF FIGURES x

CHAPTER 1: MULTIDIMENSIONAL MARKETING 1

Business has historically defined the arena in which legitimacy is conferred too narrowly. . . The marketplace is but one of many sectors in the firm's environment from which legitimacy must be won if the firm is to survive.

CHAPTER 2: MARKETING: A MANAGERIAL PROCESS Part I . . . 43

Marketing consists of those differentiating actions taken by the firm to establish its legitimacy, enhance its power, improve its negotiating ability, and to resolve conflicts in its own favor.

CHAPTER 3: MARKETING: A MANAGERIAL PROCESS Part II . . 87

As the firm attempts to maximize control over its environment, management must manipulate its finite array of tools—the marketing controllables—in such a way that legitimacy is assured even in the face of uncertainty and change . . . The marketing process is . . . a rational organization of integrated activities designed to establish enterprise legitimacy and power over time.

CHAPTER 4: MARKETING: A SOCIETAL ROLE 211

The firm and the economic system are inseparable. And the economic system is inseparably interrelated with the other social systems which constitute the institutional structure of American society . . . As the fractured goal structure of American society further complicates and confounds the problem of institutional anticipation, adaptation, and integration in their achievement, marketing management must become increasingly aware of the manner in which the process occurs and the facilitating role of marketing in their achievement.

CHAPTER 5: MARKETING: A MANAGERIAL PHILOSOPHY 262

Without examining the role of marketing in society and marketing as a philosophy of management, against the backdrop of major shifts in society's priorities and goals, the marketer is merely a technician performing functions which may compromise not simply the survival of the firm, but also the continued viability of the economic system and hence society itself.

List of Figures

		page
1.1	Lasting Legitimacy: Power	7
1.2	The Marketing Concept	8
1.3	The Marketing Concept: Keeping the Customer Satisfied	9
1.4	Hierarchy of Systems	11
1.5	Dissecting Systems	13
1.6	The Marketing Environment	14
1.7	Lasting Legitimacy and the Conventional Barometers of Enterprise and Executive Performance	16
1.8	Legitimacy-Seeking: A Balancing Act	17
1.9	Integrated Functional Divisions Within the Firm	21
1.10	Possible Conflict between Marketing and Non-Marketing Functions	22-23
1.11	"What We Have Here Is Failure To Communicate"	24
1.12	The Marketing Controllables	25
1.13	Functional versus Dysfunctional Output	27
1.14	The "Broadening" Controversy: A Collision of Conviction	32-34
1.15	Multidimensional Marketing	37
2.1	The Marketing Environment	49
2.2	The Evolution of Business Purpose	56
2.3	The Evolution of Concepts of Marketing	59
2.4	Analytical Perspectives of the Marketing Process	60
2.5	A Systems View of Marketing	67
2.6	Maslow's Hierarchy of Needs	73
2.7	An Integrated Hierarchy of Business Purpose	76
2.8	Impeding and Implementing Environmental Consciousness	80-81
2.9	The Systems Model: An Alternative to Smith and Galbraith	82
3.1	Competition for Differential Advantage	93
3.2	The Field of Competition	94
3.3	Conventional Marketing Functions	95
3.4	The Marketing Process	99
3.5	Segmentation Axes and Variables	110-111
3.6	Intra- and Interpersonal Interactions in the Consumer Decision Process	113
3.7	The Consumer Decision Process	115
3.8	Maslow's Hierarchy of Needs	116
3.9	Classes of Industrial Products: Some Characteristics and Marketing Considerations	118
3.10	Classes of Consumer Products: Some Characteristics and Marketing Considerations	119
3.11	The Adoption or Rejection Process	121

		page
3.12	The Diffusion Process	122
3.13	Market Sectors	125
3.14	The Engel, Kollat and Blackwell Model of Consumer Behavior	128
3.15	Programming the Marketing Mix	133
3.16	Marketing Myopia	135
3.17	Product Decisions	137
3.18	The Product Life Cycle	141
3.19	Rate and Level of Adoption in Three Product Life Cycles: Fad, Fashion, Durable	143
3.20	The Product Life Cycle and Categories of Adopters	144
3.21	Pricing and Price-Related Policies	150-151
3.22	A Conventional Channel versus the Vertical Marketing System	156
3.23	Characteristics of Contrasting Distribution Networks	158
3.24	Potential Channel Conflict: Differing Expectations of Channel Members	160-161
3.25	Alternative Channel Alignments for Consumer Products Manufacturers	163
3.26	Alternative Channel Alignments for Industrial Products Manufacturers	166
3.27	The Wheel of Retailing	168
3.28	Defining Characteristics of Five Major Innovations in Retailing	170-171
3.29	The Dependence Effect	176-177
3.30	Components of Communication Programs	180-182
3.31	The Communication Process: "Who .. says what . . why . . how . . and when . . to whom . . with what effect?"	183
3.32	The Process of Marketing Communication	184
3.33	Mass Media versus Interpersonal Communication	191
3.34	Advertising versus Personal Selling	193
3.35	The Multi-Stage Flow of Influence: The Web of Word-of-Mouth	195
3.36	Convergence of The Marketing Process and The Consumer Decision Process	199
3.37	Programming Implications of the Product Life Cycle	202-203
4.1	Institutional Structure of Society	217
4.2	A Constellation of American Values	222
4.3	Institutional Interrelationships through Individual Roles	229
4.4	Institutional Flows and Transactions	232
4.5	Social Integration Along the Materialistic Value Vector	236
4.6	Federal Legislation Regulating the Game of Competition	255
5.1	The Market Mechanism	275
5.2	The Invisible Hand: Profitability and Productivity = Consumer Welfare and Social Welfare	278
5.3	Social Mechanisms Regulating Market Conduct	283

		page
5.4	A Constellation of American Values	289
5.5	The Mythology of Capitalism: Four Chronic Problems	291
5.6	Key Issues and Relationships: Marketing and Society	302-303
5.7	Hierarchy of Business Purpose	306
5.8	The Process of Marketing Management: Balancing Conflicting Priorities	310

MULTIDIMENSIONAL MARKETING

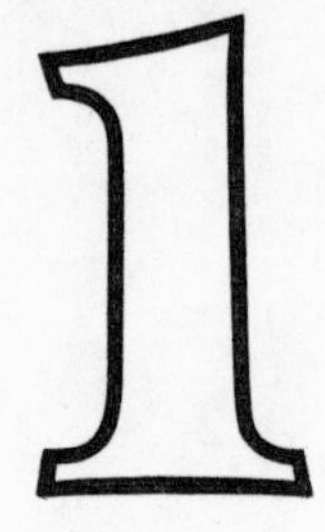

THE ENVIRONMENT AS A SYSTEM

THE ROLE OF MARKETING

THE SYSTEMS PERSPECTIVE

DISSECTING SYSTEMS

- Environment
- Goals
- Inputs
- Structure
- Processes
- Outputs
- Feedback

THE SYSTEMS CONCEPT IN PRACTICE

WHAT'S WRONG WITH MARKETING?

- Economic Applications
- Static Functions
- Anticipation and Adaptation

FORMAT

- Marketing: A Managerial Process
- Marketing: A Societal Role
- Marketing: A Managerial Philosophy

Multidimensional Marketing

Business firms have until relatively recently enjoyed a protected status in American society. Not so long ago one prominent economic analyst was able to conclude "there seems to be no general conviction abroad that [business] reform is needed." [81, p. 59] The relative calm surrounding the business enterprise is easily explained. The legitimacy of the business firm had been reaffirmed by a redefinition of business purpose following World War II: business firms were viewed as existing to serve the needs of society, *primarily the needs of consumers for material goods and services*. Profit, growth, return on invested capital, market share, stability—all the conventional measures of enterprise performance—were defined as barometers of business' responsiveness to the needs of consumers. Who could condemn an institution whose sole purpose was serving consumers' needs?

A crisis of legitimacy

But all this has changed. Today's business firm is weathering a crisis of legitimacy. "A feeling has begun to spread in the country that [business] performance has made the society uglier, dirtier, trashier, more polluted and noxious." [7, p. 7] Merely responding to changing consumer wants and needs, it seems, is no longer enough. Many firms find, often to their surprise, that governmental regulatory agencies or organized consumer activists, like Nader's Raiders, increasingly question the legitimacy of the firm's goods and services, and seek to restrict or withdraw the protected status of the firm or to force sweeping business reform. [74, p. 97] Conversely, some firms find themselves in the position of being required to provide certain goods and services, and only with great difficulty can they withdraw from activities or markets in which they have historically operated. Firms in the rail transportation industry pose a case in point. Often the railroads must maintain unprofitable rail schedules in order to provide "service" to a region.

No single event is responsible for the crisis of legitimacy business firms currently face. But among the most prominent factors are increased governmental intervention in stimulating economic activity, curbing inflation and unemployment, cornering poverty, correcting or controlling sources of environmental pollution and consumer exploitation, and conserving dwindling energy and material resources. Ralph Nader and other nameless consumer advocates too have had their effect in tightening governmental restrictions on business operations and in generating public awareness of economic malfunctions and business abuses at the consumer level. And, of course, the magnifying proportions of the economic recession, energy and other resource shortages, environmental pollution, inflation and unemployment centered in certain sectors of the economy, can no longer be ignored by even the most nearsighted. Behind these and numerous other problems of less ominous consequence is one fundamental cause: *Business has historically defined the arena in which legitimacy is conferred too narrowly.* Profitability does not insure legitimacy. *The marketplace is but one of many sectors in the firm's environment from which legitimacy must be won if the firm is to survive.*

Legitimacy

THE ENVIRONMENT AS A SYSTEM

Business firms are complex systems. And all firms function in a highly elaborate dynamic social system. The social system is itself comprised of an intricate array of social institutions made up of social organizations, of which the business firm is but one.

Outlets for outputs

In any social system the intended and unintended output of any organization must be demanded as inputs by other organizations within the system for the organization to survive. Business firms survive only so long as they can locate other organizations within the social system which demand their outputs as inputs into their own operations. Colleges educate individuals to perform desired functions in society. State and federal legislatures enact laws which presumably reflect the sentiments of the majority of society as to "right" and "wrong" behavior, laws which are translated by the judicial system into legal sanctions governing business and individual behavior. Business firms produce products and services which satisfy consumer wants and needs. *Legitimacy for any social organization is thus conferred and confirmed by other organizations or systems within the social system which demand its outputs.* The firm that is forced into bankruptcy, the college which is forced to close its doors because of inability to attract students and thus financial support for its operations, the legislator who is voted out of office, have in effect been declared "illegitimate" by the social system. Their output is simply no longer in sufficient demand to warrant legitimization by the social system.

Demand

Legitimacy: The goal of every organization

The fundamental task of any organization, whether business firm, church, governmental agency, or university, *is to establish the legitimacy of its output and,* it should be added, *the legitimacy of its methods of operation.*

The Marketplace

Legitimacy sanctified through purchase

It is generally thought that legitimacy for the business firm is conferred through the marketplace. If a firm produces output—either goods or services or both—which is demanded, the act of purchase itself is thought to confer legitimacy upon the firm, its output, and methods of operation. Such "illegitimate" business enterprises as prostitution, organized crime, gambling, "pushing" and the numbers racket are no exception. They survive so long as someone demands their output. Thus, in the extreme interpretation *the only truly illegitimate enterprise is one which can cultivate no demand for its output.* Legitimacy and legality are not synonymous. [65, p. 79]

Legitimacy versus legality

Survival for the business firm, contrary to popular mythology, hinges not simply on profitability or other measures of efficiency of enterprise or executive performance, but upon the acceptance of the organization's output and methods of operation as legitimate by relevant sectors in the firm's environment. Yet it is not simply sufficient that the firm synchronize products and methods of operation to fluctuations in consumer wants and needs. The legitimacy of the firm may be invalidated or negated by other systems within the firm's environment: competitors, governmental regulatory agencies, organized consumer activists, taxpayers, resource suppliers, or disgruntled dealers or distributors of the firm's products. The firm that ignores the legitimate demands emanating from these and other environmental sectors is compromising not simply profit, but may well be committing suicide. Nor is it sufficient that the firm merely identify and respond to the present or manifest expectations of these external systems. The quest for legitimacy is unending.

Because the environment within which the firm operates is dynamic and in a process of chaotic motion, the requirements for legitimacy are in a state of perpetual flux. Consumer wants and needs exhibit continual metamorphosis, just as the conception and application of laws governing the game of business competition are submitted to recurrent reinterpretation. Likewise, availability of material and energy resources has grown ever more restricted coincidentally as competitive pressures have intensified. Determining the requirements of legitimacy sanctioned by the systems which comprise the firm's environment is marketing management's consistent frustration and constant preoccupation. Lasting legitimacy is directly contingent upon marketing management's ability to not only *anticipate* and *adapt* the firm's output and methods of operation to the legitimate demands emanating from relevant arenas in the firm's environment, but also to *influence* other systems in the

Lasting Legitimacy
- **Anticipate & adapt**
- **Influence**
- **Facilitate**

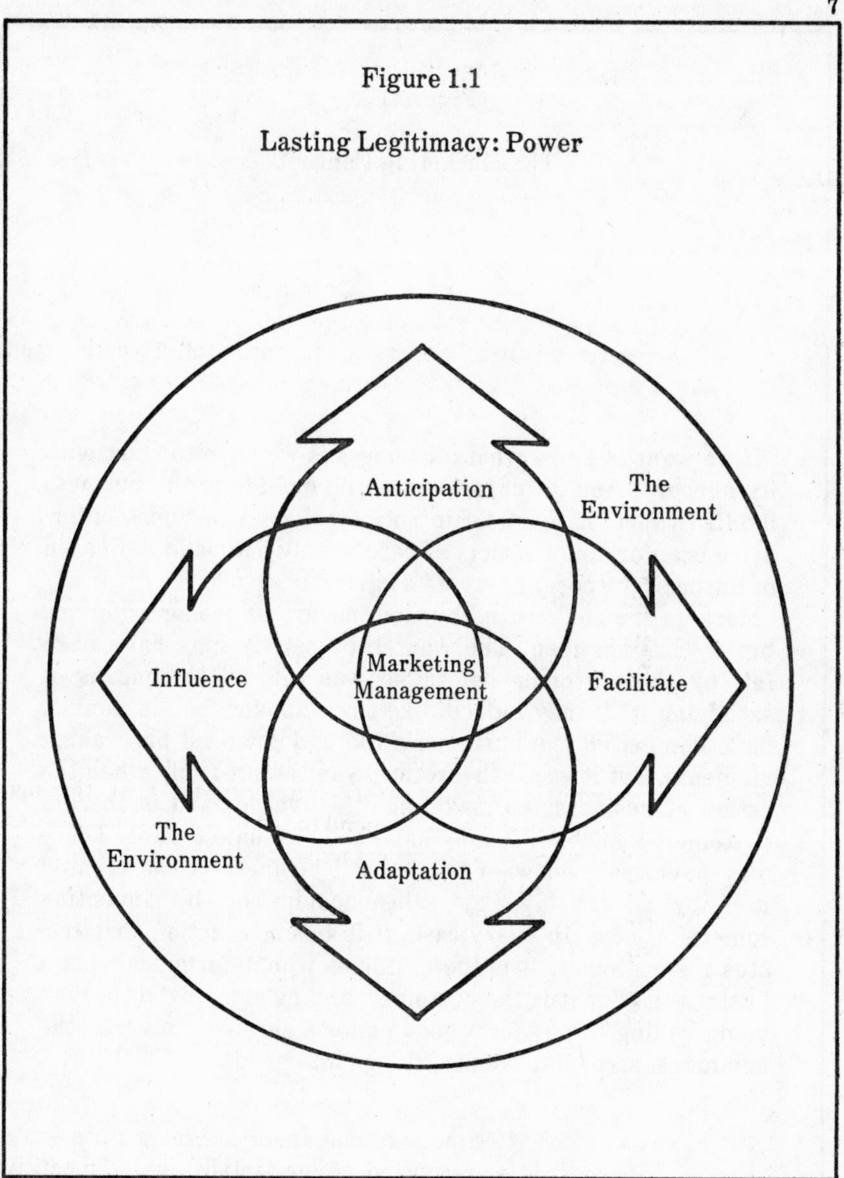

Figure 1.1

Lasting Legitimacy: Power

firm's environment to *facilitate* the establishment of positions of legitimacy (see Figure 1.1). Hence, confirmation of the legitimacy of the output or methods of operation of the firm is never assured and must be continually cultivated.

Figure 1.2

The Marketing Concept

If we want to know what a business is we have to start with its *purpose.* And its purpose must lie outside of the business itself. In fact, it must lie in society since a business enterprise is an organ of society. There is only one valid definition of business purpose: *to create a customer.*

Markets are not created by God, nature or economic forces, but by businessmen. The want they satisfy may have been felt by the customer before he was offered the means of satisfying it. It may indeed, like the want for food in famine, have dominated the customer's life and filled all his waking moments. But it was a theoretical want before; only when the action of businessmen makes it effective demand is there a customer, a market. It may have been an unfelt want. There may have been no want at all until business action created it – by advertising, by salesmanship, or by inventing something new. In every case, it is business action that creates the customer. It is the customer who determines what a business is. For it is the customer, and he alone, who through being willing to pay for a good or for a service, converts economic resources into wealth, things into goods.

Peter Drucker, *The Practice of Management*, New York: Harper & Row, 1954, pp. 37-41.

Figure 1.3

The Marketing Concept: Keeping the Customer Satisfied

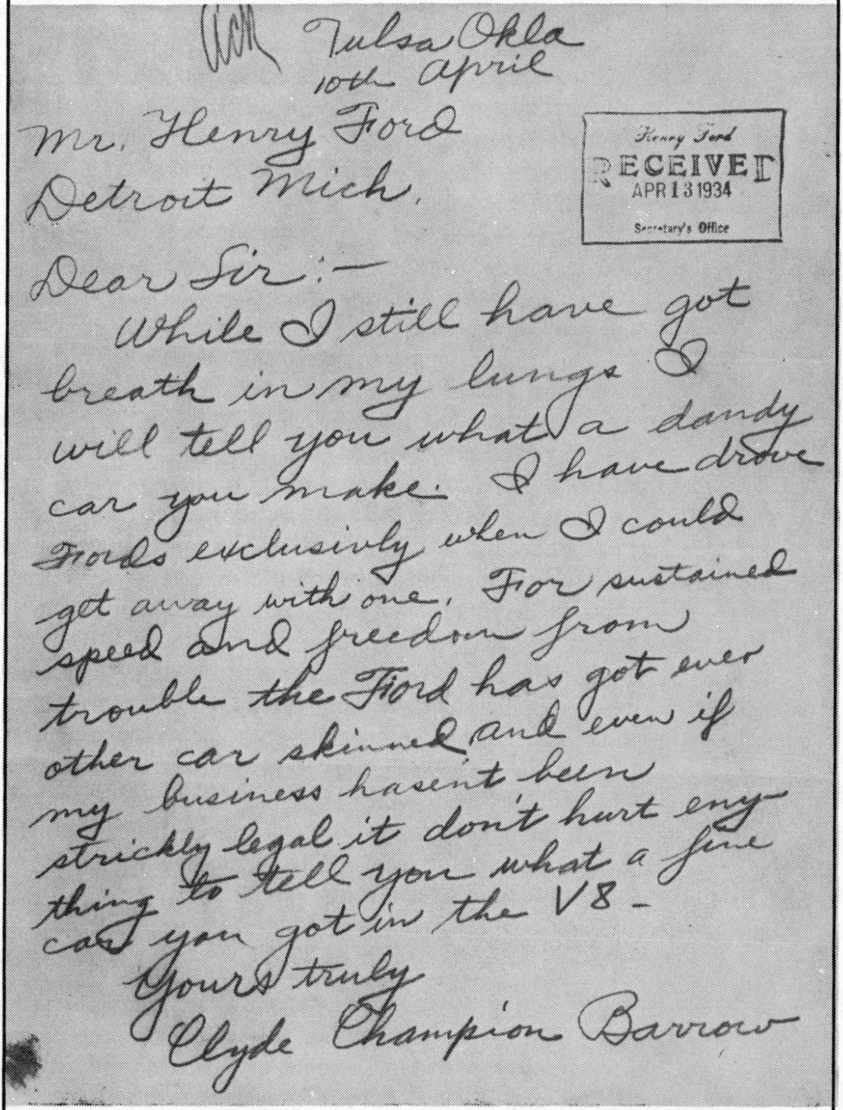

Tulsa Okla
10th April

Mr. Henry Ford
Detroit Mich.

Henry Ford
RECEIVED
APR 13 1934
Secretary's Office

Dear Sir:—
While I still have got breath in my lungs I will tell you what a dandy car you make. I have drove Fords exclusivly when I could get away with one. For sustained speed and freedom from trouble the Ford has got ever other car skinned and even if my business hasen't been strickly legal it don't hurt enything to tell you what a fine car you got in the V8 –

Yours truly
Clyde Champion Barrow

THE ROLE OF MARKETING

The contemporary push for a redefinition and reorientation of business priorities and operations is glaring evidence that business has lost contact with shifting social priorities and goals which are reflected in standards of legitimacy for the firm. Had business adjusted its output and operations more responsibly to the shifting structure of social priorities over the last half-century, the very legitimacy of business itself would not be under such serious challenge today. But businessmen have historically focused exclusively upon the things they do best — solving production, distribution, pricing or promotion problems — unable or uninspired to deal with the less tangible questions of the role, relevance, and responsibilities of business in a complex social system, and the requirements of lasting legitimacy for the firm.

Managerial Myopia

Interpretations of marketing functions and the responsibilities of marketing management have *shaped* as well as *responded* to shifts in conceptions of business priorities and purposes. In the post-World War II period marketing has contributed directly to the reorientation of business and managerial responsibility away from solving production and distribution problems toward the goal of satisfying consumer wants and needs. The orientation toward the goal of consumer satisfaction is the dominant theme underlying the prevailing philosophy of contemporary marketing management that is commonly referred to as the *marketing concept* (see Figures 1.2 and 1.3). But the myopic focus on consumer satisfaction has tended to obscure other vital arenas in the firm's environment from which legitimacy must be sought and won if the firm is to survive or prosper. Thus marketing is in no small measure responsible for the crisis of legitimacy business currently confronts.

Marketing Concept

THE SYSTEMS PERSPECTIVE

The key to the establishment of positions of lasting legitimacy or power by the business firm lies in the *systems perspective*. Systems exist in infinite variety throughout nature. Yet all systems share common characteristics.

Systems:
Elements
Objectives

All systems consist of interrelated elements or parts oriented toward common objectives or purposes.

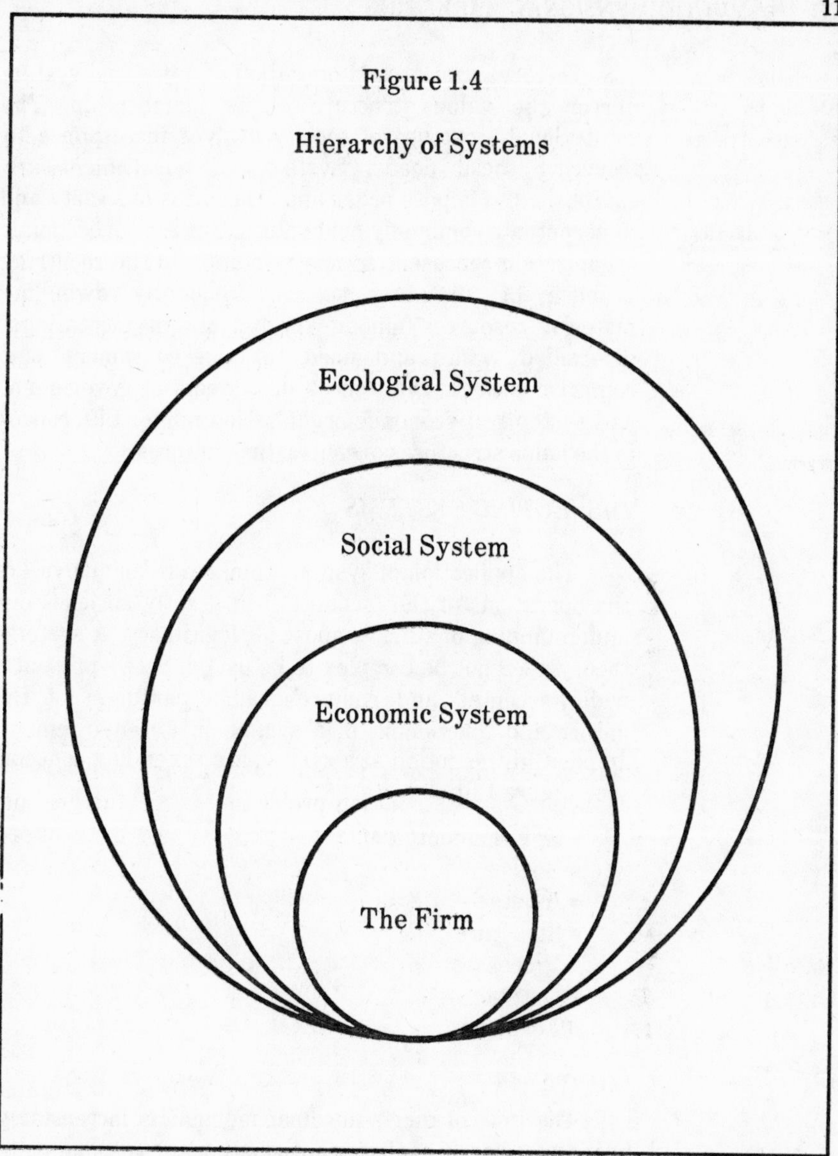

Figure 1.4

Hierarchy of Systems

System goals or purposes vary, as do their component elements or parts, but all systems share this commonality. The ecological system, the social system embedded within the ecological system, the economic system embedded within the social system, and the business firm embedded within the economic system are no exceptions (see Figure 1.4). Moreover, all are *open systems* in the sense that their structure and operations affect and are affected by forces emanating from their external environments.

Social system mirrors cultural values

Social institutions: Resolution for recurring needs

The organization and operation of any social system mirror the value structure of its membership. The institutional structure of society evolves in response to recurring social needs. Systems of government are established to impose order upon the chaos of society and to perpetuate commonly held values. Systems of economic organization represent society's solution to the recurring problem of allocating scarce, frequently dwindling material resources among the unlimited, increasingly diversified wants and needs of the consumers who comprise society. Differences in systems of government and systems of economic organization mirror differences in the value structures of contrasting cultures.

DISSECTING SYSTEMS

The application of systems thinking to an analysis of the operations of the business firm greatly enriches our understanding of a firm's quest for legitimacy. A systems theory need not be complex to be useful. So we present a widely accepted and comprehensible paradigm of the nature and functioning of a system in its environment. Implicit in the notion of a system are seven key concepts (see Figure 1.5):

- Environment
- Goals
- Inputs
- Structure
- Processes
- Outputs
- Feedback

Environment

The task of marketing management is increasingly being interpreted as that of anticipating and responding to not only shifts in consumer preferences and needs as expressed in purchase decisions, but also anticipating and adapting to these and other external forces which may confirm or deny the legitimacy of the firm's outputs and methods of operation. Among the external spheres of influence which may confirm or deny the legitimacy of the firm are consumers, competitors, governmental regulatory agencies, resource suppliers, ethical and legal sanctions on enterprise operations, and scientific and

Figure 1.5

Dissecting Systems

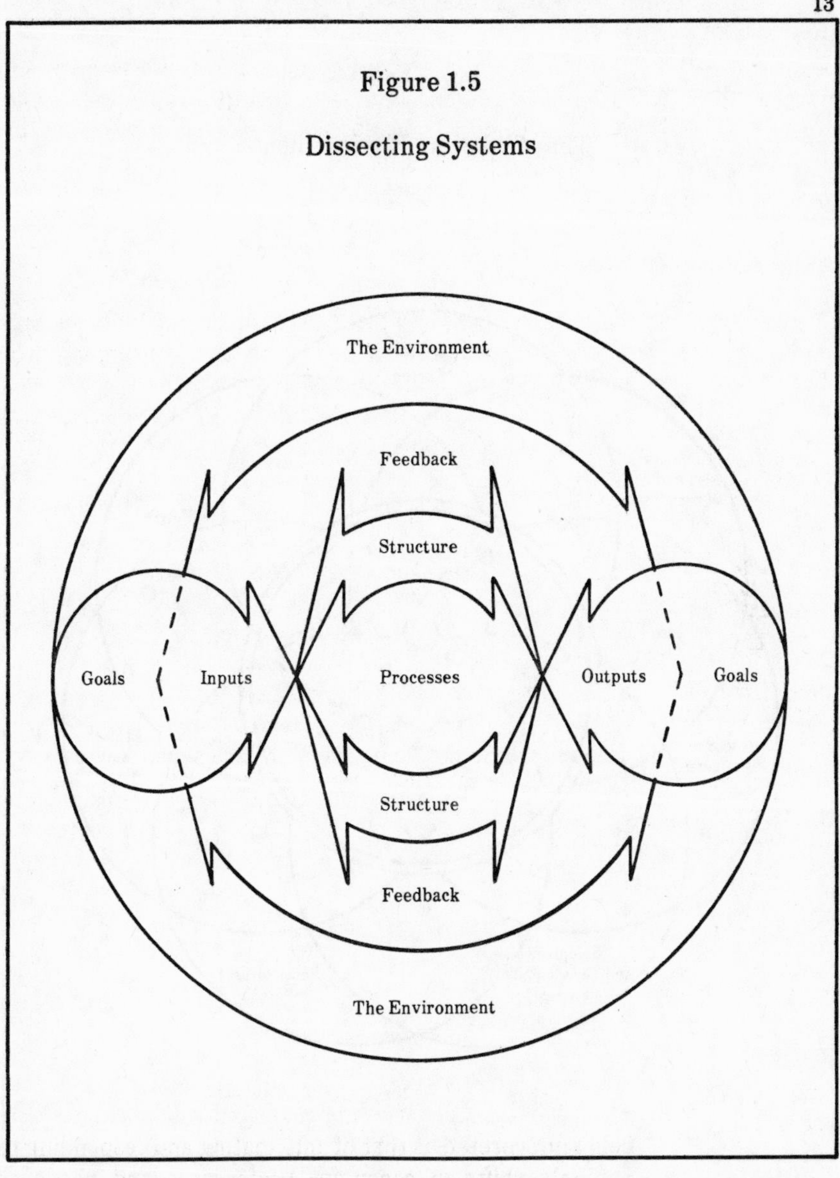

Constraints & opportunities

technological developments which may threaten or expose market opportunities (see Figure 1.6). The combination of interactive external pressures with which marketing management must deal will, of course, vary from firm to firm. And, the constraints and opportunities imposed by external spheres of influence will vary both in proximity and in strength. The small corner grocer may find competition from nearby supermarkets the most pressing

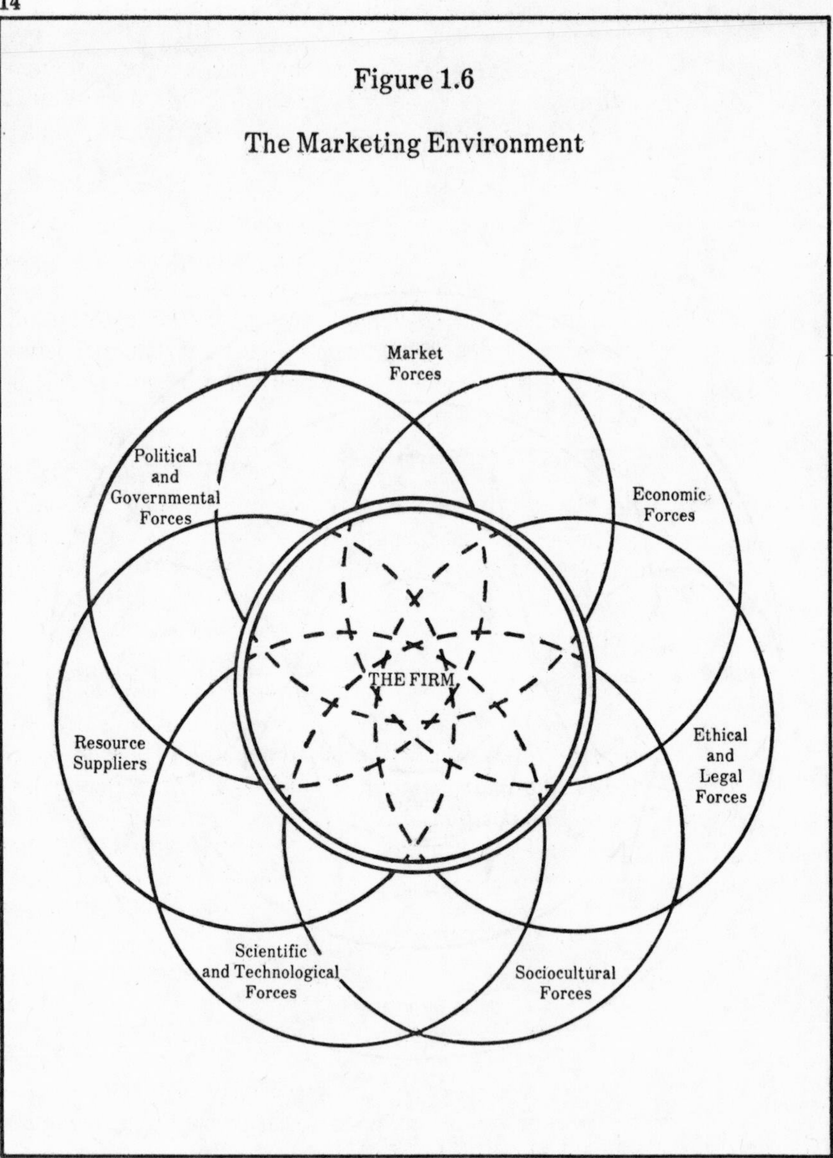

Figure 1.6

The Marketing Environment

factor in his business survival or success, seldom if ever considering the legality of his actions, or the possibility of new forms of competition, such as vending machines or nearby convenience stores, or of coordinated consumer activism directed against him. Alternatively, the giants in any industry must cope with intense competition across national boundaries in numerous spheres of industrial activity, *and* must be attuned to legal constraints at home and abroad, deteriorating energy and material resources, access to properly trained personnel, and technological developments which may make the firm's products obsolete.

Examples are endless, but the implications are clear: Myopia on the part of marketing management with respect to changes in spheres of influence in the firm's environment which may determine its legitimacy – *whether or not such changes are reflected in shifting consumer preferences and tastes* – means that marketing management is guesswork and enterprise success or death is mere accident.

Goals

We will argue throughout this text that the goal of any business firm, as with any system, is to establish its legitimacy by identifying and adapting to other systems within the social system which demand its outputs and accept its methods of operation. *Profit, growth, market share, return on invested capital, stability – all conventional criteria for gauging enterprise and executive performance – merely provide a highly imprecise, frequently misleading barometer of the extent to which marketing management is successful in securing and sustaining positions of lasting legitimacy* (see Figure 1.7).

In fact, the requirements of lasting legitimacy, as the overriding objective of the business firm, may significantly compromise the conventional measures of business performance *in the short run.* That is, the goal of legitimacy requires the recurring reconciliation of:

- The requirements of short- and long-term legitimacy or power
- Individual consumer and social priorities
- Short- and long-term social priorities (see Figure 1.8)

The simultaneous reconciliation of the frequently conflicting demands of divergent priorities will reverberate in all the conventional measures of enterprise performance: profit, growth, return on invested capital, market share, stability.

Inputs

As we have noted, the outputs from any business firm must be demanded as inputs by other systems in the

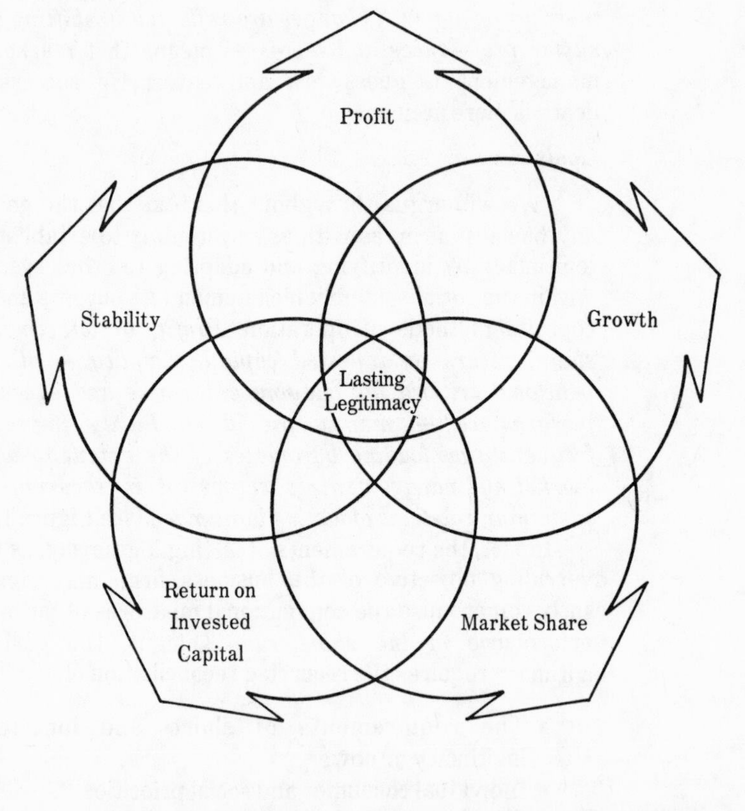

Figure 1.7

Lasting Legitimacy and the Conventional Barometers of Enterprise and Executive Performance

firm's environment if that firm is to survive. Likewise, the inputs into any business firm are outputs from many other systems within the firm's environment. Material, manpower, and energy resources constitute obvious inputs into the business firm which are critical determinants of the firm's survival, and are clearly critical to the establishment and maintenance of legitimacy. Less obvious inputs into the business firm are information concerning competitive actions and reactions, fluctuations in general

Figure 1.8

Legitimacy Seeking: A Balancing Act

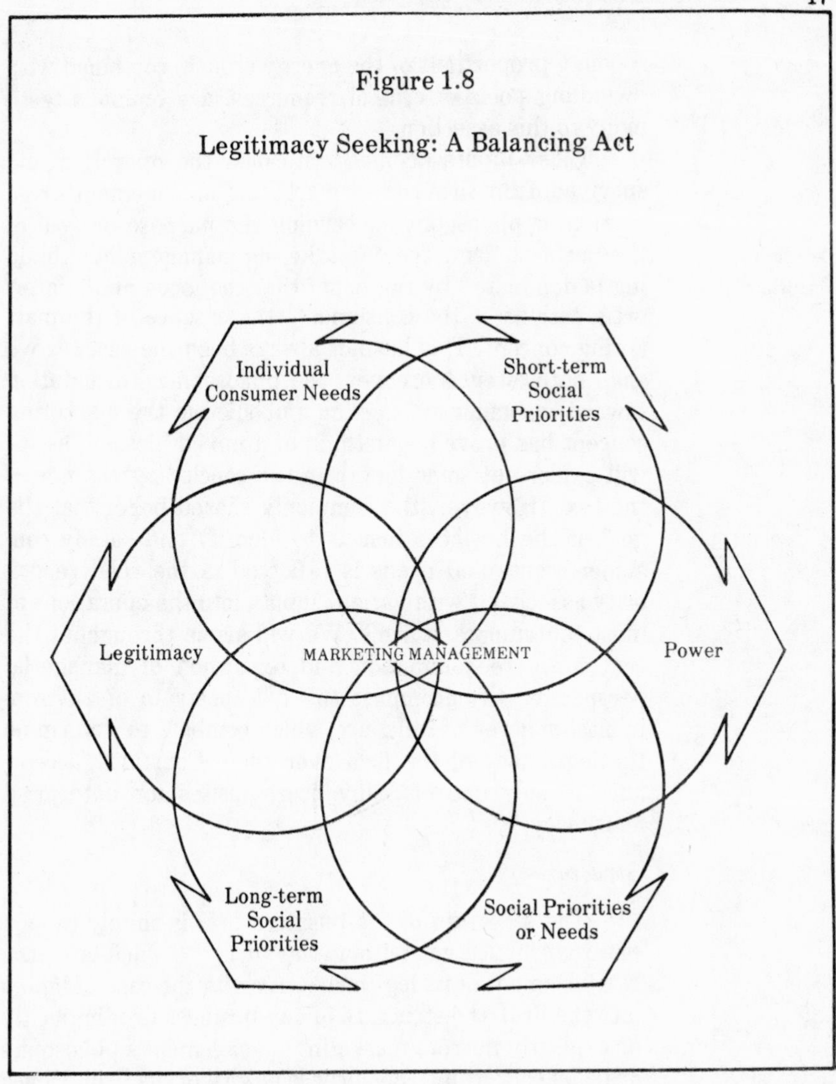

economic activity, changes in consumer tastes and preferences, laws and litigation which may impact upon the firm's operations, and innumerable other critical developments which may expose of foreclose strategic alternatives. Thus inputs into the firm's operations pose both *constraints* and *opportunities* for establishing the legitimacy of the firm. While the list of inputs into the firm is as varied as it is endless, the implications are clear: firms survive only so long as they are able to sustain flows of critical inputs into their operations. The mush-

Constraints & opportunities

Critical inputs

rooming proportions of the energy crunch, combined with dwindling pools of critical resources, are ominous testimony to this assertion.

Those inputs deemed critical in the operation and survival of the firm reflect marketing management's conception or philosophy concerning the purpose or goal of the business firm. Today marketing management's thinking is dominated by the belief that the focus of all enterprise activity is the consumer – the essence of the marketing concept. This has not always been the case, as we shall note later. Moreover, the philosophical orientation toward consumer satisfaction embodied in the marketing concept has proven something of a mixed blessing as we will explore at some length in the concluding chapter of the text. However, the commonly shared belief that the goal of the business firm is to identify and satisfy consumer wants and needs is reflected in the relative priority associated with various inputs into the operations of most contemporary firms. We will argue throughout the text for a reexamination and expansion of managerial perspective to encompass the full spectrum of environmental spheres of influence which combine to determine the legitimacy of the firm over time. Consumer acceptance is only one of many prerequisites for enterprise legitimacy.

Consumer satisfaction

Structure

The structure of the business firm is simply the apparatus instituted within the firm to facilitate the establishment of its legitimacy. As with the case of inputs into the firm, the structure of any business firm implicitly or explicitly mirrors marketing management's philosophy or belief concerning the purpose or goal of the firm. Hence the structure of business firms has shown slow transformation as conceptions of business purpose and managerial responsibility have been reinterpreted. The philosophical orientation toward consumer satisfaction embodied in the marketing concept is reflected in the structure of most firms today. This narrow orientation is no longer sufficient.

Many firms have instituted a formal hierarchy of authority and responsibility to accomplish the goal of consumer satisfaction, with rigid channels of communication and the conventional barometers of enterprise and executive performance. Yet in reality, much of the elaborate bureaucracy that encrusts most business firms is irrelevant to the establishment and maintenance of legitimacy. Many firms operate at the margin of survival because they suffer from *the triumph of style over substance*. That is, they have become so overwhelmed by structure that the performance of functions or processes which are critical in the establishment and maintenance of legitimacy for the firm is impeded or inefficient. Thus structure can either facilitate or impede the performance of functions which are requisite to the legitimacy of the firm, but ultimately the performance of specific functions is more critical to the legitimacy of the firm than the structure within which these functions are carried out.

Triumph of style over substance

Processes

Every business firm exercises direct control or influence over only a small portion of its environment. Employees, resources, and applications of resources are perhaps controllable by the firm in the short run. Energy and material resources, however, have become increasingly questionable as resource availability has deteriorated markedly, posing real constraints for marketing management charged with establishing and maintaining the legitimacy of the firm. Still other aspects of the firm's environment may be partially controllable over time. This explains why many large firms maintain lobbies in Washington to influence legislation or legislative interpretation in favor of the firm. For the most part, however, the environment lies outside management's span of direct control. Thus, *marketing management's job is essentially a process of adapting to the uncontrollable aspects of the firm's environment by manipulating the few factors under management's direct control.*

Controllables & uncontrollables

The marketing manager shoulders only a portion of the total responsibility for the firm's process of anticipating and adapting to environmental demands. Ultimate responsibility for establishing and sustaining the legitimacy of the firm is shared among the traditional func-

Legitimacy: shared responsibility

tional divisions of the firm: engineering, production, purchasing, marketing, inventory management, accounting, finance, credit (see Figures 1.9, 1.10, 1.11). Marketing management's conventional domain of authority extends primarily to the *marketing controllables*: which *products* will be offered for sale, at which *prices*, through which *distribution* systems, communicated through which *communication* vehicles (see Figure 1.12). It is principally through product, pricing, communication, and distribution decisions that the firm seeks to establish lasting legitimacy.

Marketing controllables
- **product**
- **price**
- **communication**
- **distribution**

The domain of authority and responsibility which marketing management accepts, and the manner in which marketing decisions are carried out, mirrors marketing management's philosophy concerning the purpose or goal of the firm. Hence marketing responsibility extends far beyond the conventional controllables. *Marketing constitutes the interface between the firm and the environment*. Decisions made in all functional divisions of the firm are translated through marketing, underscoring the need for internal coordination in the achievement of enterprise objectives. For example, product strategy decisions require close coordination among marketing, production, engineering, finance, and purchasing. Likewise, the performance of all functions which influence the process of enterprise adaptation necessitates integrated decision making among functional divisions of the firm.

Interface

Integrated decision making

As in the case of inputs and structure of the firm, performance of marketing functions or manipulation of marketing controllables is today dominated by the philosophical orientation toward consumer satisfaction embodied in the marketing concept. We will have a great deal more to say about the performance of marketing functions and the philosophy which guides their performance in succeeding chapters. It is essential to keep in mind, however, that both *interpretations* of appropriate marketing functions and the *performance* of marketing functions directly reflect marketing management's conception of the goal of business, a goal which should extend beyond consumer satisfaction.

Interpretation

Performance

Outputs

In the process of anticipating and adapting to the demands imposed by the systems comprising its external

Figure 1.9

Integrated Functional Divisions Within the Firm

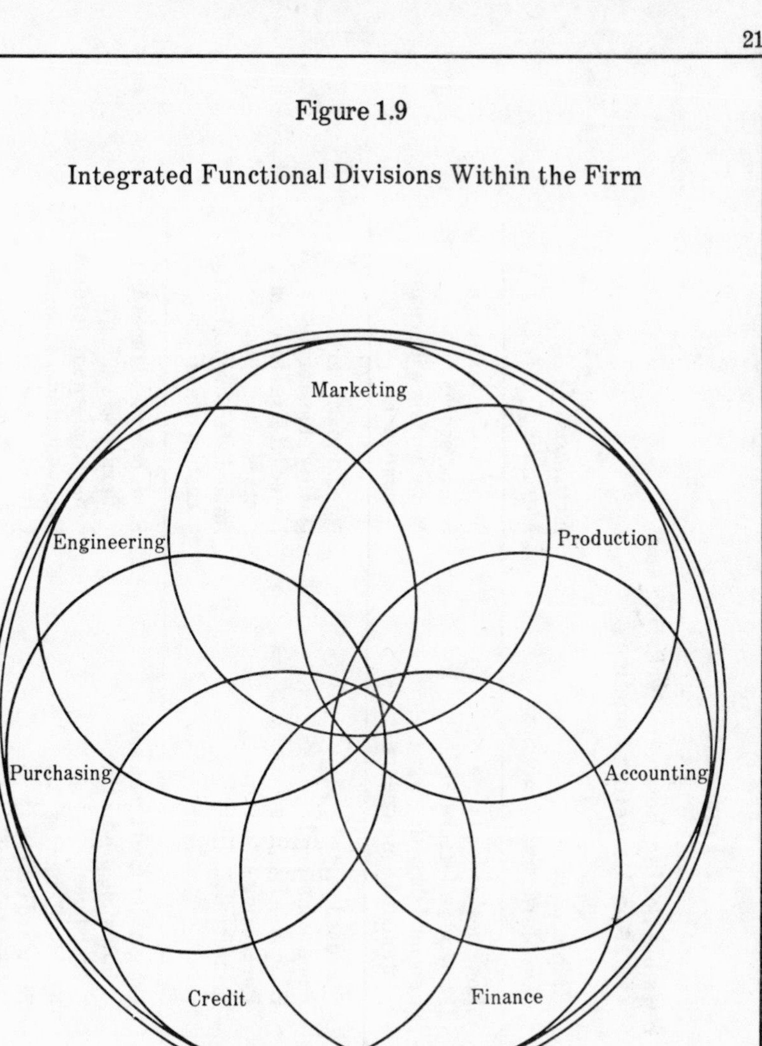

environment, the firm produces a variety of outputs which are either sanctified or rejected by environmental spheres of influence. The most obvious functional output produced by any business firm consists of those products, services, or promotional appeals oriented toward the satisfaction of the needs of consumers comprising selected target

Figure 1.10

Possible Conflict between Marketing and Non-Marketing Functions

Non-Marketing Functions	*Emphasis of Non-Marketing Functions*	*Emphasis of Marketing*
Engineering	Long design lead time Functional features Few models with standard components	Short design lead time Sales features Many models with custom components
Purchasing	Standard parts Price of material Economic lot sizes Purchasing at infrequent intervals	Nonstandard parts Quality of material Large lot sizes to avoid stockouts Immediate purchasing for custom needs
Production	Long order lead times and inflexible production schedules No model changes Standard orders Ease of fabrication Average quality control	Short order lead times and flexible scheduling to meet emergency orders Frequent model changes Custom orders Aesthetic appearance Tight quality control

Inventory Management	Fast-moving items, narrow product line Economic levels of stock	Broad product line Large levels of stock
Finance	Strict rationale for spending Hard and fast budgets Pricing to cover costs by customers	Intuitive arguments for spending Flexible budgets to meet changing needs Pricing to further market development
Accounting	Standard transactions Few reports	Special terms and discounts Many reports
Credit	Full financial disclosure of customers Low credit risks Tough credit terms Tough collection procedures	Minimum credit examination of customers Medium credit risks Easy credit terms Easy collection procedures

Adapted from Philip Kotler, "Diagnosing the Marketing Takeover, *Harvard Business Review* (November-December, 1965), p. 72. Reprinted with permission of publisher.

Figure 1.11

"What We Have Here Is Failure To Communicate"

As marketing requested it

As sales ordered it

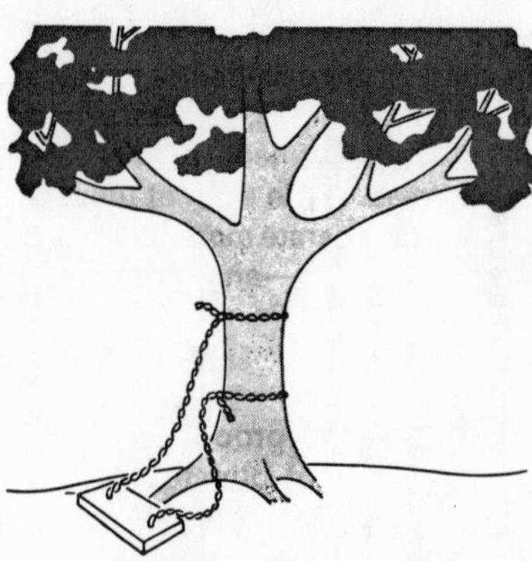

As engineering designed it

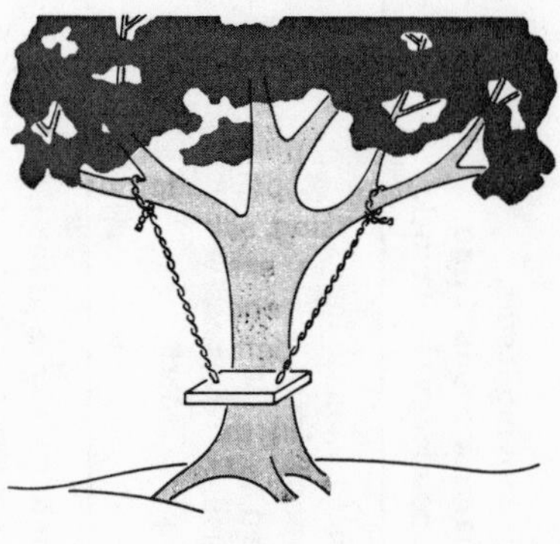

As manufactured

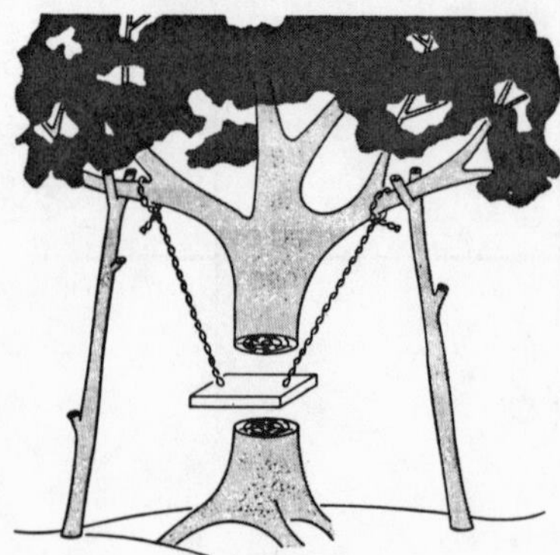

As installed

What the customer wanted

Figure 1.12

The Marketing Controllables

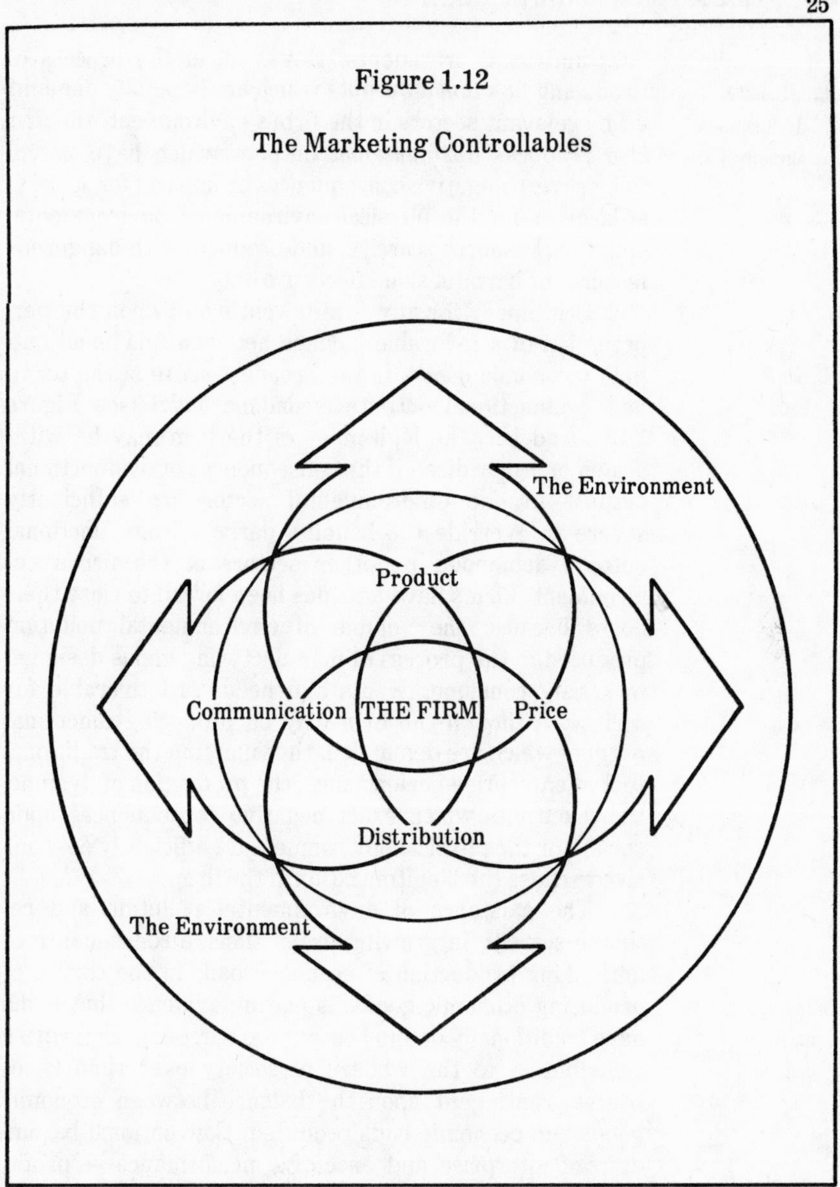

markets or market segments. These either find acceptance among their intended markets, thus establishing the legitimacy of the firm, its output, and methods of operation, or fail to meet with receptive markets. Less obvious outputs from the firm's operations are vast volumes of information, employment and employee morale, financial inputs into community development, and sometimes laws and legal precedents. However, in the process of

Functional & dysfunctional outputs

producing *functional* outputs which are hopefully demanded by relevant sectors in the firm's environment, the firm also produces *dysfunctional* outputs which have potentially severe negative consequences or impacts for society-at-large or for the physical environment. Environmental pollution, resource scarcity, and products with dangerous features or harmful side-effects are only a few.

Goods & bads

Legitimacy for any firm is contingent upon the perpetuation of a favorable balance between functional outputs (economic *goods*, in the broadest sense of the term) and dysfunctional outputs (economic *bads*) (see Figure 1.13). And yet, the legitimacy of the firm may be withdrawn or jeopardized if the consequences of dysfunctional outputs in one environmental sector are sufficiently severe to override the benefits derived from functional outputs demanded by other sectors of the firm's environment. Firms have at times been forced to close their doors because the volume of environmental pollution produced in the process of manufacturing goods designed to satisfy consumer wants and needs is intolerable for society. Although the firm may be producing functional outputs which are demanded, thus meeting the traditional test of enterprise performance, the production of dysfunctional outputs which exact negative consequences upon society or the physical environment is sufficiently destructive to cause the illegitimization of the firm.

Output too narrowly defined

The existence of environmental pollution and resource scarcity in growing proportions, a consequence of unthinking production of economic bads in the course of producing economic goods, is glaring evidence that firms have traditionally defined output too narrowly. Enterprise contribution to the welfare of society over time is, of course, contingent upon the balance between economic goods and economic bads produced. Conventional barometers of enterprise and executive performance — profit, growth, return on invested capital, market share — only serve to deepen the problem because they have traditionally ignored economic bads altogether. Clearly, however, the establishment of lasting legitimacy requires that marketing management's attention be directed to the negative reverberations upon society and the physical environment of producing outputs which are demanded by other environmental sectors. The pursuit of legitimacy in

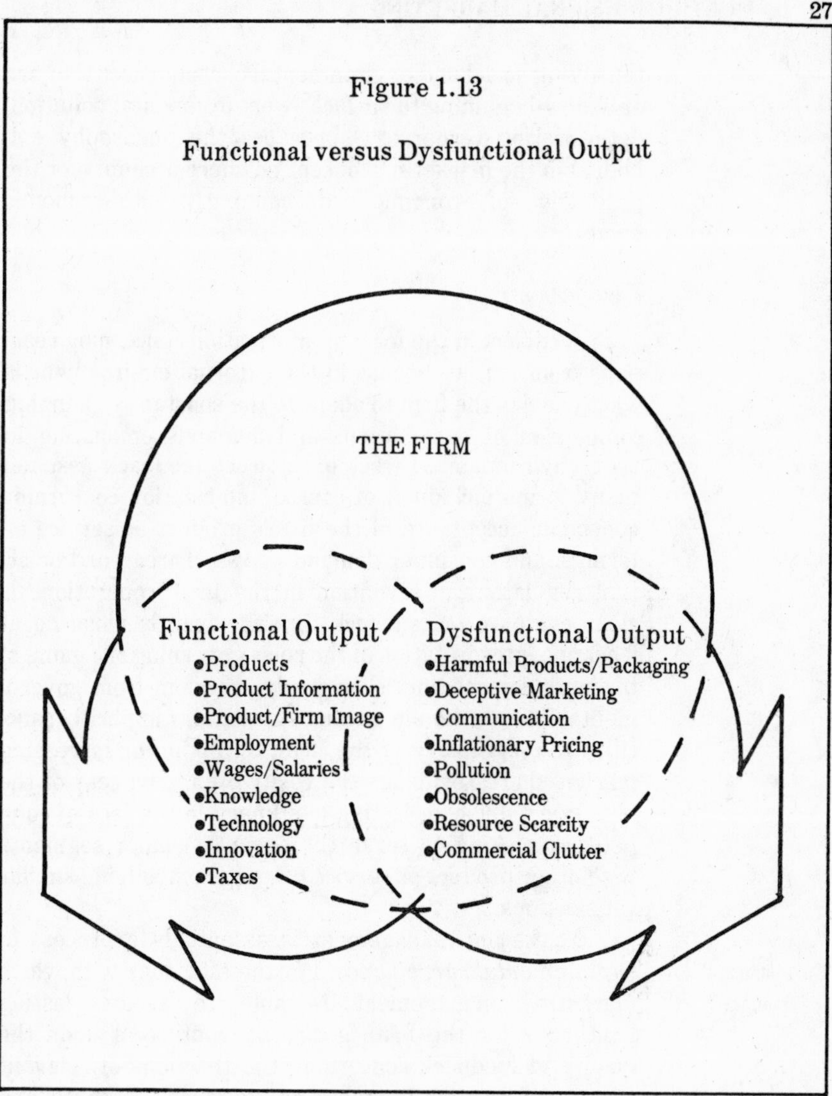

Figure 1.13

Functional versus Dysfunctional Output

the short-run may compromise the goal of lasting legitimacy. The production of dysfunctional outputs today may disallow the establishment of legitimacy in the future. Again, marketing management's conception of the goal of business will be reflectd not only in the relative priority placed upon certain inputs in the firm's operations, structure, and processes, but also in the nature of outputs from the firm's operations.

The exclusive focus on production of goods and services to serve consumer wants and needs has led to intensifying social and environmental consequences that are only now beginning to surface — environmental pollution, deteriorating resources — because the philosophy embodied in the marketing concept nowhere accounts for the production of economic bads conjointly with economic goods.

Feedback

Feedback in the form of information concerning reactions from various arenas in the external environment is what enables the firm to adapt to the constantly changing complexion of expectations and demands emanating in that environment. Direct or indirect feedback assumes many forms including, of course, information concerning consumer acceptance of the firm's product or service offerings, and consumer demand *per se*. Threatened or actual regulatory intervention in the firm's operations is clear evidence or feedback that the firm is violating at least one interpretation of the rules governing the game of business competition. Conversely, freedom from governmental intervention in business operations implicitly sanctifies the legitimacy of the firm. Shrinking or increasing market shares evidence the relative effectiveness of the firm in establishing lasting legitimacy in the face of competitors seeking to serve the same consumer segments with other product or service offerings embodying similar satisfactions.

Environmental surveillance

Marketing management is essentially a process of *environmental surveillance*. For the efficiency with which marketing management is able to secure lasting legitimacy for the firm is directly contingent upon the quality of feedback concerning the reactions of relevant sectors of the environment to the firm's outputs and methods of operation. The nature of feedback into the firm varies with conceptions of the goal of the firm. The marketing concept suggests that feedback from consumers is of paramount importance in shaping adaptive strategy. However, this exclusive focus on consumer reactions to the firm's products and services may obscure the legitimate demands arising in other arenas in the firm's environment. These demands, if unanswered, may threaten the legitimacy of the firm.

THE SYSTEMS CONCEPT IN PRACTICE

Although marketing management is increasingly aware of the necessity of anticipating change and adapting the firm's output and methods of operation to the possible impacts of widely diversified environmental forces, systems thinking has not yet gained widespread adoption. Marketing management, it seems is simply too overburdened with day-to-day operating problems. Of more immediate concern than the possible impact of economic, political, governmental, scientific, or technological forces upon the firm's operations, is the availability of human, financial, physical and energy resources, and the actions and reactions of competitors, consumers, and stockholders to the firm's marketing activities. Virtually ignored by marketing management are the multiple reciprocal impacts of the firm's operations in various noneconomic arenas in its environment.

In cases where the systems viewpoint has been incorporated into marketing decision making, marketing management's exclusive concern has been confined to those factors which most directly figure in legitimizing strategies in the short run. Where governmental regulations limit product, pricing, communication or distribution strategy options, as in the case of periodic price ceilings and freezes or full disclosure of the composition of pharmaceutical products, such constraints will be accommodated in planning marketing operations. Where technological developments imply obsolescence of the firm's current products, they will likely be rapidly adopted by the firm. The focus of marketing management, for the most part, remains consumer satisfaction, and understandably so, for the short-run prosperity of the firm is largely contingent upon its ability to cultivate customers for its products and services.

Performance measures

Also, conventional measures of enterprise and executive performance tend to obscure managerial consideration of the reciprocal impacts of environmental forces and enterprise operations, including the simultaneous production of economic *bads* along with the production of economic *goods* demanded by consumers.

For example, consumer preferences have shown a steady shift away from returnable beverage containers toward "throw-aways." Beer and soft drink bottlers have responded by switching production and distribution facilities to the preferred "throw-away" containers, apparently unmindful of the fact that rusting beer and soft drink cans and nonbiodegradable bottles would multiply into a major mountain of litter and pollution. Responding to manifest consumer preferences for "throw-away" packaging is, of course, an application of the marketing concept, the belief that the consumer sanctifies the legitimacy of the firm by the act of purchasing its products or services. However, the dysfunctional consequences for society, the economy, and the environment of shortsighted marketing decision making have grown to such proportions that they can no longer be ignored. Hence some far-sighted firms have completed the feedback loop in their legitimacy-seeking activities by replacing bottles and steel cans with aluminum cans and instituting reclamation centers for retrieving and recycling aluminum. The establishment of a feedback loop in the channel of distribution has proven sensible on both economic and ecological grounds. Curiously, the recycling movement initiated by a regional beer brewer, *Coors* of Golden, Colorado, quickly spread to other regional brewers, finally prompting the national distributors to join the parade. Marketing management's apparent immunity from systems thinking is only slowly responding to treatment, the result of intensified environmental pressures.

WHAT'S WRONG WITH MARKETING?

Functional focus

Marketing has historically been interpreted and defined almost exclusively in terms of those functions required to distribute goods and services and more recently in terms of those functions required to identify and serve consumer wants and needs. Improving distributive efficiency and refining techniques for anticipating and responding to consumer demands for goods and services remains the overriding objective of most marketing practitioners and analysts. Even where the systems perspective of marketing has been implemented, emphasis has largely been restricted to the possible impact of environmental forces on the performance of functions required to identify and satisfy consumer wants and needs, rather than upon the multiple impacts of the firm's operations upon its environment. There is something seriously wrong with this nearsighted focus on marketing functions.

Marketing, as conventionally defined and practiced, has left gaping areas of social concern largely neglected. The results are as numerous as they are distressing: environmental pollution in endless variety, deteriorating energy and material resources, a skewed distribution of material goods across society, and immeasurable frustration and resentment arising from the dramatic contrasts between the *haves* and the *have nots*, mirrored in distrust, suspicion, and sometimes outright revolt.

It is understandable that marketing management and marketing thought are contaminated by the same shortsightedness. Improving techniques for obtaining and serving consumer demand is a highly absorbing and intricate job, and one that produces (at least partially) measurable results: sales. The impact of marketing activity on society, the economy, and the environment is often less tangible, and thus less quantifiable, frequently delayed, and often so diffused as to obscure its effects. But this intense functional orientation produces a marketer who is not simply myopic, he is blind. Even within the conventional domain of marketing management, the performance of marketing functions required to identify and satisfy consumer wants and needs, a number of blind spots are apparent.

Economic Applications

First, marketing functions tend to be considered only in an economic context. Yet, as prominent marketing analysts have observed, "The modern marketing concept serves very naturally to describe an important facet of all organizational activity. All organizations must develop appropriate products to serve their sundry consuming groups and must use modern tools of communication to reach their consuming publics." [50, p. 15] Marketing functions are increasingly being translated into nonconventional noneconomic applications, including the marketing of political candidates, universities, hospitals, police departments, social action groups such as Nader's Raiders, charitable organizations, even the U.S. Postal Service, but not without controversy (see Figure 1.14). In the political arena, for example, *voting block* translates

Figure 1.14

The "Broadening" Controversy: A Collision of Conviction

Case

. . . Whether marketing is viewed in the old sense of "pushing " products or in the new sense of "customer satisfaction engineering," it is almost always viewed and discussed as a business activity.

. . . marketing is a pervasive societal activity that goes considerably beyond the selling of toothpaste, soap, and steel.

All organizations are formed to serve the interest of particular groups: hospitals serve the sick, schools serve the students, governments serve the citizens, and labor unions serve the members.

Marketing is that function of the organization that can keep in constant touch with the organization's consumers, read their needs, develop "products" that meet these needs, and build a program of communications to express the organization's purposes.

. . . The modern marketing concept serves very naturally to describe an important facet of all organizational activity. All organizations must develop appropriate products to serve their sundry consuming groups and must use modern tools of communication to reach their consuming publics. The business heritage of marketing provides a useful set of concepts for guiding all organizations.

The choice facing those who manage nonbusiness organizations is not whether to market or not to market, for no organization can avoid marketing. The choice is whether to do it well or poorly, and on this necessity the case for organizational marketing is basically founded.

Excerpted from Philip Kotler and Sidney J. Levy, "Broadening the Concept of Marketing," *Journal of Marketing* (January, 1969), pp. 10-15, published by the American Marketing Association.

Fig. 1.14 Continued

Rejoinder

If a definition were framed to meet the authors' contentions, marketing no longer would be bounded in terms of either institutions or the ultimate purpose of its activities. If a task is performed, anywhere by anybody, that has some resemblance to a task performed in marketing, that would *be* marketing.

Before becoming so proprietary, it should be recognized that the marketing profession did not originate most of the concepts noted by the authors. For example, the authors indicate that the re-examination of "target groups, differential advantage, communication channels and messages" constitutes a *marketing* audit—wherever this is performed. However, it should be noted that political leaders and parties were conducting these activities thousands of years before marketing existed as a field of serious study. Marketers' self-image may be pleasurably inflated by claiming that political campaigns are just another part of marketing, but what progress is to be gained by such reasoning?

A church does not sell its religious and redemptive services. Political parties do not sell specific services (unless corruptly committing illegal acts). The Heart Fund does not sell donations: there is no established price or terms of sale, and the donor is given no specific *quid pro quo.* Thus, a particular act must be related to an eventual or intended offer to buy and/or sell a specified good or service—with the terms of sale specified between the parties—or that act is not a *marketing* act, regardless of its nature.

Attenuate marketing's definition to make it almost universal, and it will wholly lose its identity.

A manageable, intelligible and logical definition of marketing can be fashioned when its scope is bounded within those processes or activities whose ultimate result is a *market transaction.*

Excerpted from David J. Luck, "Broadening the Concept of Marketing—Too Far," *Journal of Marketing* (July, 1969), pp. 53-55, published by the American Marketing Association.

Fig. 1.14 Continued

Reply

. . . the scope, methods, and aims of any discipline are determined more by *tradition* than by anything intrinsic in the name.

The . . . possible difference between business marketing and other types of marketing might be in what Professor Luck calls the *market transaction*. He says that the aim of marketing is "the ultimate purchase-and-sale of a product or service." This criterion is not as unambiguous or acceptable as it might appear at first glance.

The fact that spiritual and educational services are usually paid for in other ways than outright purchase reflects convenience and tradition. Is anyone deceived that there is not a *quid pro quo?*

The crux of marketing lies in a *general idea of exchange* rather than the narrower idea of market transactions. Exchange involves two (or more) parties who voluntarily agree to enter into a "trading" relationship. The trade may consist of one product for another, a product for a service, a service for a service, or a product or service for money. Each party enters into the exchange because he wants something other than he gives. Each party tries to emphasize the value of what he is giving in order to consummate an exchange that is mutually satisfactory, and which perhaps will lay the basis for a continuing relationship.

Marketing is a universal process carried on by individuals, groups, and organizations. Basically, it describes those efforts to win the support of others through offering value. This process is termed marketing for two reasons: First, a better term for this generic and endemic process has not been found. Second, we think that a single theory can ultimately be forged to describe this process no matter where it occurs and no matter what it is called.

Excerpted from Philip Kotler and Sidney J. Levy, "A New Form of Marketing Myopia: Rejoinder to Professor Luck," *Journal of Marketing* (July, 1969), pp. 55-57, published by the American Marketing Association.

into *market segment*, *election* into *sales campaign*, *candidates* into *products* or *images*, *campaign strategy* into *marketing mix*, and *voters* into *consumers*.

> It is not surprising . . . that politicians and advertising men should have discovered one another. And, once they recognized that the citizen did not so much vote for a candidate as make a psychological purchase of him, not surprising that they began to work together. [64, p. 27]

The future should see an even more rapid spread of conventional marketing methods into unfamiliar, noneconomic territory. New applications will necessitate an alteration or adaptation of conventional marketing functions to the unique demands and constraints imposed by nontraditional marketing problems. Today, however, most marketers remain sharply focused on the traditional economic applications of marketing functions: identifying and satisfying consumer wants and needs, "keeping the customer satisfied."

Static Functions

The functional orientation in marketing, in addition to being restricted to economic applications, is also highly static. Refinements in marketing techniques and methods tend to be confined to those functions which are appropriate to the existing economic system. But the economic system changes, and will change, and marketing functions must change with it. Marketing and marketing management, it seems, have been content to passively react to changing economic realities and environmental conditions. As a consequence many business firms have faced a succession of severe malfunctions and inefficiencies: radical recessionary cycles, serious unemployment among the echelons of white collar occupational categories, magnifying energy and material resource shortages, spiraling inflation. The examples are endless. As changing economic and environmental conditions have dictated altered functions for marketing, marketing has been reinterpreted, reorganized and reapplied, belatedly at times, always *reacting* to externally-imposed pressure. Yet, as we have noted, the key to lasting legitimacy for the firm lies in *anticipating* as well as *adapting* to the possible impact of changes in environmental forces, before they occur.

Reactive marketing

Anticipation and Adaptation

The implication of systems thinking for marketing is that marketers must be increasingly attentive to the probable pace and course of evolution of society, the environment, and the economic system, and must decipher the impact of such changes for marketing functions. In addition, marketing management must anticipate the possible impact of marketing activity on society, the environment, and the economic system. One extremely likely consequence of further evolution of the economic system is increased interdependence between economic institutions and other institutions within the social system. Accordingly, marketers must not only examine how marketing fits into the economic system and the environment, but how the economic system fits into society as a whole and the environment. In addition to their traditional functional perspective, marketers must develop a societal perspective of marketing, and a philosophy which is compatible with marketing's expanded role and responsibility within the firm, society, and the environment. Marketers must adopt a *societal* and *philosophical* perspective, as well as a functional or *managerial* perspective of marketing (see Figure 1.15). The price to the firm of ignoring these important alternative perspectives of marketing is no longer profit. The price may well be survival.

Managerial (Functional) Societal Philosophical perspectives

FORMAT

The purpose of the remaining sections of this text is to present a balanced analysis of marketing encompassing three essential perspectives: marketing as a *managerial process*, as a *societal role*, and as a *managerial philosophy*. The societal and philosophical aspects of marketing have been virtually ignored by marketing practitioner and marketing analyst alike. Yet a more comprehensive understanding of the *multidimensional* nature of marketing, particularly of its societal and philosophical dimensions, is increasingly essential in understanding and responding to the highly intricate, rapidly unfolding interdependent physical, social, and economic system that forms the environment for the firm. All three perspectives are implicit in the definition of marketing proposed in this text. Moreover, all three perspectives are reconciled within the

Figure 1.15

Multidimensional Marketing

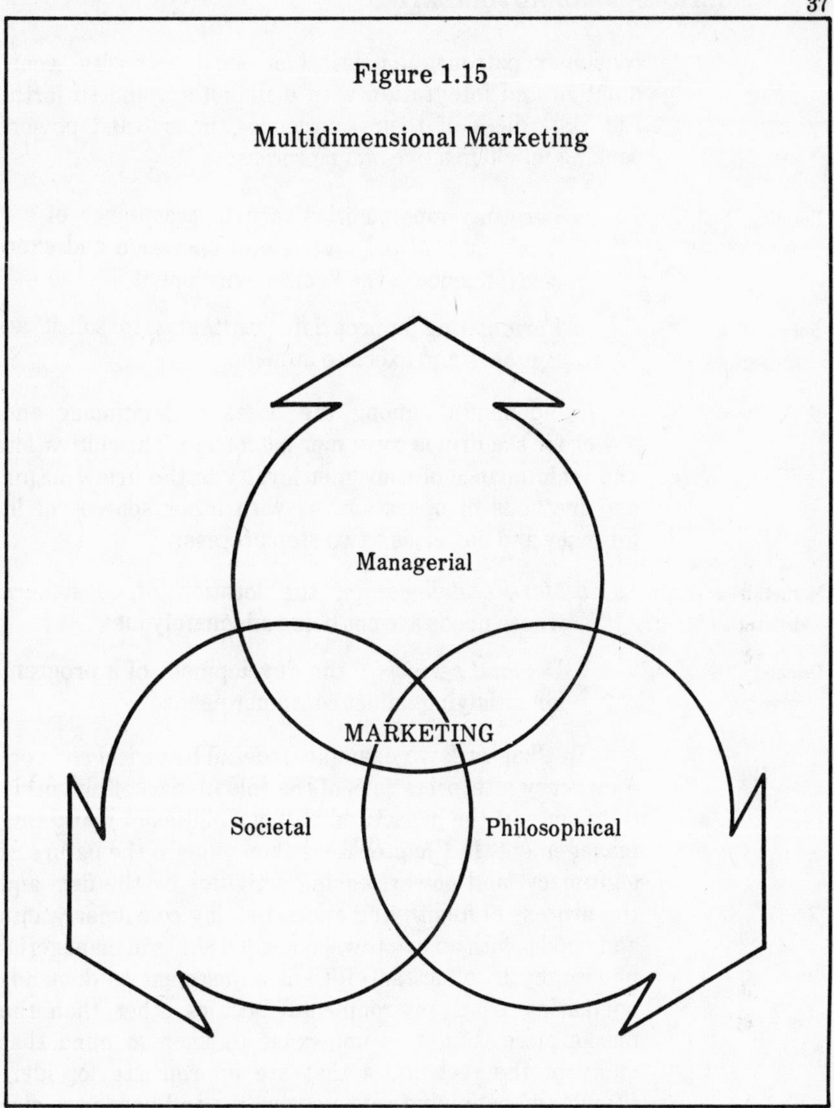

systems definition of marketing explored in subsequent sections.

Marketing: A Managerial Process

Marketing from a managerial perspective is essentially a process of legitimacy seeking by the firm. Legitimacy, or acceptance of the firm's output or methods of operation by relevant sectors within the firm's environment, can derive from any of a variety of sources:

consumer patronage, political or legal authority, coordination and integration with distributors, and so forth. But regardless of their source, legitimacy- and power-seeking unfold in a two-stage process:

Locating opportunities

- Locating opportunities to gain acceptance of the firm's output and methods of operation and exercise influence in the firm's environment

Formulating strategies

- Formulating appropriate strategies to solicit acceptance and exercise influence

Fundamental among the bases of legitimacy and power for the firm is consumer patronage. The cultivation and maintenance of consumer loyalty to the firm's output and methods of operation, as with other sources of legitimacy and power, is a two-step process:

Market delineation

- *Market delineation*, the location of consumers whose needs are not being adequately met

Demand servicing

- *Demand servicing*, the development of a program for satisfying unmet consumer needs

In Chapter 2 we examine in detail historical and contemporary interpretations of the role of marketing within the firm and the associated responsibilities of marketing management. In Chapter 3 we then explore the nature of legitimacy- and power-seeking activities by the firm and the process of identifying and satisfying consumer wants and needs, with an eye toward needed shifts in managerial philosophy to effect an efficient adjustment to demands emanating from environmental sectors other than the marketplace. But it is important to keep in mind that many of the techniques that are appropriate for identifying and satisfying consumer wants and needs are also appropriate for legitimacy- and power-seeking efforts in other arenas: political, charitable, consumerist, revolutionary, criminal, religious. Equally essential to understanding the processes and techniques discussed is a grasp of the firm as a legitimacy-seeking system, a characteristic the firm shares with all systems. An understanding of this essential notion underscores the necessity of organization and coordination in the performance of marketing processes or functions, and the necessity of integrating into the process of marketing a managerial philosophy reflective of a systems orientation.

Marketing: A Societal Role

Chapter 4 explores the nature of American society and in particular the nature of its economic institution. A basic understanding of the social system is critical in comprehending the role, relevance, and responsibilities of marketing in American society.

Social institutions

American society can best be understood as a complex of highly interdependent social institutions. These comprise the environment within which all firms function and from which all business firms seek to establish and maintain positions of legitimacy. To ignore the environment, to fail to understand and consider its complexity in marketing decision making, is very likely to result in the restriction or withdrawal of legitimacy from the firm.

Marketing cannot be studied in a vacuum. A thorough understanding of the rapidly evolving interdependent social system within which the firm operates is essential if the legitimacy of the firm is to be established and sustained through farsighted marketing decision making. Initially, then, an overview of the principal elements of American society is presented. Since such concepts as institutions and culture are likely to be unfamiliar to many marketing students, basic approaches and concepts essential in the analysis of social systems are examined. Then, the underlying structure of the American social system is sketched with particular emphasis on institutions and values. Next, the American economic system is profiled. This, of course, is the specific context within which marketing management operates. Finally, to emphasize the systems aspect of society, the interrelationships among social institutions are explored.

Marketing: A Managerial Philosophy

Reactive marketing

Marketing has been interpreted almost exclusively as an *adaptive* or *reactive* process. The unfortunate consequence of this view is that it obscures the reciprocal impacts of marketing activity upon the firm's environment and those of the environment upon marketing activity. Where in past shortsightedness on the part of marketing management concerning the dysfunctional, social, economic, and environmental consequences of marketing activity may have been excusable, or at least explainable, the stakes are increasing. Inflation, recession, environmental pollution, energy and material resource scarcity, unemployment, and poverty are all too real. Marketing management can no longer afford to ignore the social, economic, and environmental consequences of its decisions. The legitimacy of business itself and the continued viability of the American economic system are in the balance.

Mythology of capitalism

To underscore the importance of this needed shift in managerial perspective, Chapter 5 examines the fundamental tenets of the *mythology of capitalism* under which the American economic system and the firms which comprise the economy have long operated. We then examine the role of marketing in perpetuating the mythology of capitalism in America and the severe social, economic, and environmental consequences of continued adherence to capitalistic fiction. By contrasting capitalistic fact and fiction several chronic problems are brought to light which pose severe consequences for the continued viability of the economic system. These critical problems serve to underscore the necessity of a shift in managerial philosophy toward a more balanced multidimensional perspective of marketing which reconciles the reciprocal impacts of the firm on its environment and the environment upon the firm. The functional, societal and philosophical perspectives of marketing converge in the definition of marketing proposed in the text.

CHAPTER 1: REVIEW QUESTIONS

1. What factors combine to explain the "crisis of legitimacy" currently confronted by American business firms? Is the crisis likely to subside? How should businessmen in general and marketers in particular respond to the crisis? Is it the government's job to solve the crisis? Is it the responsibility of business?

2. What is meant by the concept of "legitimacy" for any system? For any social organization? For the business firm? What qualifies an enterprise as "illegitimate?"

3. What is the role of marketing in securing the legitimacy of the firm? How responsive have marketing, marketers, and marketing analysts been to this role?

4. What is the *marketing concept*? What's wrong with the marketing concept? What's wrong with marketing?

5. What is a system? How do the ecological environment, society, the economic structure, and the firm qualify as systems? What are their component parts and goals?

6. What are the major features of systems? How do they interrelate? How do these relate to the business firm? To marketing?

7. How does the goal of legitimacy relate to the conventional barometers of enterprise and executive performance – profit, growth, market share, return on invested capital, and stability?

8. We have referred to the process of legitimacy seeking as "a balancing act." For whom? What must be reconciled or balanced? How does this interpretation jibe with the marketing concept?

9. Legitimacy must be shared responsibility. By whom? Where does marketing fit in? What are the "marketing controllables?" How do they relate to the goal of legitimacy?

10. What are the principal functional and dysfunctional outputs of the firm? How does the balance between functional and dysfunctional outputs relate to enterprise legitimacy?

11. Why has the systems concept of the firm been so little implemented in actual business operations?

12. What's wrong with marketing? How generalizable are marketing techniques to noneconomic applications? Why are conventional interpretations of marketing functions essentially "static?" Why must marketers develop *societal* and *philosophical* perspectives of marketing, in addition to their more conventional *managerial* perspective?

MARKETING: A MANAGERIAL PROCESS

PART I

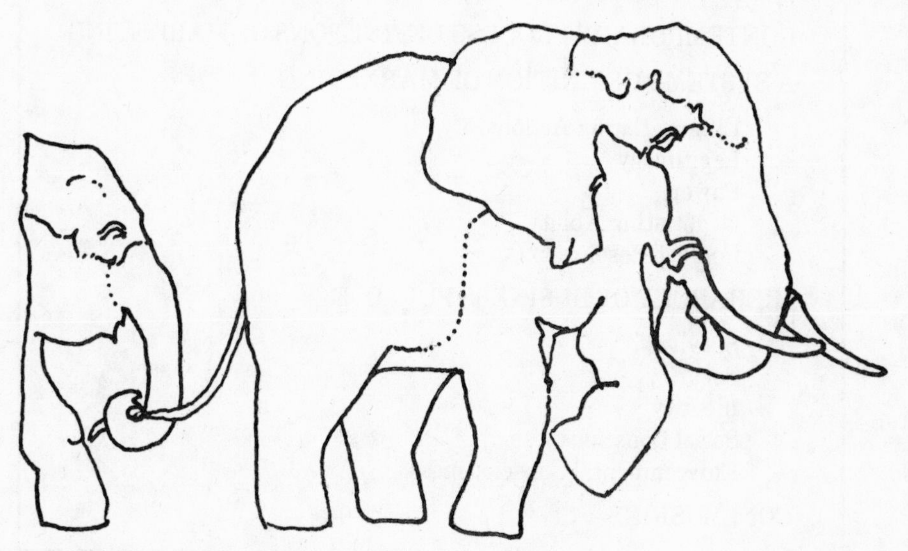

THE ENVIRONMENT FOR MARKETING

THE ROLE OF MARKETING IN SOCIETY

BUSINESS PURPOSE AND MANAGERIAL RESPONSIBILITY: AN HISTORICAL PERSPECTIVE

- Production Orientation
- Sales Orientation
- Marketing Orientation

THE EVOLUTION OF CONCEPTS OF MARKETING

- Marketing as Distribution
- Marketing as Selling
- Marketing as Adaptation to Consumer Needs

CONTEMPORARY PROCESS DEFINITIONS OF MARKETING

A SYSTEMS DEFINITION OF MARKETING

- Differentiating Actions
- Legitimacy
- Power
- Negotiating Ability
- Conflict Resolution

HIERARCHY OF BUSINESS PURPOSE

- Survival
- Security
- Identity
- Social Consciousness
- Environmental Consciousness

CONCLUSIONS

Marketing: A Managerial Process

In Chapter 1 we introduced the notion of a *system*, a collection of interdependent structures and functions which are oriented around some common goal and which produce outputs which reflect the attempt to achieve that goal. In introducing the concept of legitimacy, we concluded that in any social system the output of any organization must be demanded by other organizations within the system for the organization to survive. Legitimacy for any social organization, indeed for any system, is conferred and confirmed by other organizations within the larger social system which demand its output.

At a minimum, the business firm, and consequently marketers, must produce and distribute products and services which satisfy at least some consumer wants and needs some of the time. Legitimacy of *output*, however, is

Output

Methods of operation

no longer the firm's sole prerequisite for survival. It is also necessary that the firm establish the legitimacy of its *methods of operation* in the eyes of relevant sectors of its environment, whether they be capable of imposing legal sanctions, imposing resource restrictions, or withholding their dollar votes. This second essential aspect of legitimacy is the thrust of the crisis of corporate "social responsibility" in which American industry, and particularly marketing management, has been embroiled in the decades of the 1960's and 1970's. Firms are not simply expected, but often mandated to conduct their affairs in a manner which is responsive to the priorities and needs of society-at-large. In this sense, legitimacy must be conferred and confirmed by suppliers, regulatory agencies, consumer advocates, investigative bodies, stockholders, taxpayers, as well as by the conventional conferees of enterprise legitimacy, consumers themselves.

Marketing management: A balancing act

Surviving this challenge to the legitimacy of business enterprise requires that the firm add a *societal* dimension to the traditional profit and efficiency measures of success in the marketplace. The process of marketing management is essentially a balancing act, and requires the most refined sensitivity to the possible conflicts between short- and long-term enterprise objectives, individual consumer needs and societal imperatives, and short- and long-term social priorities.

If firms do not *themselves* synchronize their output and methods of operation to the legitimate demands which emanate within relevant sectors of the environment, they run a severe risk of being absorbed under the aegis of the political or governmental sectors, of finding their legitimacy restricted or withdrawn. The very thought of governmental intervention in business operations is antithetical to the American conceptualization of "free enterprise" or the "commonwealth of the market." [87, p. 14] On the other hand, many firms have been found guilty of activities antithetical to the well-being of the intricate and delicately balanced social system in which they operate. It is increasingly clear that American business has historically defined the arena in which legitimacy is conferred too narrowly. The marketplace is but one of many environmental arenas from which legitimacy must be sought and won if the firm is to survive or succeed in the attainment of its goals.

Firms market themselves

Anticipation Adaptation

In this chapter we will elaborate on the nature of the environment within which the marketing process unfolds, and then examine the role of marketing in that environment. We will present an overview of the manner in which interpretations of marketing functions have shaped as well as responded to shifts in business priorities. Since World War II marketing has been viewed essentially as a process of adaptation to the wants of consumers, a focus which obscures other environmental interactions and pressures which impact upon the firm's operations. We will present a number of conventional definitions of the marketing process, some more insightful than others. We will then present in elaborate detail an alternative conceptualization of the role and process of marketing based on the systems concepts presented in the introductory chapter. Finally, we will argue that in order to overcome the myopia which has historically plagued American business, firms must recognize that the structure of consumer demand has evolved along with the evolution of the American social system. It is no longer sufficient that firms view their products in a merely functional sense. The firm's output includes not only any physical products it may manufacture and market. *The firm markets itself*, a notion which has been painfully long in surfacing. Consumers now demand the satisfaction of wants and needs which are an integral component of lifestyle, self-concept, self-actualization. Firms must respond by ascending a hierarchy of self-defined business purpose which parallels the ascent of the American consumer from biogenic needs to psychogenic needs as a result of affluence. In short, the nature of the environment for marketing has changed radically in the last century, and business has been slow in responding. What is required is a redefinition of the marketing process in terms of *environmental responsiveness* – anticipation and adaptation.

THE ENVIRONMENT FOR MARKETING

Social system

Viewing the firm as a system requires that we avoid the tendency to perceive the firm as a discrete entity – albeit a dynamic one – which can be lifted out of its environment and dissected into its component parts. Firms function in an elaborate and constantly changing social system which is itself comprised of multitudinous subsystems. The business firm is but one of many systems which are interwoven in the fabric of society. This intricate array of social organizations, institutions, norms and sanctions constitutes the environment for marketing.

Multiple impacts

The widely divergent interactive systems which comprise the firm's environment impact upon the firm in equally diversified ways. For example, suppliers of physical, financial, and energy resources constantly test the ingenuity of marketing management to sustain flows of critical inputs into the firm's operation, thus determining in large measure the success of legitimacy-seeking efforts. The technological base on which the social system's (and the firm's) scientific and material progress hinges is in a state of constant, sometimes revolutionary flux and must be monitored on an almost daily basis. Thus the firm can capitalize upon, or at least accommodate technological breakthroughs and innovations which may *expose* or *foreclose* market opportunities. The uncertain state of health of the economy is a highly unpredictable force in the firm's environment which must be anticipated in outlining enterprise objectives and focusing marketing operations. As events of the mid-1970's have dramatically demonstrated, the establishment of enterprise legitimacy through the cultivation of loyalty relationships with consumers may be radically affected by the redistribution of income resulting from inflation, recession, or fiscal and monetary policies of the government. These and innumerable other convolutions of the firm's environment form a highly intricate backdrop against which the firm's legitimacy-seeking efforts are carried out. It is the role of marketing management to decipher some pattern in the chaos of the firm's environment in order to provide a foundation for the design of marketing programs to establish the lasting legitimacy of the firm.

Deciphering patterns

Strategies of adaptation

Formative

Adaptive

Evidence suggests that firms are growing increasingly aware of the *formative* and *adaptive* manner in which the firm interacts with its environment. The contemporary business literature, for example, reflects the recognition that the viability of an enterprise over time hinges upon its ability to not simply adapt to, but also anticipate an ever-changing *kaleidoscope* of environmental forces. The extent to which systems thinking has pervaded the world of the marketing practitioner, however, is open to question as we have noted.

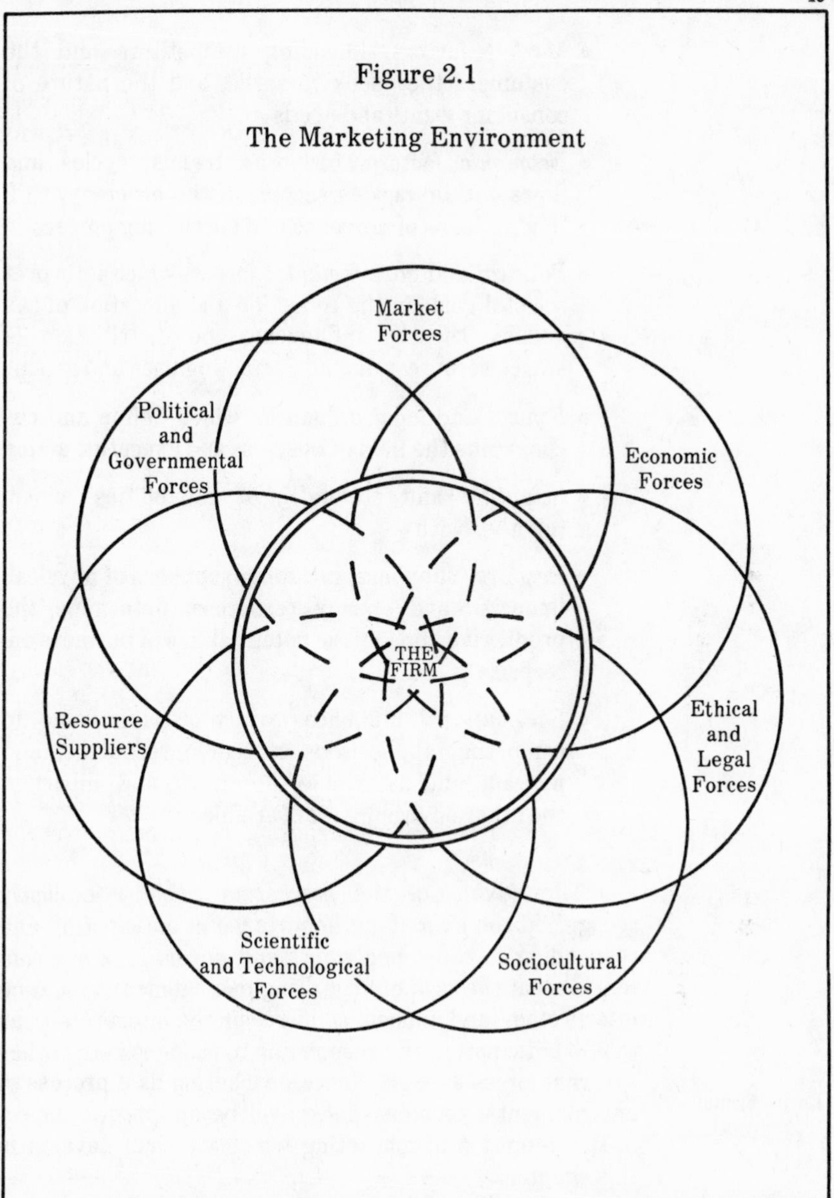

Figure 2.1

The Marketing Environment

While the array of environmental forces which impact upon the firm's operations may be conceptualized in a number of meaningful ways, among the major external spheres of influence which may confirm or deny the legitimacy of the firm are (see Figure 2.1):

- *Market* factors, including competitors and the customers they seek to serve, and the nature of consumer wants and needs
- *Economic* factors, including trends, cycles and flows within various sectors of the economy, shifting patterns of affluence and purchasing power
- *Political* and *governmental* forces, which interpret societal goals in the collection and allocation of tax dollars, thereby influencing the distribution of scarce resources among competing uses and groups
- *Ethical* and *legal* influences which define and circumscribe the field of business and executive action
- *Scientific* and *technological* capabilities which, together with
- *Resource* suppliers, including suppliers of physical, financial, and energy resources, determine the productive and logistic potentialities of business enterprise
- *Sociocultural* influences which ascribe value to competing applications of scarce resources, and pervade and determine the nature and impact of the other environmental variables

The advent of the *marketing concept* explicitly recognized the overriding importance of anticipating and responding to consumer wants and needs. It is our contention that the task of marketing management should be interpreted (and indeed *is* increasingly interpreted) as that of anticipating and responding to changes in the other external forces as well. Hence, marketing as a process of environmental responsiveness will be an integral aspect of the definition of marketing which we shall develop in this chapter.

Environmental responsiveness

Not only are the various environmental influences inseparable from the firm, they are also inseparable from each other. The fact that the firm and its environment are interactive, interdependent and inseparable implies that the firm and its environmental context qualify as a true *ecological system*, or *ecosystem*. Ecology is the study of the mutual relations among organisms and their environments, relations which exist in very delicate balance.

Ecosystem

[49, p. 54] As the environment or ecosystem surrounding the firm changes, the firm must adapt or respond in creative, farsighted ways lest its survival be threatened. It's that simple. Firms acquire *learned* patterns of response, as do people, to certain recurrent patterns and pressures in the environment. It is difficult to *unlearn* responses which are invalidated by altered conditions in the environment. Firms, like people, tend toward an inherent conservatism in that they *react* to change rather than *anticipate* change before it occurs. Moreover, organizational structure imposes additional inflexibility on the adaptive capabilities of the firm which reinforces their reactive nature.

React versus Anticipate

To say that environmental change is occurring at an accelerating rate is a gross understatement. Predicting change with accuracy is almost an impossibility, but remains among marketing management's highest priority responsibilities. With the current trend toward multinational business, hosts of American firms have discovered that they must now deal with a vastly expanded, intricate, and largely unknown environment. This trend has greatly compounded the problems and ability of marketing managers in making rational and farsighted decisions. Who could have predicted only a few years ago, for example, the way in which economic, political, legal, physical, technological and cultural factors would converge to create the worldwide fuel crisis of the 1970's? Who would have forecast active trade with the Soviet Union and Communist China? The systems comprising the firm's environment interact in ways which are readily apparent, and in ways too subtle and complex for even the astute marketer or trained social scientist to comprehend. The ability to predict change is certainly a plus for the firm for it provides a foundation for reorganizing outputs and methods of operation within the firm. But the ability to *control* environmental elements does not necessarily follow from the ability to predict.

THE ROLE OF MARKETING IN SOCIETY

Firms – and marketing – do not operate in a vacuum. Firms interact with and are interdependent with the various systems which comprise their environment.

The legitimacy, relative power position, and indeed the very survival of the firm depend on the degree to which managerial strategies provide for adjustment to the ever-changing demands imposed on the firm by society, the economy, and the physical environment.

Recurrent needs

Any society is confronted by certain recurring needs and wants, be they biological or psychological, that must be fulfilled. At a minimum, the members of a society require a dependable supply of food, clothing, and shelter. When these basic needs are fulfilled, desires for security, love, group membership, and intellectual stimulation are activated. Material goods fulfill both the biological needs and many of the psychological motives, since "products" or "things" possess both *utilitarian* or functional attributes and *social-symbolic* ones.

Product attributes
- **Utilitarian**
- **Social-symbolic**

Social institutions

Social institutions arise in any culture in response to the articulation or manifestation of a society's recurrent needs and wants. While social institutions differ as to form and function, all social institutions mirror the fundamental value structure of the culture.

Value structure

Like all social institutions, the economic system mirrors the underlying value structure of society. In American society immense value has historically been placed on the primacy of individual rights and needs. One of our founding principles was that every individual in American society has a right to have his unique wants and needs fulfilled, insofar as this is possible under the constraints imposed by limited resource capabilities and the demands of society-at-large. Hence the economic system which has emerged in this country is a competitive *market mechanism*, or what some analysts have termed "*the commonwealth of the market*":

Market mechanism

> The commonwealth of the market, although it has elements of intrinsic conflict and power seeking, has its roots in a free society. The moment individuals are free to engage in those activities they wish, the creative spirit of men will manifest itself. Some will be more creative than others or creative in different ways. In the economic sector, the creativity of individuals and firms results in a division of labor in which necessarily we would have more than we need of some things and not enough of others. Hence, so that each may participate in the output of the other,

> exchange is essential; this characterizes the commonwealth of the market. And as free individuals will have differing values, the exchange must be a bargaining process, in which values are equated. Each will bargain in such a way as to enhance the outcome in his own favor. [87, p. 14]

Capitalism: Political and economic systems independent

A guiding principle of the American culture is that the political system and the economic system should operate independently. The market mechanism should control the allocation of resources, and government merely provide the rules by which the game of competition is played, *at least in theory*. At the opposite end of the ideological spectrum are the socialist countries, in which the political and economic systems converge. In socialist systems, the economic institution is *synonymous* with the political/governmental institution. The power to allocate resources and determine economic priorities resides in the government bureaucracy or central planning authority. Socialist systems of economic and political organization also mirror the value structure of society, or at least the value structure of those in a position to enact political and economic policy. In such systems the welfare of society-at-large prevails over the needs and rights of the individual. If necessary the individual is subordinated to the goals of society. Both capitalistic and socialistic systems of economic organization, however, share a common purpose: to achieve an efficient allocation of society's scarce material resources among the unlimited wants and needs of the consumers who comprise society, in conformance with the value structure of the culture.

Socialism: Political and economic systems converge

Resource allocation

Individual versus societal needs

The relative priority associated with individual, as opposed to societal needs has been a major differentiating feature of socialist and capitalist systems historically. However, the differences have been obscured in recent decades. Many of the socialist countries, notably the Soviet Union, have permitted a limited market system to evolve for certain types of products to provide a mechanism for responding to individual consumption priorities and preferences. Public utilities, agricultural subsidies, oil depletion allowances and wage and price controls are all examples of sectors of the American economy in which private enterprise and public policy have converged under the alleged purpose of protecting the interests of society-at-large from the abuses of individual consumption interests. The implications of these trends are that capitalist and socialist systems of social organization have moved toward greater convergence in practice if not in theory.

Market mechanism
- **Roles**
- **Functions**

The responsibility of the economic system in allocating resources to diverse groups of consumers is interpreted and facilitated by a set of *roles* or *functions* which we have previously termed the market mechanism. *Marketing is the process of decision making which performs the resource allocation function.* Hence, *marketing decisions made at the micro or firm level collectively determine how the economic system performs at the macro or societal level, and vice versa.*

Micro decisions
↓
Macro performance

Firm
↕
Environment

We have emphasized that the firm cannot properly be viewed as distinct from its environment. The dependency relationship works both ways. Marketing managers and indeed all managers in business organizations make decisions in an effort to acquire a competitive edge over other firms engaged in similar enterprise. In the process of jockeying for competitive advantage and simultaneously confirming the legitimacy of the firm, marketing management fulfills the roles delineated and required by the economic system, and ultimately facilitates the allocation of goods and services throughout the various strata of society.

Facilitate
versus
Impede

Since decisions at the *micro* level collectively register major ramifications for the efficient functioning of the economic system at the *macro* level, marketing management's prevailing conceptualizations and interpretations of its role and responsibilities within the economic system determine the extent to which society derives satisfaction and welfare from the distribution of resources. The manner in which the role-players perceive their roles determines the degree to which their roles *facilitate* rather than *impede* the efficacy of the economic system in allocating resources among competing applications. Currently marketing managers appear to perceive their role as predominantly that of identifying and then satisfying consumer wants and needs. Hence the measure of the success or legitimacy of the market mechanism or the firm is the spectrum of consumer wants or needs which it satisfies.

It appears intuitively obvious that this role definition is far more appropriate than the ones which preceded it, since firms survive only so long as they can cultivate consumers for their products. Strangely, however, firms have not always conceived of their role as one of identifying and satisfying consumer wants and needs. The philosophical and tactical evolution of American enterprise has been a long and sometimes painful one. Moreover, and perhaps most importantly, we will argue throughout this text that marketing management has historically defined its role and responsibilities too narrowly, even in the dawning era of consumer activism — *consumerism.* Consumers constitute but one of many arenas in the firm's environment from which legitimacy must be sought and won if the firm is to survive.

BUSINESS PURPOSE AND MANAGERIAL RESPONSIBILITY: AN HISTORICAL PERSPECTIVE

Marketing and business purpose

Interpretations of marketing functions and of the responsibilities of marketing management have *shaped* as well as *responded* to shifts in business priorities and purposes. Prior to World War II the role of marketing was primarily defined and delineated in response to prevailing philosophies of business management. In the post-World War II period, however, marketing as a discipline and as a managerial focus or philosophy has had direct inputs into the reorientation of business and managerial responsibility toward the goal of consumer satisfaction. While this shift has certainly led to greater business responsiveness to fluctuations in consumer tastes and preferences, *the myopic focus on consumer satisfaction has tended to obscure other vital arenas in the firm's environment from which legitimacy must be sought and won. Thus marketing in no small measure is responsible for the crisis of legitimacy currently confronted by American business.* The following sections will briefly trace the evolution of interpretations of business and managerial responsibility and explore how interpretations of marketing have displayed a parallel pattern of evolution (see Figure 2.2).

Production Orientation

Interpretations of business purpose and managerial responsibility have been markedly influenced by the rapidly accelerating pace of technological progress since the Industrial Revolution of the late Eighteenth Century.

Figure 2.2

The Evolution of Business Purpose

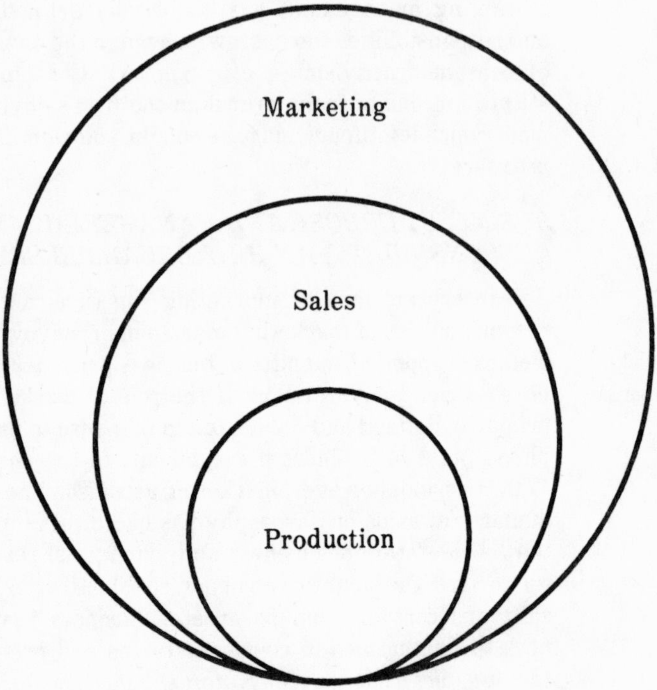

Demand > supply

Division and specialization of labor and factory production methods largely supplanted domestic, hand, or craft manufacturing and promoted ever higher levels of productive efficiency. Steam and motor driven machinery were major technological innovations with far-reaching ramifications for material productivity. But the real impetus to productive efficiency emerged with the conception of a system of organization which determined the optimally efficient placement and interrelationship of men and machines: the *corporation*. The materièl requirements of the War Between the States provided additional impetus to innovation and industrialization, and later the dis-

The corporation

covery of electricity and the invention of the automobile signaled the dawning of the era of high technocracy.

Technology

By a quirk of historical serendipity, these and other major innovations were translated into an accelerating rate of technological progress by men gifted both with great vision and extraordinary pragmatism, like Andrew Carnegie and Henry Ford. The combination of these two factors led to what has been called the Watershed Era of the late Nineteenth Century. Encouraged by advancements in productive efficiency, and with consumer demand and discretionary income growing exponentially, these and other financial and business leaders were instrumental in gearing the country for an explosion in productive activity. In the *era of scientific management* which heralded the Twentieth Century, the goal of business and indeed of society-at-large was to produce more and more for less and less. Managerial responsibility was defined in terms of *productive efficiency*. In a sense this focus on productive efficiency was a form of environmental responsiveness, since consumers concurred with the goal of business. It can be argued that the innovations and innovators which emerged in this era were the major reason the United States was propelled into the Twentieth Century in a position of unprecedented technological and economic strength.

Productive efficiency

Sales Orientation

Intensified competition

By the late 1920's and early 1930's widespread productive efficiency signaled intensified and even predatory competition in many industries and initiated a shift of managerial concern to the problems of capturing customers from competitors and efficiently moving output from points of production to points of consumption. Supply caught, and even outstripped demand in many industries. Manufacturers could no longer sell everything they produced. Distribution channel innovations like the supermarket method of merchandising gained a quick competitive foothold and consumers were confronted with concentrated, comprehensive arrays of goods offered via self-service, a distinctive break with tradition. Problems of *efficient distribution* and *effective salesmanship* became managerial priorities as many companies adopted a sales orientation, focusing upon those factors which influence, impede or trigger the exchange process. For the most

Supply ≥ Demand

Distributive efficiency

Effective salesmanship

part, however, selling and distribution activities continued to take a back seat to production. The consumer remained a shadowy figure in the background, his needs and characteristics still a nebulous unknown in the eyes of most businessmen.

Marketing Orientation

Following the experience of the Great Depression and World War II, demand for consumer goods was at record high levels. The horizons of the American consumer were tremendously enlarged by the general affluence following the war and the internationalizing of those who had served overseas. The purchasing power and expectations of the lower income strata of American society were greatly elevated in the economic upswing of the late 1940's and early 1950's. The result was the creation of mass markets for consumer items previously confined to the affluent few. Items formerly considered luxuries were now considered necessities. The introduction of radios and televisions into millions of homes radically altered the ability of producers to communicate with customers.

Mass markets

The dawning of mass marketing paralleled the growth of mass media and the rapid expansion of channels of distribution to accommodate the phenomenal demand for goods that possessed not only physical, functional and sociopsychological utility, but also time and place utility. Competition took on the added dimensions of promotional and locational or *nonprice* competition. In the 1950's, with accelerating competition, industrial expansion and diversification, distribution and selling evolved into *marketing* — the synchronizing of all organizational operations toward serving consumer wants and needs. [60] The focus of all organizational activity shifted to the consumer. Peter Drucker expressed it most succinctly: "The purpose of the company is to *create a customer*." [22, p. 37] Marketing activities provided the integrative and coordinative focus for the firm, pinpointing the firm's consumer orientation and detailing its process of adjustment to the demands of increasingly vocal consumers. The sense of business purpose emerging from this frame of reference was termed the *marketing management philosophy*, the *marketing orientation*, the *consumerist orientation*, and most popularly — the *marketing concept*.

Supply>demand

Create a customer

Efficiency in serving consumers

Figure 2.3

The Evolution of Concepts of Marketing

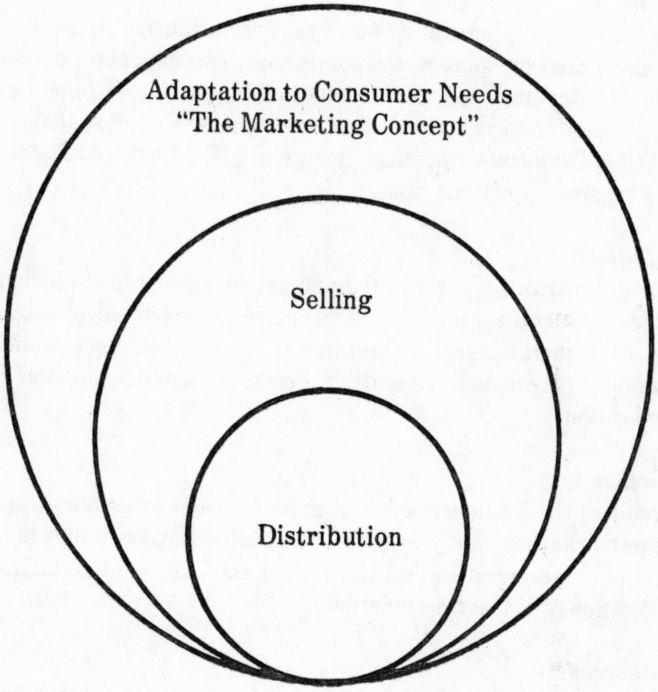

Disposing of manufactured output was proving increasingly difficult; ignoring consumers, impossible.

THE EVOLUTION OF CONCEPTS OF MARKETING

Interpretations of marketing functions and the responsibilities of marketing management have closely paralleled definitions of business purpose in the post-Industrial Revolution era (see Figure 2.3). Moreover, *analytical perspectives* of marketing have reflected interpretations of marketing functions and responsibilities

Figure 2.4

Analytical Perspectives of the Marketing Process

Commodity
Categorized products and services into arbitrary classification systems based on sources and conditions of supply, the extent and nature of demand, common channel alignments, and functions of agencies and institutions relevant in the marketing of specific commodities. Oriented toward the design of efficient distribution systems for specific commodities.

Institutional
Focused on the operation of independent institutions—including wholesalers and retailers—and agencies in a channel of distribution, their significance in the marketing of specific commodities, functions performed, operating costs, economic position and competition.

Functional
Examined the nature, need, and importance of functions essential in the marketing of any product. Facilitated measurement of marketing effectiveness and efficiency and elimination or reduction of duplication of marketing functions.

Managerial
Reformulated marketing functions in conformance with marketing management's strategic task of identifying and serving distinguishable segments of consumer demand. Focused on managerial decision making, and operationalization of the *marketing concept.*

Systems
Interprets marketing management as a process of reconciling controllable variables with the actions of consumers and competitors in the marketplace, in an environment conditioned by an array of interactive forces, to effect enterprise legitimacy and power over time. Views marketing as a functional element of the firm, the firm as a functional element of the economic system, and the economic system as a functional element of the social system and the culture.

(see Figure 2.4). The role of marketing in defining, expressing, and attaining business goals has been slowly expanded, until today marketing provides the organizing and integrative focus for all functional areas within many firms.

Marketing as Distribution

When problems of productive efficiency were the preoccupation of management, marketing as conventionally defined was of little significance in the operations of the firm. Throughout the Nineteenth Century and up to World War II, demand for most manufactured goods greatly outstripped supply. Thus marketing responsibility was largely confined to problems of physical distribution through the early decades of the Twentieth Century, and later to locating markets for manufactured output. This emphasis on physical distribution and locating markets is clearly reflected in the proliferation of substantial channel innovations which characterized the early decades of the Twentieth Century. Chain stores, supermarkets, and large department stores emerged to serve a national market for consumer goods which had developed as a result of the convergence of the many factors outlined above. Level of affluence, and hence disposable and discretionary income, was rising steadily (with the exception of the worst years of the Great Depression), as were the material expectations of consumers even in the relatively disadvantaged socioeconomic strata. The automobile was beginning to manifest profound and irreversible effects on the habits and mobility of the American consumer. As a consequence, consumers demanded an ever wider array of consumer goods, convenient both in place of purchase and in use. As a result, channels of distribution were geared to provide increasingly varied assortments of goods in massive quantities, assembled in locations convenient to consumers. *Distributive efficiency* was the overriding focus and responsibility of marketing management, although marketing itself remained subordinate to production in the priority structure of the firm. Producers perceived demand and raw materials to be virtually limitless. The only constraint appeared to be the firm's ability to meet the demands of distributive efficiency — a *logistics* problem.

Physical distribution

Identifying markets

Distributive efficiency

Marketing as Selling

During the early decades of the Twentieth Century, the American economic system had been transformed from an economy of relative scarcity to an economy of potential abundance. *Consumption* replaced production and distribution as the key constraint on economic growth. As early as the 1930's, firms in some industries encountered the blunt realization that competition had intensified to threatening levels and demand was not infinite. In spite of vastly improved channels of mass distribution, the problems of reaching the market had escalated in complexity. Consumers were more articulate and ardent in expressing their wants and needs, and firms began to organize marketing intelligence systems to determine more precisely the nature and extent of demand. In fact, the very definition of demand had undergone radical redefinition. Demand was no longer interpreted as an inverse function of price, the traditional economist's view. *Demand* was instead viewed more appropriately as *a social and economic phenomenon*. Retailers paid more attention to store atmosphere, made more rational location decisions, and engaged in sales promotion and advertising on a local and occasionally a national scale. Firms which produced and/or marketed consumer goods utilized aggressive salesmanship and advertising, made possible by the widespread ownership of radios, television, and automobiles. *Market segmentation* became an operational as well as a theoretical concept and *marketing research* came into its own as a tool for deciphering the nature and composition of consumer demand. The consumer was viewed primarily as an outlet for disposing of the firm's products. His needs were relevant insofar as they facilitated the movement of output and contributed to sales volume.

Consumption

Demand
- **Social**
- **Economic**

Market segmentation

Marketing research

Marketing as Adaptation to Consumer Needs

The explosion in material productivity following World War II prompted a reorientation of business priorities and brought marketing – or selling – to the forefront of business activity. In many industries productive capacity had exceeded the market's capacity for consumption. It was no longer sufficient for the firm to simply locate markets for its products, since frequently such markets were either saturated with competition or nonexistent. Buying power was at an all time high, but spiraling technology and intense competition had resulted in such high levels of production that *demand* had supplanted *supply* as the key constraint on economic and enterprise growth. Firms slowly came to the realization that they must now design products to meet specific consumer needs. The increasing activity of consumers, both as individuals and as interest groups, reinforced the need for a redefinition of the role of marketing within the firm. Consumers, government agencies, and responsible businessmen were unanimous in their conviction that American business must adopt a more responsive stance relative to the needs and wants of consumers. Thus the *consumer*, rather than the demands of productive efficiency, became the focus or orientation of business operations and the principal basis of legitimacy for the firm.

Demand

Consumer orientation

As the consumer emerged as the focus of business operations, previously separate exchange, distribution, and facilitating functions were synthesized under a single center of responsibility, marketing. The task of identifying and serving distinguishable segments of consumer demand became the objective and overriding responsibility of marketing management. Marketing management itself figured more and more significantly in defining corporate priorities and allocations of corporate resources. Profit, growth, return on invested capital, and market share were reinterpreted as indices of the level of consumer satisfaction marketing management attained through the proper performance of the marketing functions of identifying and serving consumer wants and needs. The process of establishing legitimacy became the province of marketing management, and the consumer became the focus of legitimizing efforts.

The notion that the legitimacy of the firm was contingent upon achieving some measure of consumer satisfaction, and that therefore all functional areas within the firm should be oriented, integrated and coordinated toward serving consumer wants and needs, was termed the *marketing concept*. In simple terms, the marketing concept merely meant that firms exist only so long as they are able to attract customers for the firm's products. Maximizing consumer satisfaction should therefore be the

Marketing concept

central priority of any firm, for by maximizing consumer satisfaction the firm simultaneously confirms its legitimacy. Implementation of the marketing concept requires that the goals of the firm and the philosophy of marketing management converge, an evolution which has been very painful for many firms in American business.

CONTEMPORARY PROCESS DEFINITIONS OF MARKETING

Interpretations of marketing roles and responsibilities as formulated both by analysts and practitioners, naturally reflect the prevailing philosophy of marketing. Interpretations of the role and function of marketing have multiplied and broadened considerably in the past few decades.

> Certainly there is no lack of divergent viewpoints concerning the nature of marketing. It has been described by one person or another as a business activity; as a group of related business activities; as a trade phenomenon; as a frame of mind; as a coordinative, integrative function in policy making; as a sense of business purpose; as an economic process; as a structure of institutions; as the process of exchanging or transferring ownership of products; as a process of concentration, equalization, and dispersion; as the creation of time, place, and possession utilities; as a process of demand and supply adjustment; and as many other things. [60, p. 43]

Representative "managerial" or "functional" definitions of marketing still in widespread use include the one formulated by the marketing staff of The Ohio State University:

> Marketing is the process in a society by which the demand structure for economic goods and services is *anticipated*, or *enlarged* and *satisfied* through the *conception*, *promotion*, *exchange*, and physical *distribution* of such goods and services. [6, p. 4]

The authors of this definition clearly intended marketing to be viewed as "a subject of much broader scope than the compilation of functions or managed activities commonly identified as marketing responsibilities in individual companies." [60, p. 43] The definition is commendable in that it explicitly recognizes the *formative* and *adaptive* nature of the marketing process. Firms and marketing strategies must adapt to the shifting pattern of consumer tastes and preferences in the marketplace. The formative influence is the result of "the aggregate impact of product offerings, marketing communications and institutions" as they "contribute to the formulation of attitudes or values" that affect consumption patterns and consumer preferences. [60, p. 44]

According to E. Jerome McCarthy, the author of the most widely adopted principles of marketing textbook:

> Marketing is the performance of business activities which direct the flow of goods and services from producer to consumer or user in order to satisfy customers and accomplish the company's objectives. [63, p. 19]

Functional focus

In McCarthy's definition, as in the Ohio State conceptualization, note that the emphasis is clearly upon the performance of those *functions* required to *identify* and *serve* unsatisfied consumer wants and needs: exchange, distribution, and the various facilitating functions. With the adoption of a "functional" or "managerial" perspective in marketing, the earlier goal of distributive efficiency was reinterpreted as *marketing efficiency*, or the gearing of all organizational operations to shifting patterns of consumer wants and needs — the now familiar marketing concept.

The emphasis on consumer satisfaction as the *raison d'être* of the firm represents a major advancement in marketing thought. The drawback of the functional, managerial, or consumerist conceptualizations of the nature of marketing is their failure to recognize that *enterprise legitimacy is contingent upon more than consumer satisfaction*. While the consumer remains the central focus of marketing management, the process of maximizing consumer satisfaction is directly or indirectly influenced by a host of additional external pressures. The potential impact of such influences must be anticipated in planning and organizing to fulfill consumer expectations concerning both products *and* producers. As we noted earlier, among the external spheres of influence which may confirm or deny the legitimacy of the firm are:

Environmental influences

- Market factors
- Economic factors

- Political and governmental forces
- Ethical and legal influences
- Scientific and technological capabilities
- Resource suppliers
- Sociocultural influences

These factors compose the environment or the larger system within which marketing operates. Clearly this array of environmental forces encompasses more than the wants and needs of consumers.

A SYSTEMS DEFINITION OF MARKETING

The growing awareness that enterprise legitimacy hinges not only on satisfying at least some consumers some of the time, but also upon anticipating and responding to the possible impact of numerous other environmental forces, has prompted development of a "systems" view of the firm. The firm, like any organism, is a system interacting with other systems within a larger social system, its environment. As such, the firm is influenced by, and in turn influences other systems in its environment. Every action the firm takes has direct and indirect impacts on other systems in its environment, even systems relatively remote from the firm. Customers won by one firm, for example, are at the expense of the firm's competitors. An increase in prices charged by manufacturers to wholesalers and retailers is typically reflected in higher prices to ultimate consumers. Production of products to meet consumer wants and needs is accompanied by production of wastes which pollute the environment. Hiring the so-called "hard core" unemployed helps remove a possible cause of social upheaval, by eliminating a major source of frustration and resentment. Every enterprise action brings about a corresponding reaction in some sector of the firm's environment. Thus the firm must calculate the multiple impacts of its outputs and operations on all aspects of the environment, and become an active, positive agent, rather than merely reacting to waves of influence as they occur.

Interdependent systems

Action ↕ Reaction

Marketing, then, is a formative, anticipatory, and adaptive process in which the enterprise interacts with the environment in ways which are mutually beneficial,

Figure 2.5

A Systems View of Marketing

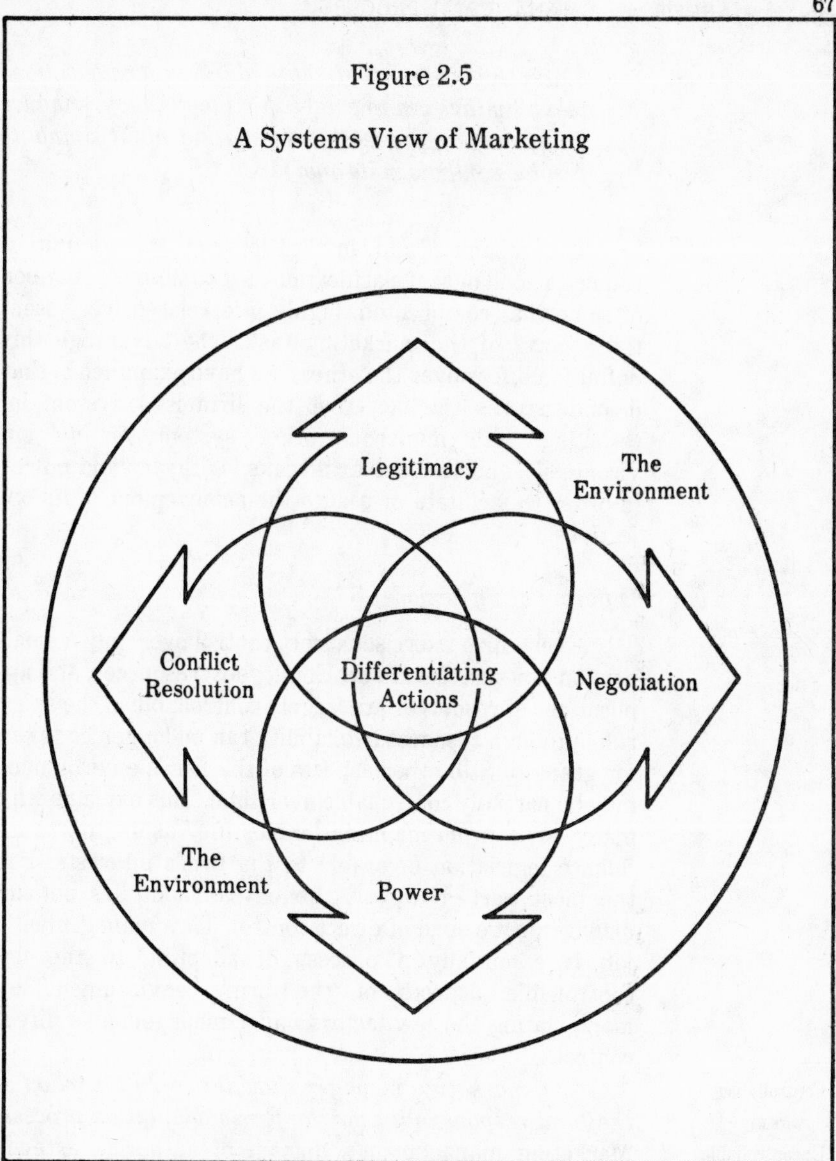

and which result in positions of legitimacy and market power over time. The notions of legitimacy, power, and environmental responsiveness are central to the definition of marketing we will use throughout this text (see Figure 2.5):

*Marketing consists of those differentiating actions taken by the firm to establish its legitimacy, enhance its power, improve its negotiating ability, and to resolve conflicts in its own favor.**

The meaning and implications of this definition require a good deal of clarification as it combines a number of somewhat complicated, highly interrelated, yet essential aspects of the marketing task. The advantage this definition offers over the others we have examined is that it underscores the fact that the firm is a system interacting with numerous other systems in its environment, and that the firm seeks legitimacy and power in order to facilitate or assure the achievement of its objectives.

Differentiating Actions

Every firm exercises direct control over only a small portion of its environment. Employees, resources, and applications of resources are largely controllable in the short run, although resource availability can no longer be taken for granted. Still other aspects of the firm's environment may be partially controllable over time. This explains why many large firms maintain lobbies in Washington to influence legislation favorable to the firm's interests. For the most part, however, the environment lies outside management's span of direct control. Thus management's job is essentially a process of adapting to the uncontrollable aspects of the firm's environment by manipulating the few factors under management's direct control.

Controllables versus Uncontrollables

The marketing manager shoulders only a portion of the total responsibility for the firm's adaptation process. Marketing management's domain of authority extends primarily to the marketing controllables:

---

*This definition of marketing is adapted from one suggested by Dr. Donald A. Taylor, Professor of Marketing, Michigan State University. Dr. Taylor's concepts were based upon ideas earlier formulated by Wroe Alderson, Frederick A. von Hayek, and Joseph A. Schumpeter.

Differentiating actions
• Product
• Price
• Distribution
• Communication

- which *products* will be offered for sale
- at what *prices*
- through which *distribution* systems
- communicated through which *communication* vehicles

It is principally through positive differentiation in product, pricing, distribution, and communication strategies that the firm seeks to establish differential advantages over competitors by cultivating and maintaining favorable relationships with consumers and with other relevant sectors in the firm's environment. This is what we mean by *differentiating actions* of the firm: *competition for differential advantage*. Favorable consumer relationships may involve consumers actually purchasing the firm's products or simply viewing the firm or its products in a more favorable light. It is through such actions as well that the firm seeks to establish legitimacy in competitive, regulatory, investigatory, governmental and other arenas. Thus marketing management performs an essential legitimizing function for the firm. Yet coordination with other functional areas within the firm is equally vital in order to identify areas where legitimacy is essential or beneficial and to formulate strategies for cultivating positions of legitimacy in the firm's environment.

Legitimacy

Legitimacy = acceptance

In order to *establish its legitimacy* any organization must gain *acceptance for its output and methods of operation* from relevant systems in its environment. For the business firm, legitimacy derives principally from consumer acceptance of the firm's output, whether goods or services, but also from the acceptance of the firm's methods of operation by suppliers, regulatory agencies, stockholders, investigating boards, taxpayers, and a great many others in the firm's environment. The requirements for legitimacy imposed by any of these external systems will shift over time. One obvious shift to which the firm must adjust will be consumer expectations for product performance. Today's products provide standards by which tomorrow's products are evaluated, and tomorrow's products are expected to provide higher levels of satisfaction across a broader spectrum of evaluative criteria, for example, ecological considerations. By implication, firms must be continually attentive to shifting standards of legitimacy in all of these arenas. This responsibility falls largely to marketing management.

Power

Power = influence = lasting legitimacy

By *power* we mean the *ability* of the firm *to influence other systems in the firm's environment to facilitate the establishment of positions of legitimacy.* Power = *lasting* legitimacy. Power may derive from any of a number of sources. One vital source of power is consumer loyalty. Profit, growth, share of market, and return on invested capital all index the extent to which the firm is able to offer products which in some measure satisfy consumer wants and needs in the short run. But to attain survival, not to mention profit, growth, a stable or increasing market share, or a desirable rate of return on invested capital, the firm must continue to offer its present or prospective customers greater satisfaction than can competing firms. Thus, consumer confirmation of the legitimacy of the output or methods of operation of the firm is never assured and must be continually cultivated. Hence, power is a function of the ability of the firm to find and foster *loyal repeat customers*.

Another possible basis of power derives from the ability of the firm to influence legislation or judicial interpretation in its favor. Many firms maintain lobbies in state and federal legislatures and governmental agencies to influence laws or legal interpretations which favor the firm.

A third basis of power might derive from convincing the firm's distributors that their interests, as well as those of the supplying firm, are best served by coordinating operations and avoiding unnecessary duplication of effort to assure higher levels of consumer satisfaction than can competing marketing systems.

Negotiating Ability

Negotiating ability
- **Anticipating**
- **Accommodating**
- **Adjusting**
- **Reconciling**

By *negotiating ability* we mean the capacity of the firm for *anticipating, accommodating, adjusting or reconciling itself to the demands of external sources of influence which may impede or promote the establishment of positions of legitimacy.* Negotiation is inherent in the notion of the firm as a system interacting with other systems in a dynamic environment. The impact of external or countervailing sources of power or influence upon the firm may be felt in innumerable ways, calling for highly varied and innovative responses on the part of marketing management. Competing firms negotiate through their products. In effect, the prospective customer constructs an array of product specifications against which product alternatives are evaluated. That firm whose products best conform to consumer specifications will likely win a customer, at least in the short run. To maintain loyalty relationships with customers over time, and hence augment or maintain legitimacy and power, the firm must continually anticipate and respond to changes in consumer expectations and needs.

Negotiation over price and access

Another example of negotiation is the acquisition of material, manpower, and energy resources, supplies and equipment to support production and marketing activity. Firms negotiate with suppliers for resources and materials to provide continuity to production and marketing effort. In addition, of course, the price paid for resources and other supplies has a direct impact on the profitability of the firm.

Conflict Resolution

System ⟹ conflict

In order to *resolve conflicts* in favor of the firm marketing management must understand the nature of the many sources of conflict which the firm is likely to confront. Conflict is inherent in the notion of the firm as a system serving unlimited needs with scarce resources. One obvious form of conflict arises out of competition among firms seeking to serve the same customers with substantially similar products. Another less obvious source of conflict is that arising out of enterprise actions which may come under legal scrutiny or possible litigation.

Influence

The key to resolving conflict in favor of the firm lies in the power of the firm to exercise influence to establish positions of legitimacy in the firm's environment. Power, whether based on loyalty relationships with consumers, political influence, financial resources, or any other basis, enables the firm to compete successfully with other firms which may seek legitimacy in the same environment.

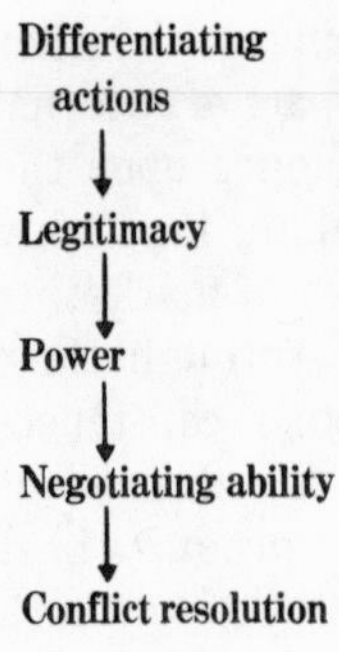

These five central concepts — *differentiating actions, legitimacy, power, negotiating ability,* and ability to *resolve conflicts* in favor of the firm — are highly interdependent. It is through differentiating actions that the firm seeks to establish and maintain positions of legitimacy and power. Power facilitates enterprise negotiation for survival and conflict resolution in favor of the firm. Thus the legitimacy and power of the firm determine its continued ability to attain the common business objectives of profit, growth, stability, share of market, or return on invested capital, and simultaneously maintain a delicate symbiosis with the macroenvironment.

HIERARCHY OF BUSINESS PURPOSE

Social/environmental responsibility ↕ Business goals

At the heart of the issue of business responsibility facing management today is the question of the degree to which social and environmental consciousness or responsibility are consistent with the attainment of business goals. Historically, management has circumvented or ignored the issue, or has interpreted "social responsibility" as being in conflict with the traditional criteria for gauging enterprise performance. Increasingly, however, businesses are being called to account for their actions, either by the government, consumers, or their own management. Because of shifting environmental demands and changing social priorities, and growing pressure from consumers both individually and collectively, indifference to socially responsible behavior increasingly will be reflected in challenges to the legitimacy of the firm. The welfare of consumers and of society can no longer be separated. Consumers *are* society.

Consumers ↕ Society

Exchange myopia

The *exchange myopia,* or the focus on the exchange of dollars for products, which characterizes much of the marketing literature and permits the distinction between the consumer and society is a manifestation of the now dated notion that firms sell physical/functional products only. In the final analysis, *firms market themselves.* Products represent but one dimension of the total market offering the firm makes to prospective customer-citizens. *The product, its functional attributes and performance features, merely provides the communication vehicle through which the total image and impact of the firm are conveyed.* Both the product attributes of concern to the prospect *and* the configuration of enterprise attitudes and actions determine the image of the firm embodied in its

Product = vehicle

Figure 2.6

Maslow's Hierarchy of Needs

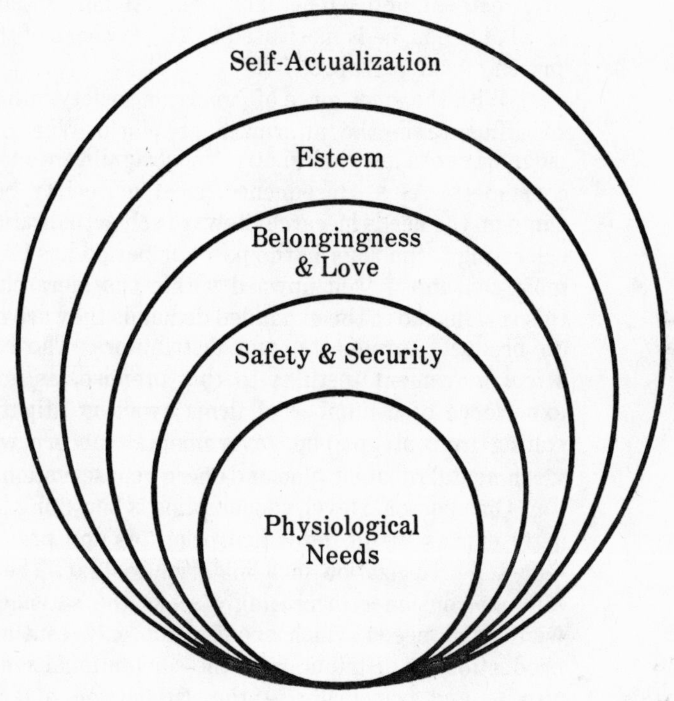

Adapted from Abraham H. Maslow. *Motivation and Personality.* New York: Harper & Row, 1954, pp. 80-92.

Image⟶ Legitimized or rejected

market offering. It is this total image which the consumer-citizen either legitimizes or sanctions through repeat purchasing or rejects.

Consumer expectations have evolved rapidly in the past quarter-century. To aid in understanding the new consumer and how he has evolved, a familiar conceptual framework is highly useful (see Figure 2.6). Abraham H. Maslow has characterized human behavior as intrinsically

Needs
• Biogenic
• Psychogenic

self-serving and *goal directed.* He contends that individuals seek satisfaction of inborn *biogenic* and higher-order *psychogenic* needs which may be arranged in order of primacy. Basic level needs (physiological, safety and security) are *prepotent* and demand fulfillment prior to the satisfaction of higher level needs (belongingness and love, esteem, and self-actualization). As man satiates one level of needs, he is motivated to satisfy those of the next priority level. [61, pp. 80-92]

Hierarchy of prepotency

With the emergence of American society into the era of affluence in the aftermath of World War II, basic biogenic needs lost their motivational significance for most consumers. As a consequence, most of society began a climb up the needs hierarchy toward self-actualization. Accelerating technology in the postwar period has propelled most consumers well upward within the hierarchy, and this is reflected in the expanded demands they are making on products, producers, and distributors. The *consumerism* movement testifies to this premise, as does the experience of a number of firms awaiting litigation resulting from stepped-up governmental concern with environmental rehabilitation and energy conservation.

Expressive

On a personal level, consumption is becoming increasingly expressive of individual priorities and preferences —or self-actualization in a material context. The newly affluent consumer increasingly seeks the satisfaction of wants and needs which require not only consumption, production, or distribution in the conventional sense, but also — and principally — the satisfaction of aesthetic needs of a higher order. [28] Eugene J. Kelley, former editor of the *Journal of Marketing*, puts it this way:

Aesthetic needs

Lifestyle

> People are not as likely to see themselves as consumers in the future, but as something else — perhaps as individuals creating their own style of living by using the services of business. [43, p. 170]
>
> . . . marketers are not selling isolated products which can be viewed as symbols; they are selling, or consumers are buying, a style of life or pieces of a larger symbol. [43, p. 168]

Standards for assessing product value will shift with altered lifestyle requirements and businessmen cannot afford to ignore them. Consumer sensitivity to shifting dimensions of product value ultimately is reflected in sales and profit figures. These new consumers comprise the sociocultural context of the firm. They have not suddenly appeared but have evolved over the last three decades. Business firms, then, have had time to adjust to the demands manifested as a result of the increased importance of higher level needs. The record of their adjustment, however, warns of impending crises for many firms.

Inertia of adjustment

The extent to which the firm maintains open surveillance of changing consumer expectations as related not only to "products," but to the social and environmental citizenship or legitimacy of the enterprise, and makes appropriate adjustments in its total market offering, will be mirrored in its stream of income and its long-term survival. The *integrated hierarchy of business purpose** discussed in the next paragraphs *highlights the fundamental consistency which exists between organizing for enterprise goal attainment and meeting the demands of shifting societal goals and environmental responsibilities.* Enterprise adjustment to changing consumer societal expectations is prerequisite to enterprise goal attainment. Adjustment is facilitated through the adoption of the integrated hierarchy of business purpose.

Priority of purposes & needs

The integrated hierarchy of business purpose reflects the basic premise underlying Maslow's hierarchy of needs (see Figure 2.7). Purposes are arrayed in order of priority, business purposes mirroring the priority structure of consumer needs.

As is the case with individuals, firms typically move up the integrated hierarchy of business purpose, but they move in response to the shifting structure of consumer priorities and goals. An enterprise whose purpose is dominated by survival — to produce something and sell it somehow — will find its products, and thus the firm itself, rejected by consumers whose purchases are motivated by the need for self-actualization. Businesses must adopt a hierarchy of purpose which is responsive to the evolving structure of consumer needs.

---

*W. Thomas Anderson, Jr., Louis K. Sharpe and Robert J. Boewadt, "The Environmental Role for Marketing," pp. 69-72, *MSU Business Topics*, Summer 1972. Used by permission of the publisher, Division of Research, Graduate School of Business Administration, Michigan State University.

Figure 2.7

An Integrated Hierarchy of Business Purpose

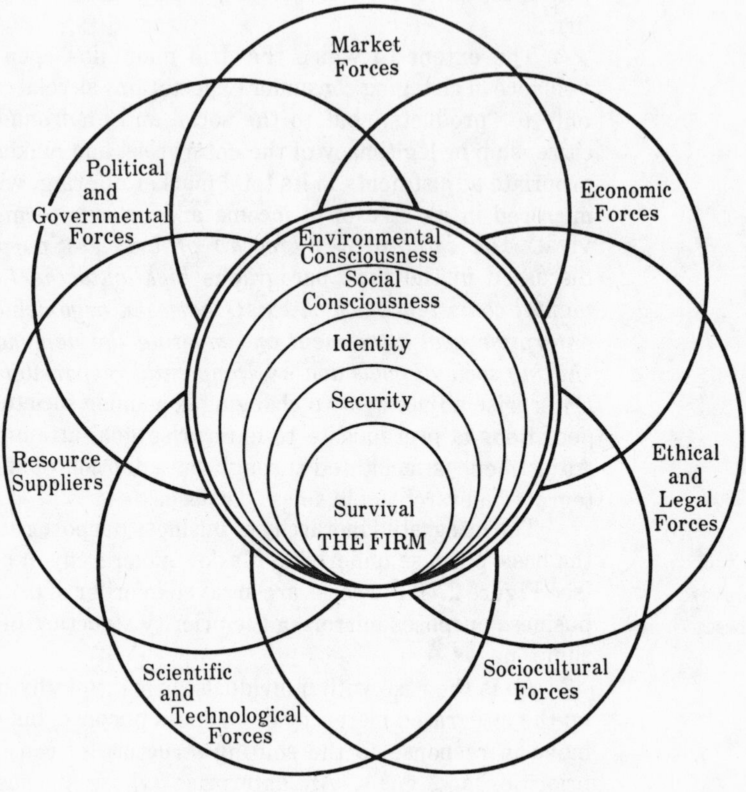

Market Forces

Political and Governmental Forces

Economic Forces

Environmental Consciousness

Social Consciousness

Identity

Security

Resource Suppliers

Ethical and Legal Forces

Survival

THE FIRM

Scientific and Technological Forces

Sociocultural Forces

Survival

Black ink

Paralleling Maslow's hierarchy, the firm's fundamental purpose is concerned with survival. In the short run this may be equated with black ink on the ledger. But more than this, survival in a competitive business environment means doing something right, at least minimally, from the standpoint of satisfying consumer needs. A survival orientation, however, is not tenable over the long run because it ignores the necessity of continually fitting products to the altered requirements of shifting consumer priorities.

Security

Once short-run survival has been attained, security objectives predominate. In most firms this goal is met by forecasting, long-range planning, and programming processes. The firm scans the environment for threatening actions by competitors and attempts to sustain revenue flows sufficient to support required enterprise functions.

Stability → market orientation

Security as a unifying focus for corporate action implies a closer correspondence of product offerings to consumer specifications than survival simply because stabilizing flows of sales revenue necessitates the adoption of a market orientation. However, security does not necessarily lead to growth, increasing profitabiity, or higher levels of return on invested capital. A market focus is shortsighted if it relates to achieving consumer satisfaction through performance features and functional attributes of products solely. Consumer expectations for enterprise performance extend far beyond these.

Identity

Cultivating consumer loyalty

Identity objectives constitute the third hierarchical level. These may be evidenced by the development of consumer brand loyalty and/or competitive recognition of the firm as a distinct market power. Brand loyalty, of course, signifies the successful cultivation of consumer loyalty over time and evidences the firm's standing commitment to the goal of consumer satisfaction. Consumer loyalty gives rise to competitive power, and power facilitates organizational goal attainment. But the achievement of identity does not exempt the firm from the responsible exercise of its power. Consumers expect it and governmental and regulatory agencies demand it. *Identity objectives seem to characterize most major firms today.*

Social Consciousness

The responsible use of market power necessitates the adoption of a social awareness extending beyond the consumer satisfaction embodied in product attributes. Increasingly, firms find themselves thrust into the arena of social consciousness, the fourth purpose level. Social consciousness may evolve from three sources:

Social consciousness
- Intrafirm
- Public attitude
- Governmental-regulatory

- *Intrafirm pressures* – conscious introspective examination by the firm's leadership of the responsibility of the organization in a societal context
- *Public attitude pressures* – society's expectations of business conduct as interpreted and formalized by leaders and shapers of public opinion
- *Governmental-regulatory pressures* – formalized legal prescriptions of ethical business conduct or informal suasion via contractual awards or negative sanctions

Ideally, intrafirm pressures will be the dominant influence at this level. Traditionally, the latter two forms of pressure have been the fundamental precipitator of action within the business community. There currently is evidence that businessmen are engaged in active soul searching within the domain of social responsibility. Hopefully, this effort will bear fruit before their role is legislated for them.

Organizations may work closely with governmental agencies in social, environmental or economic problem areas, encourage their employees to participate in public leadership activities, donate grants-in-aid, or involve themselves in any number of other social enterprises. While greater social involvement represents a giant step forward from the Robber Baron era of the late Nineteenth Century, it is not enough.

Environmental Consciousness

The counterpart of self-actualization for the individual may be termed environmental consciousness on the part of the firm. Environmental consciousness on the part of business is a natural response to society's emergence into the era of high technocracy, where society increasingly is made aware that economic progress has a social cost which is exacted from all of society.

Social costs

At the level of environmental consciousness, the firm's leadership recognizes the potential impact of its decisions or actions on an interdependent global community as well as the impact of forces external to the firm upon enterprise operations. This impact may be economic, cultural, or ecological. It may be tangible or as intangible as the quality of life. The firm must fully accept the responsibility for disruptions it may cause in these arenas, not for altruistic reasons but rather for its own long-term survival motives. It is this type of thinking which is implied by the systems approach in marketing.

When a firm's actions and market offerings reflect attainment of the apex of the hierarchy of business purpose – the level of environmental consciousness – the firm is truly *applying the systems approach* to its operations (see Figure 2.8). Systems thinking implies that marketing management is constantly cognizant that business legitimacy hinges not only on satisfying at least some customers some of the time, but also upon anticipating and responding to the impact of numerous other environmental forces (see Figure 2.9). The firm is totally inseparable from and interdependent with its environment. Fortunately for American society, many firms are reinterpreting their priorities in light of the multiple and multiplying influences which comprise their environment. For firms like these, who are behaving *responsibly* and *responsively* now and are planning for the future, the integrated hierarchy of business purpose represents a comprehensive framework for interpreting the role and responsibilities of the enterprise in its complex interactive setting. This schema also provides a standard for gauging the potential effectiveness of alternative marketing and survival strategies.

Responsible
Responsive

Each successive level within the hierarchy subsumes all subordinate levels. Hence, translated into business practice, it would be impossible to achieve environmental consciousness without simultaneously satisfying the demands of survival, security, identity, and social consciousness. Lasting legitimacy is the barometer of the extent to which the hierarchy successfully has been interpreted in planning and programming enterprise operations. Within this frame of reference the term "profit" loses many of its negative connotations, because when the firm profits, so does society-at-large. The firm that profits at the expense of society faces eventual restriction of profits and withdrawal of legitimacy.

Lasting legitimacy

Figure 2.8

Impeding and Implementing Environmental Consciousness

Boo!

Executives assigned to planning all too often remain sealed off in their departments—consulted occasionally by someone who wants extrapolations of the past rather than troublesome departures from convention.

The result is a dismaying abundance of corporate problems that could have been avoided, and not just in hindsight. For several years, for instance, there have been indications that something of fundamental importance was happening in the oil business. If U.S. automakers had studied the distribution of world petroleum reserves and the course of politics in the Middle East, they might have been better able to anticipate the big price rise. If they had then turned their full resources to designing cars that would run on less gasoline, they would probably be selling more cars today.

The troubles of Reserve Mining Co. provide another case in point. When Reserve's owners, Armco and Republic Steel, chose to fight for the freedom to continue dumping taconite tailings into Lake Superior, they must have been counting, against all probability, on the evaporation of environmentalism. Since 1969, Reserve has earned a reputation for flagrantly opposing the public interest, has spent $6 million in legal battles, and is bound to spend a lot more. It could have filtered the water supplies of affected communities in the first place for an estimated $12 million.

Fig. 2.8 Continued *Yea!*

Du Pont seems to be handling the fluorocarbon issue with dexterity. Fluorocarbons are a class of chemical products that includes the Freons, the principal gases used as aerosol propellants, as well as in refrigeration and air-conditioning systems. Freons are an invention of Du Pont and have become one of its many profitable businesses. The company estimates that the industries directly dependent on fluorocarbon production contribute $8 billion to the economy and employ 200,000 people.

During the past year, several scientists have, on the basis of computer models, suggested that fluorocarbons rising into the upper atmosphere may damage the ozone layer that shields the earth from excessive ultraviolet radiation. The scientists warn that the consequences would probably be disastrous—including increased incidences of skin cancer and substantial biological and climatic changes. Their work is highly speculative at this point, however, as they themselves have acknowledged.

No rational manager would halt production of a major product on mere speculation. Not with the premature and costly elimination of phosphates from most laundry detergents still fresh in his memory. "The fluorocarbon issue troubles me greatly," says Du Pont Chairman Shapiro. "I hear the theory doesn't hold water, but there is great alarm that the atmosphere will be destroyed."

Under these trying circumstances, Du Pont appears to be doing about the best it can. Along with other fluorocarbon manufacturers, it is supporting research sponsored by the National Academy of Sciences and the Manufacturing Chemists Association. The latter group alone has funded, to the tune of $1.5 million, atmospheric measurements to test the hypothesis, and it plans to begin work in the stratosphere this year. Finally, Du Pont has made it unmistakably clear that it will stop production if, as it says, "any creditable scientific data show that any fluorocarbons cannot be used without a threat to health."

Particularly now, when their credibility is so low, corporations need to show convincingly that they can move quickly and conscientiously when such problems of potential public concern arise. Environmentalists tend to set standards of minimum or even zero risk to public health and safety. But decisions about risk are too important to be weighed in an atmosphere that pits environmental crusaders against corporate villains. The crusaders are apt to win most of the battles, and society will pay enormously for unrealistically risk-free production.

Excerpted from Charles G. Burck, "The Intricate 'Politics' of the Corporation," *Fortune* (April, 1975), pp. 112, 188, 190. Used with permission of the publisher.

Figure 2.9

The Systems Model: An Alternative to Smith and Galbraith*

Characteristic	*Adam Smith's Classical Market Model*	*John Kenneth Galbraith's Managerial Model*	*Systems Model*
Nature of the economy	**Perfectly competitive**	**Monopolistic-oligopolistic**	**Constrained competition**
Level of Profits	**Normal**	**Supernormal**	**Satisfactory**
Enterprise goal	**Short-run profit maximization**	**Security and growth of business volume**	**Legitimacy**
Locus of decision-making power	**Entrepreneurs**	**Management**	**Management**
Medium of competition	**Price**	**Price Product Selling costs**	**Price Product Distribution Communication Resources Costs**
External constraints on enterprise behavior	**Markets**	**Markets**	**Markets Economy Political/governmental Ethical/legal Scientific/technological Resource suppliers Sociocultural**
Determinants of social/environmental sensitivity	**None**	**Social and charitable propensities of management**	**Management perceptions of social/environmental pressures**

*Adapted from Charles G. Burck, "The Intricate 'Politics' of the Corporation," *Fortune* (April, 1975), p. 111.

CONCLUSIONS

A systems perspective of marketing requires a refined sensitivity to the multiple impacts of the firm's environment on marketing activities and to the impacts of marketing activities on the firm's environment. Marketing unfolds within a multifaceted mosaic of constraints and opportunities. Historically the firm's proximate environment has been delineated by marketing analysts as the economic system, or the unregulated play of competitive forces, in which the role of marketing was considered to be distribution or selling. Expanding our conception of the environment in which marketing activity unfolds necessitates a reconceptualization of the role of marketing. The expanded role of marketing management is interpreted as a process of reconciling controllable variables with the actions of consumers and competitors in the marketplace, in an environment conditioned by an array of interactive external forces, to establish enterprise legitimacy and power over time.

Interpretations of the role and responsibilities of marketing have paralleled interpretations of business priorities and purposes, from the days of intense production orientation, to the era of generating mass markets for distributed products through efficient salesmanship, to the dawning of the age of consumer activism – *consumerism*. Intense focus on consumers to the exclusion of other environmental sectors, however, can be as myopic as the marketing philosophies that preceded it. This is the principal weakness of contemporary definitions of marketing. What is needed is a definition of marketing which explicitly recognizes the multiple reciprocal impacts of the firm and the environment, and the manner in which the firm depends on the environment – in all its manifestations – for legitimization of the firm's output and methods of operation. Notions of legitimacy, power, and interdependency with the environment are implicit in the definition used throughout this text:

> *Marketing consists of those differentiating actions taken by the firm to establish its legitimacy, enhance its power, improve its negotiating ability, and to resolve conflicts in its own favor.*

This definition explicitly recognizes that firms do not merely market physical/functional products. In the final analysis, *firms market themselves*. To market themselves effectively — to achieve legitimacy — firms must ascend a hierarchy of business purpose which propels them out of myopic interpretations of products, consumer needs, and the marketing process. Environmental awareness — anticipation and adaptation — is the key.

Environmental awareness

Chapter 3 will operationalize this expanded definition of marketing and translate it into appropriate areas of managerial decision making, into strategies of enterprise adaptation which simultaneously contribute to the welfare of the firm and the welfare of society-at-large.

CHAPTER 2: REVIEW QUESTIONS

1. What are the two general areas in which the business enterprise must confirm its legitimacy?

2. Why is adaptation to the firm's external environment insufficient to assure legitimacy? What must the firm do in addition to adaptation?

3. What are the seven major sectors in the firm's environment? Give examples of ways in which each environmental sector specifically impinges on the firm's activities.

4. What is an ecosystem? Is the business firm an ecosystem? Why?

5. Why do firms tend to react to change rather than anticipate it?

6. Describe the commonwealth of the market.

7. How do capitalist and socialist systems differ in their views of the relative priority associated with individual and societal needs?

8. How does the market mechanism in the United States reflect the underlying value structure of American culture?

9. What is the common purpose of socialist and capitalist systems?

10. Why is the marketing concept myopic?

11. How have business priorities and purposes evolved since the late Eighteenth Century?

12. How have conceptions of the role of marketing in the business firm evolved in concert with conceptions of business purpose?

13. What factors combined to necessitate a marketing orientation rather than a production or selling orientation?

14. How do the commodity and institutional approaches to the analysis of marketing differ?

15. What is the nature of contemporary but conventional definitions of marketing like that of the marketing staff of The Ohio State University?

16. In general, what do conventional definitions of marketing fail to account for?

17. Briefly describe the systems definition of marketing presented in this text, including a brief analysis of each of its component parts. What does this definition recognize that is absent in conventional definitions?

18. With whom does the firm negotiate?

19. What permits the firm to resolve conflicts in its own favor?

20. What are the levels of the hierarchy of business purpose?

21. What is meant by the "integrated hierarchy of business purpose?"

22. How does the integrated hierarchy of business purpose facilitate anticipation and adaptation?

23. Along what dimensions does a systems model of marketing differ from a classical marketing model or Galbraith's managerial model?

24. What is the measure of the firm's achievement of the level of environmental responsiveness in the hierarchy of business purpose?

MARKETING: A MANAGERIAL PROCESS

PART II

ORGANIZING FOR MARKETING: A CONVENTIONAL VIEW

ORGANIZING FOR MARKETING: IMPLEMENTING THE SYSTEMS PERSPECTIVE

GOAL AND RESOURCE SPECIFICATION

- Resource Specification
- Goal Specification
- Social Auditing

DELINEATION

- Targeting by What?
- Targeting by Whom?
- Market Segmentation
  - Criteria for Evaluating Segmentation Variables
  - Why Segment?
- The Consumer Decision Process
  - Perceived Need
  - Pre-decision Activity
  - Adoption or Rejection Decision
  - Use Behavior
  - Post-decision Evaluation
- The Marketing Research Process

PROGRAMMING

PRODUCT/PRICING STRATEGY

- Product Strategy
  - Product Strategy Decisions
  - Company Objectives and the Product Mix
  - The Product Life Cycle
  - Addition and Deletion Decisions: The Product Audit

- Pricing Strategy
    - Controllable versus Uncontrollable
    - Internally-determined Prices
    - Externally-determined Prices

DISTRIBUTION STRATEGY

- Channel of Distribution
- Vertical Marketing Systems
    - Negotiation and Conflict Resolution
    - Vertical and Horizontal Integration
    - Contractual Arrangements
- Channel Alignments
- Channel Structures
- Innovations in Retailing
    - Supermarket Merchandising
    - Planned Shopping Centers
    - Automated Merchandising
    - Convenience Stores
    - Boutiques

COMMUNICATION STRATEGY

- The Role of Marketing Communication in Society
- The Role of Marketing Communication in the Firm
- The Communication Process
    - Communication System
    - Prerequisites to Communication
    - Communication Effectiveness
    - Communication Fidelity
    - Communication Efficiency
    - Mass Media versus Interpersonal Communication
    - The Process of Social Influence
    - The Image of the Firm

TRANSACTION

REPROGRAMMING

- Reprogramming and the Product Life Cycle
- Anticipation and Adaptation

CONCLUSIONS

Marketing: A Managerial Process

Part II

We have suggested (how could you forget!) that *marketing* is most appropriately viewed as:

> Those *differentiating actions* taken by the firm to establish its *legitimacy*, enhance its *power*, improve its *negotiating ability*, and to *resolve conflicts* in its own favor.

How does the firm simultaneously accomplish all these things? How does the firm minimize uncertainty, maximize the prospect of long-range survival, and ultimately entrench itself in positions of power relative to its competitors? In the American economic system *entrepreneurship*, or the ability to predict the likely impact of change in environmental forces on enterprise operations, and *competitive strategy formulation* are the keys to establishing the lasting legitimacy of the firm.

Power is sought through differentiation. And attempts to differentiate the firm from competitors seeking to serve the same markets result in competitive strategy formulation, or the firm's *one best attempt* at responding to the demands emanating from relevant sectors in the firm's environment. Firms may manifest differentiation in any of a variety of ways. For example, a firm may have earned the distinction of producing the worst products in an industry. Clearly, this is not what we, or marketing management has in mind. It's positive differentiation that counts.

The four P's
- **product**
- **price**
- **promotion**
- **place**

Differentiating actions or competitive strategies manifest themselves in many dimensions. Traditionally, differentiation has been viewed within the mnemonic of *the four P's* or *the marketing mix:* product, price, promotion and place. *Product* differentiation, once considered only applicable to the physical and functional attributes of products, is now considered legitimate in the psychological and sociopsychological dimensions as well. Varying channel alignments and careful attention to such intangibles as store image compose the *place* or *physical distribution* component of the marketing mix. Differentiation in *price* and terms of sale is critical, and pricing strategy no longer reflects conventional economic conceptualizations of *rational economic man* and predictable price/quantity relationships. Finally, the *promotion* mix is now viewed more accurately as a total communications mix, rather than merely an advertising or selling problem. It is these differentiating activities that the firm engages in to acquire power to overcome the risks of uncertainty that comprise the system we term *competition.* A more succinct statement of the firm's mission is *competition for differential advantage* (see Figure 3.1). [87, p. 13]

Competition = differentiating actions

Given that differentiation leads to market power, and hence more positive differentiation (uniqueness) leads to *more* market power, pure competition symbolizes the worst of all possible worlds for the marketer and monopoly signifies the best of all possible worlds. The game of business competition is played on a field resembling a continuum ranging from pure competition to monopoly (see Figure 3.2). It is through differentiating actions that the firm seeks to establish its legitimacy and power and simultaneously improve its competitive position. Lasting legitimacy is synonymous with power, and absolute power

The game of business competition

Figure 3.1

Competition for Differential Advantage

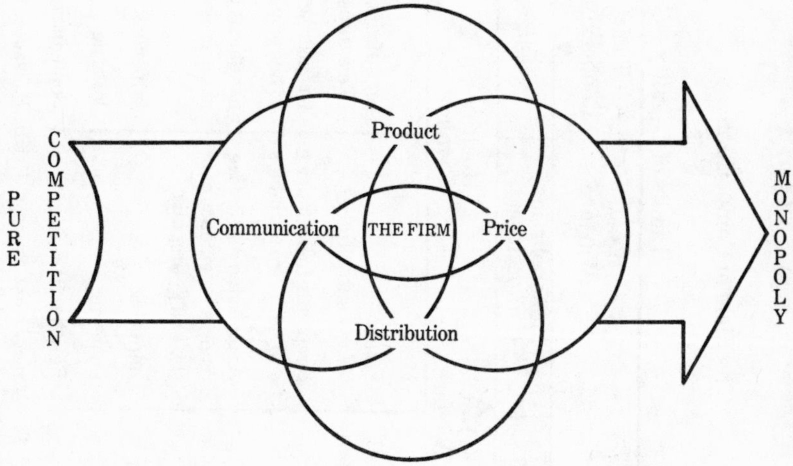

is synonymous with monopoly. Therefore, through positive differentiation the firm improves its competitive position and simultaneously registers points toward lasting legitimacy in the game of business competition.

Limits of legality

While political and legal forces define the rules of the game of competition and attempt to perpetuate a system of more or less free competition, all business incentives point in the opposite direction. Competitive strategies by their very nature attempt to minimize competition and maximize the firm's position of power. Firms which

Figure 3.2

The Field of Competition

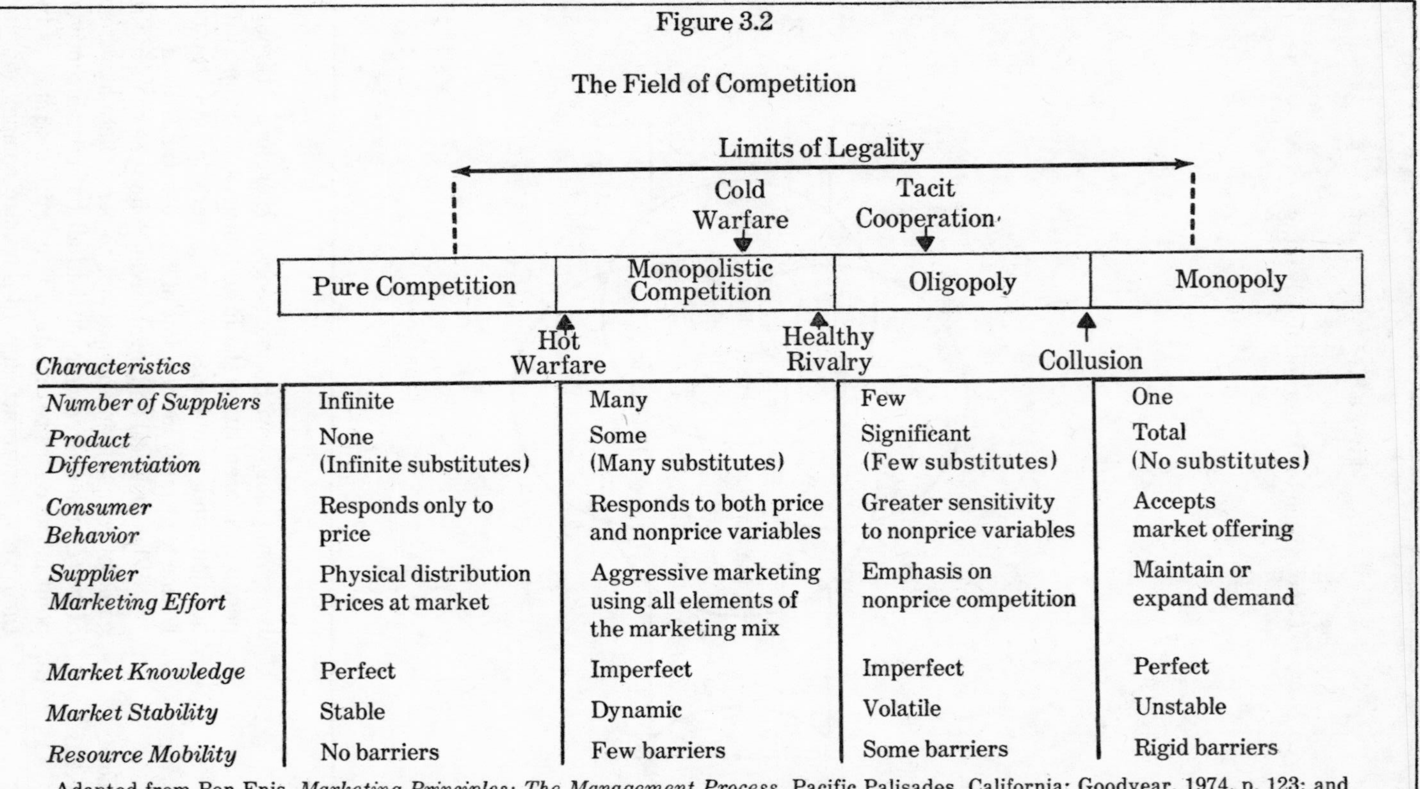

Characteristics	Pure Competition	Monopolistic Competition	Oligopoly	Monopoly
Number of Suppliers	Infinite	Many	Few	One
Product Differentiation	None (Infinite substitutes)	Some (Many substitutes)	Significant (Few substitutes)	Total (No substitutes)
Consumer Behavior	Responds only to price	Responds to both price and nonprice variables	Greater sensitivity to nonprice variables	Accepts market offering
Supplier Marketing Effort	Physical distribution Prices at market	Aggressive marketing using all elements of the marketing mix	Emphasis on nonprice competition	Maintain or expand demand
Market Knowledge	Perfect	Imperfect	Imperfect	Perfect
Market Stability	Stable	Dynamic	Volatile	Unstable
Resource Mobility	No barriers	Few barriers	Some barriers	Rigid barriers

Adapted from Ben Enis, *Marketing Principles: The Management Process*, Pacific Palisades, California: Goodyear, 1974, p. 123; and Philip Kotler, *Marketing Management: Analysis, Planning and Control*, Englewood Cliffs, New Jersey: Prentice-Hall, 1972, p. 252.

Figure 3.3

Conventional Marketing Functions

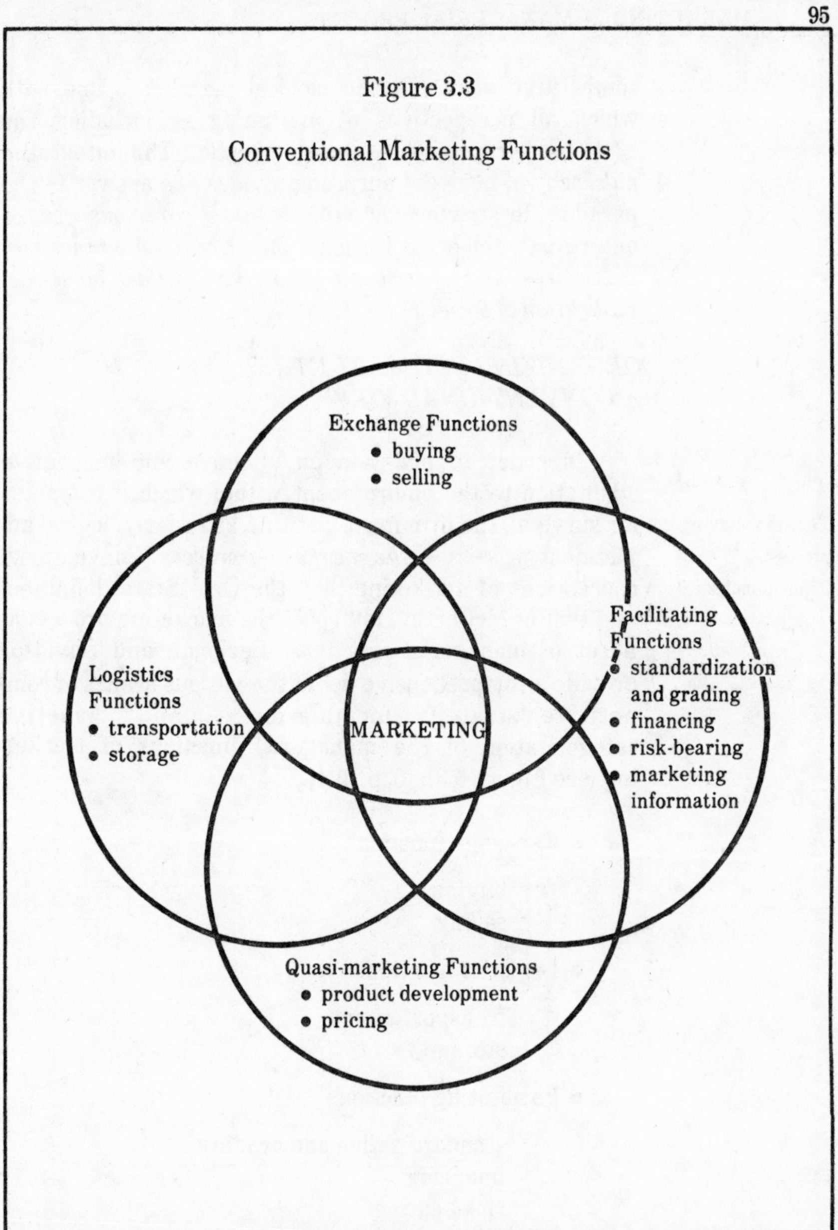

manage to successfully differentiate in most aspects of the marketing process or through marketing programming are those which enjoy the numerous advantages of the monopolist's end of the competitive continuum. This notion that monopoly is Nirvana directly contradicts the notion of classical economists that pure competition is the competitive ideal. This ideological paradox is one with which all perspectives of marketing – including the systems perspective – must wrestle. The integrated hierarchy of business purpose provides one answer to the paradox. In striving for *environmental consciousness*, or enterprise self-actualization, *the firm simultaneously maximizes its contribution to the welfare and actualization of society.*

ORGANIZING FOR MARKETING: A CONVENTIONAL VIEW

The marketing process: functionalism

In order to maintain an effective and innovative adaptation to the environment within which it competes for survival, the firm must institute an orderly, logical adjustment process – *the marketing process*. Conventional conceptions of marketing, like the Ohio State definition, and that of McCarthy, interpret the marketing process as a set of managerial *functions*. Beckman and Davidson provide a comprehensive list of the various arenas of competitive strategy formulation – an exhaustive categorization of the managerial functions of marketing (see Figure 3.3): [6, p. 424]

- Exchange functions

  buying
  selling

- Logistics functions

  transportation
  storage

- Facilitating functions

  standardization and grading
  financing
  risk-bearing
  marketing information

- Quasi-marketing functions

  product development
  pricing

This system of categorization suffers many glaring deficiencies. However, the relegation of product development and pricing to the status of quasi-marketing activities reflects three basic inadequacies in this type of functional analysis:

Deficiencies:
- **product narrow**
- **price determined**
- **information**

- The product is viewed very narrowly as merely a physical product rather than a means of need satisfaction
- Pricing is viewed as strictly determined by market forces in a system circumscribed by intense competition
- Marketing communication is interpreted as an information function rather than a persuasive process

All three assumptions are, of course, highly unrealistic. The major weakness of such functional approaches, however, is their *failure to view marketing as a dynamic, interactive process* incapable of being separated from the firm's totality of adaptive activities and from environmental influences. Beckman and Davidson even acknowledge this weakness in functional analysis very briefly, and yet devote several hundred pages to meticulous functional analysis:

> There is no doubt that even in marketing there has been a strong tendency toward overemphasis of functional specialization. Consequently, the weaknesses in coordination and teamwork may have offset the advantages of specialization in many instances . . . there is a need for moderating emphasis on functionalization. It has admittedly been carried too far at times. Second, there is need for more emphasis on coordination, probably by the systems approach, within an establishment or enterprise, within a channel of distribution, or within whatever part of the marketing process is involved. [6, p. 420]

Finally, such functional analyses provide no orderly framework for establishing the goals of the firm and realizing them through sound competitive strategy. According to a systems or environmental responsiveness interpretation of the marketing process, the various components of competitive strategy are not discrete, autonomous entities. On the contrary, they bear logical, largely predictable and occasionally inevitable relationships to each other and to their constellation of environmental influences. Instead of being a set of functions, *the marketing process is more appropriately viewed as a rational organization of integrated activities designed to establish enterprise legitimacy and power over time.*

ORGANIZING FOR MARKETING: IMPLEMENTING THE SYSTEMS PERSPECTIVE

The differentiating actions taken by the firm to achieve competitive advantage bear logical relationships to each other and to the environment, and compose a logical sequence (see Figure 3.4):

Systematic framework

- Goal and resource specification
- Delineation
- Programming

  Product/pricing strategy
  Distribution strategy
  Communication strategy

- Transaction
- Reprogramming

Strategic tools:
• control
• legitimacy
• power

These processes suggest the *strategic tools* available to marketing management in its attempt to gain some degree of *control* over its environment, to achieve *legitimacy* over time, and to acquire positions of enduring *power* relative to the firm's competitors in the marketplace. In the following sections we will discuss briefly some of the relevant decisions required at various stages in the sequence. We will also try to give you a hint of the theoretical tools available for marketing decision making within this framework. You should study this section with the following limitation in mind:

Theoretical tools

We do not suggest that this section provides an exhaustive account of the fundamentals of planning and managing marketing effort. We merely suggest that the sequence or framework is appropriate to and facilitates the implementation of the systems concept — marketing

Marketing effort:
• systems thinking

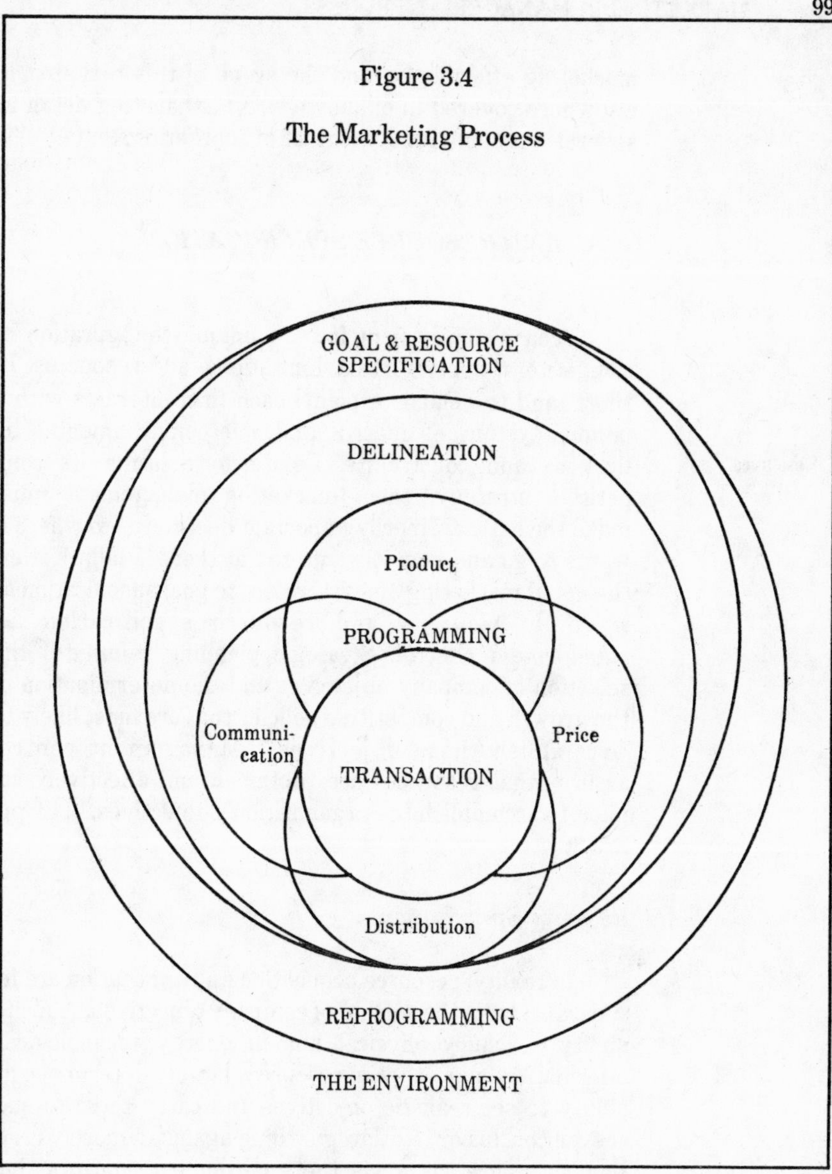

as environmental responsiveness. It is unfortunate that most texts which espouse the systems concept and extoll its virtues also fail to infuse its spirit and dynamism into the managerial process of marketing. What you read in the following pages is our attempt to incorporate an explicit *recognition of firm/environmental interrelationships* into the marketing decision-making process. A detailed explication of the numerous technicalities involved in a total marketing effort is beyond the scope of this text, but is elsewhere covered in exhaustive and exhausting detail in several excellent fundamentals of marketing texts.

GOAL AND RESOURCE SPECIFICATION

Goals ↕ Resources

Each business firm faces a unique configuration of competitors, opportunities, limitations, and resources. In short (and to belabor a point) each firm interacts with a unique system of macro- and microenvironmental influences and constraints. Before formulating its competitive strategy, then, marketing management must make the extraordinarily important decision as to where it wants to go and how it wants to get there. Philip Kotler, the noted marketing analyst, refers to goal specification as *strategic planning* and resource specification as *management control.* Strategic planning refers to "the selection of company objectives and the determination of the growth and competitive policies that are most likely to accomplish these objectives." Management control assures that resources are "obtained and effectively applied to accomplish the organization's objectives." [49, pp. 229-30]

Resource Specification

Mutually profitable relationship

In reality, resource acquisition and application are inseparable from the setting of company objectives. A firm's ability to acquire physical, human, energy, technological, information, and financial resources largely determines its ability to set realistic objectives and carry them to successful conclusion. Kotler, guarding against a merely reactionary stance vis à vis the environment, concurs that "each company faces the challenge of synthesizing a uniquely productive and profitable relationship with its environment." [49, p. 229] If the setting of company objectives and the specification and acquisition of resources facilitate not only a "productive and profitable" relationship with the environment, but rather a *mutually* productive and profitable relationship, then the firm could truly be said to be implementing the spirit as well as the dynamism implicit in systems thinking.

Goal Specification

Redefinition of business goals

In the process of reappraising their interpretation of business purpose and the role of marketing within the firm, marketing management is beginning to redefine business goals and measures of business success or performance as well. Since World War II, business firms have viewed their role as one of serving the needs of consumers for material goods and services, presumably in an arena circumscribed by regulative forces pushing to perpetuate an approximation of pure competition. Theoretically at least, the condition of pure competition mitigated against competitive excesses in the marketplace and assured that in their attempts to maximize their firm's self-interest (profits), businessmen would simultaneously maximize the welfare of society-at-large. The primary barometer of success in the simultaneous achievement of self-interest and contribution to social welfare was *profitability*, and in fact profit was re-legitimized as an enterprise goal with the coining of the *marketing concept*. Other traditional measures of enterprise success and legitimacy include *return on invested capital, growth, stability,* and *sales volume*. These measures suffer serious limitations from a systems viewpoint, not the least of which is their gross inability to register or reflect any negative impact the firm's activities may have on the environment or upon society. Moreover, the shortsighted pursuit of profitability, productivity, growth, and the like may seriously compromise the long-term legitimacy or survival ability of the firm. The demands of legitimacy may directly conflict with the requirements of power, a difficult concept with which we will wrestle at length in Chapter 5. One obvious example is the dangerous and shortsighted drain on finite energy resources required to satisfy virtually insatiable consumer demands for material goods.

Invisible hand

Conventional measures:
- limitations
- shortsighted

Legitimacy versus power

Short-term versus long-term

Systems thinking requires the reconciliation of short- and long-term enterprise priorities, of legitimacy and power (lasting legitimacy). It requires that management balance short- and long-term enterprise objectives, and weigh enterprise priorities against social/environmental exigencies. Profit, productivity, and sales are generally calculated in the short run, and they reflect legitimacy seeking in only one narrow arena: consumer demand for material goods. Systems thinking demands farsighted measures of enterprise performance which account not only for the welfare and health of the firm, but also of consumers as individuals and as a societal whole.

Social Auditing

Other dimensions

Much as been written in recent years about *social accounting* or *social reporting*, that is, measuring enterprise performance on dimensions other than material or economic output. An enterprise social report or *social audit* would reflect the ability of the firm to respond to societal as well as economic needs in its environment. A social audit would measure the impact of the firm on its community and larger environment – the impact of its products, its methods of operation, and its internally and externally oriented programs and policies. The firm's legitimacy- and power-seeking activities would be subjectively measured in all their various manifestations. Social auditing does not suggest that costs incurred in these activities be ignored, or that financially profitable activities are bad. On the contrary, a firm which fails to assure its own health, longevity, and stability produces only dysfunctional outputs, from any perspective.

Environmental impact

The term *social auditing* has been bandied about for years, but is still in the embryonic stages of implementation. Measures of the degree of a firm's environmental responsiveness and legitimacy do not readily lend themselves to quantification. They are largely qualitative and highly subjective, and for that reason alone foreign to business managers. It is far simpler to cite percentage return on investment figures to anxious stockholders than to cite cases where the firm has contributed to the quality of life or alleviated economic or social injustice. These sorts of contributions need to be measured against appropriate norms, and frequently the norms do not exist.

Hard to quantify

Appropriate norms

One attempt to identify areas in need of measurement – or, to use our terminology, arenas from which legitimacy must be sought and won – was made by Frank Cassell, noted marketing analyst at Northwestern University.* [14, p. 23] He acknowledges the difficulties of making a systematic analysis of enterprise activities which reverberate upon society and the environment, and

*Frank H. Cassell, "The Social Cost of Doing Business," p. 23, *MSU Business Topics*, Autumn 1974. Reprinted by permission of the publisher, Division of Research, Graduate School of Business Administration, Michigan State University.

of their relationship to the long- and short-term economic health of the organization. Cassell suggests that the following items be evaluated in terms of their environmental impact:

Environmental impact

- The level of performance of a corporation in its primary *economic* function –

  producing goods and services that people need
  creating jobs
  paying fair wages
  ensuring worker safety
  earning a decent profit
  doing all this in a lawful and reasonable manner

- The conduct of these operations in ways that improve the *quality of life* rather than degrade it –

  maintaining a high quality of goods and services
  dealing fairly with customers, employees, suppliers, and shareholders
  providing genuine equality of employment and career opportunity
  making efforts to conserve the natural environment

- Social investments of both money and manpower in *problem solving community agencies* –

  participation of company employees in community organizations
  funding of educational, charitable and cultural activities

- A deeper and less traditional involvement in *dealing* not just with the symptoms of social ills but *with the causes* –

  comprehensive research and data base available nowhere else
  participating in cooperative planning
  undertaking experimental social projects in areas of mutual benefit to company and community

Where the company is

Cassell suggests that the measurement and goal specification process begins "just where the company is," with an analysis of existing programs and policies that have social and environmental impact, including the studying of individual attitudes within the organization. [14, p. 24] Each company's assessment will be different, since each company possesses a unique array of material and human resources and, we might add, faces a unique configuration of environmental forces. Costs and benefits of existing programs should be reevaluated, and new expenditures weighed critically.

Where the company is going

A final point, which returns us to the very essence of systems thinking and environmental responsiveness, is this: A firm cannot and should not set goals for itself which benefit society, consumers, and/or the environment at the expense of its long-term viability. To leave you with this impression would be misleading, if popular in some circles. Firms should set goals, measure effectiveness, and establish policy such that the needs or demands of *all* environmental sectors — including the firm — can be met at least adequately if not optimally. The welfare of the firm is inseparable from and interdependent with the welfare of society. True systems thinking requires that enterprise goals be specified with this interdependency firmly in mind.

Enterprise welfare ↕ Societal welfare

DELINEATION

Every marketer of any product, service, or idea must determine who are his potential and actual consumers or market. Gone are the good old days when demand was sufficient to insure profitability to the firm that could merely produce and distribute products. An integral aspect of the new conception of marketing which arose with the advent of the *marketing concept* was the realization that serving consumers required that they first be located and identified. Implicit in this realization is the notion that consumers are not all alike. They react to products and firms in idiosyncratic ways and hence cannot be considered one homogeneous market. On the other hand, any collectivity of consumers shares certain common characteristics which means that they are capable of being grouped along some dimensions. Even if such groupings are imprecise — and they usually are — they nonetheless permit the marketer to allocate resources and determine target markets in a much more scientific, less "seat-of-the-pants" manner.

Serving consumers:
- **locating**
- **identifying**

Scientific vs. "seat-of-the-pants"

Targeting by What?

Market delineation actually requires two types of targeting. First, the firm must delineate its market by identifying the generic function or set of utilities or *anticipated satisfactions* associated with its product offerings (and don't forget that a "product" is much, much more than merely a physical/functional entity). Systems thinking requires that a firm consider the utilities, benefits, or satisfactions embodied in its product offerings, rather than the tangible items it markets. This is the thesis of Theodore Levitt's classic article on "marketing myopia," in which he contends that most businesses define their business (market) too narrowly. [56] For example, if Hollywood had defined its business as entertainment rather than movies, movie makers would have viewed the introduction of television as a welcome growth opportunity rather than a dangerous source of competition. Toro Corporation, on the other hand, defines its market as the lawn and garden care market rather than the lawn mower market, a broad market definition which permits recognition of a multiplying array of diverse market opportunities. Sometimes a narrower market definition is in order. R. J. Reynolds Tobacco Co., for example, positioned *Winston* firmly in the filter cigarette market, supplanted *Kent* cigarettes as the filter king, and made no attempt to compete in other types of tobacco markets like unfiltered cigarettes or cigars.

Generic function: product positioning

Marketing Myopia

The firm, then, in determining the aggregate demand of potential buyers of a commodity or service, should *define the market sufficiently broadly that all potential competition is taken into consideration, and yet narrowly enough so that it can offer a viable product alternative in its chosen market(s).* A firm which defines its market too broadly runs the risk of spreading its resources too thin in an attempt to meet the challenge of many diverse competitors.

Broad
Narrow

Targeting by Whom?

After the firm has defined or delineated its relevant market according to the types of utilities or satisfactions it provides through its product offerings, it must determine *who* specifically constitutes the market for the particular set of utilities or benefits implicit in its products. *Gross market* refers to all consumers who could conceivably have a need — conscious or unconscious — for a product, service, or idea. Gross market can be a useful concept if a firm ultimately hopes to reach all potential consumers.

Potential need vs. Potential purchase

However, such a strategy is usually infeasible. A more useful concept is

> *market*, defined as *a group of buyers (and sellers) within a specific geographical area, for a particular product, service, idea, or reasonable substitute, at a particular stage in the trade channel, at a particular point in time.*

This definition operationalizes the concept of market and makes target marketing much more feasible. This permits the firm to concentrate its efforts on those consumers who not only *need* the product, but who are likely to *buy* it.

The market should be viewed as a *spectrum of demands*, and a product as a *collection of utilities* or benefits with the ability to satisfy these demands. In systems terms, the segmentation phase of market delineation facilitates legitimacy seeking and conferral by isolating that subset of the population which will demand the firm's output, and then focusing marketing efforts on those consumers.

Market Segmentation

Segmentation
↓
Programming

The purpose of segmentation, then, is to determine differences and similarities among consumers which may be consequential in designing marketing strategies to reach them and satisfy their demands. Programming or tailoring of marketing effort to consumer expectations follows from segmentation of potential buyers. Otherwise, why bother to find differences among consumers? For this reason, a market segment is not merely a group of people with shared characteristics.

> *A market segment is a group of individuals whose expected reactions to the marketer's efforts will be similar during a specified time period.*

A market segment is defined in terms of the expected reactions of its constituents to a particular marketing strategy.

Whenever a market consists of two or more consumers, that market is capable of being segmented or divided into meaningful consumer groups. The maximum number of segments a market can theoretically consist of is the total number of consumers constituting the market. Each consumer is a separate market in principle, because his needs and desires are unique. Ideally, a marketer might study each individual consumer in order to tailor an optimum marketing program to his needs. This would result in total market segmentation. At the opposite extreme, if there were no segmentation at all, the entire market would be a segment — the only segment.

Total segmentation

No segmentation

The broadest market division is that which separates the *consumer market* from the *industrial market*. [18, p. 104] This division results in two groups — *ultimate consumers* and *industrial users* — which differ significantly in terms of motives and events surrounding the purchase, but which are too broad to be properly considered market segments. It is appropriate to segment industrial markets as well as consumer markets, although the bases or axes for segmentation will likely differ.

In reality, most sellers do not find it worthwhile or economically feasible to study each individual consumer and customize the product, price, communication, and distribution mixes to satisfy each individual's needs. The exception might be the industrial marketer who faces a few very large buyers, or a specialty goods broker dealing in highly exclusive, extravagantly priced products, such as original art works or fine jewelry. Normally, the seller searches for classes of consumers who differ in product expectations or anticipated satisfactions prompting product purchases.

Industrial market: rifle approach feasible

Criteria for Evaluating Segmentation Variables. The basic question becomes: How can the seller determine which consumer characteristics produce the best partitioning of a particular market? Certain key criteria are highly useful for determining the practicality of a particular set of consumer characteristics for segmentation purposes: [49, p. 167-68]

- *Measurability* — Is the segment measurable and identifiable? Measurability is the degree to which information exists or is obtainable on various consumer attributes or behaviors *which relate to the probable purchase of the product*.
- *Accessibility* — Will focusing marketing efforts on a particular market segment have a positive impact in eliciting desired responses? Accessibility is the

degree to which the firm can effectively focus efforts on a market segment. For example, is the segment accessible with certain types of media campaigns? If the segmentation dimension were opinion leadership, it is probable that the segment could be reached through specific media since media habits differ between opinion leaders and followers.

- *Substantiality* — Is the segmentation variable shared by a sufficiently large number of potential customers to justify the expense and effort of focusing marketing efforts on the segment? Substantiality is the degree to which segmentation variables are shared among a sufficiently large number of potential customers to justify separate market cultivation. A segment should be the smallest group of consumers for which it is practical to tailor a separate marketing program.

- *Reliability* — Are the consumer characteristics stable indicators of demand potential? Reliability is a question of stability over time. If a segmentation variable remains stable, marketing strategies will have a cumulative effect and different strategies for different segments will be cost-justified.

Subjective, but critical, determination

Whether a given market segment may be effectively characterized according to these criteria is often a subjective determination of management, although the determination of appropriate segments is becoming more scientific and less hit-or-miss.

Segmentation variables

Benefit segmentation

The choice of appropriate segmentation variables or consumer characteristics which relate to the probable purchase of the product is critical. The thoughtless choice of criteria for market segmentation can lead to vast inefficiency in marketing effort and to compromised or hedged objectives. Major segmentation variables include: *geographic*, *demographic*, *psychographic*, *behavioral*, and *benefits sought*. Figure 3.5 lists some of the major segmentation axes and gives examples of specific consumer characteristics which could be utilized. Benefit segmentation is particularly interesting because it is a logical extension of market delineation in terms of benefits or utilities potentially implicit in the product. An example of benefit segmentation might be a toothpaste manufacturer who targets his efforts at consumers who want white teeth. The campaign would focus on the ability of the product to provide white teeth, and other benefits such as cavity prevention would be secondary. Benefit segmentation greatly enhances the ability of a firm to satisfy specific consumer wants and needs, and is no more difficult to research or implement than other forms of market segmentation.

Why Segment? The advantages inherent in market segmentation can be broken down into three broad categories: [49, p. 168]

- *Market segmentation provides the marketer with a better perspective to spot and compare marketing opportunities.* Through segmentation research, the marketer can examine the distinct needs of each market segment and compare them against current competitive product offerings. If there exists a disparity between the benefits provided by current market offerings, and the needs of consumers comprising a given segment, then customer satisfaction is less than optimal. Segments with low levels of satisfaction – unmet needs – may represent excellent marketing opportunities for the firm willing to research and meet those needs. Segmentation research and segmentation strategies represent concrete examples of environmental responsiveness in the consumer arena.

- *Knowledge of market response differences acquired through segmentation research enables the marketer to guide allocation of the marketing budget in such a manner that peak cost-efficiency is derived from each dollar spent.* A stengthened market and profit position is the likely result.

- Finally *segmentation permits the marketer to fine-tune product adjustments, distribution alignments, and the communication mix to the specific needs of particular consumer groups.* Instead of using a single marketing program aimed at all potential buyers – the "shotgun" approach – separate marketing strategies can be created to meet the diverse needs of different groups of buyers – the

Shotgun

Figure 3.5

Segmentation Axes and Variables

Axis	*Variables*	*Examples*
Geographic	Region	Southwest, Pacific, Mountain, South Atlantic, New England
	County Size	Under 5,000; 5,000-20,000; 20,000-50,000; 50,000-500,000; 500,000 +
	City Size	Same
	Population Density	Urban; suburban; rural
	Climate	Tropical; arid; cold
Demographic	Sex	Male; female
	Age	1-4; 5-10; 11-18; 19-34; 35-49; 50-64; 65 +
	Family size	1; 2-3; 4-5; 6 +
	Income	Under $5,000; $5,000-$7,999; $8,000-$9,999; over $10,000
	Occupation	Professional, Managerial, Technical (White collar); Craftsman, Foreman, Clerical, Sales (light blue collar); Operative, Service Worker Laborer (blue collar)
	Education	Grade school or less; some high school; high school graduate; some college; college or advanced degree
	Social class	Lower-lower; upper-lower; lower-middle; upper-middle; lower-upper; upper-upper
	Family life cycle	Young single; young married, no children; young married, oldest child less than 6; young married, oldest child over 6; older married with

Figure 3.5 Continued

		children; older married, no children; older single
	Race	White; Black; Indian; Oriental
	Nationality	American; British; French; German; Eastern European; Latin American; Asian
Psychographic	Alienation	Alienated; nonalienated
	Conservatism	Conservative; liberal; radical
	Cosmopolitanism	Cosmopolitan; local
	Dogmatism	Dogmatic; open-minded
	Authoritarianism	Authoritarian; democratic
	Leadership	Leader; follower
Behavioral	Rate of use	Heavy; average; light
	Search	Sources of information
	Shopping	Frequency; patronage; loyalty
	Product use	Intended versus unintended uses
Benefit	Economy	Initial cost; operating cost; obsolescence
	Function	Performance; comfort
	Status	Prestige; conspicuous consumption
	Style	Fad; fashion; ego-expression
	Sociability	Visibility; acceptance

Rifle

"rifle" approach. Segmentation breaks a heterogeneous market down into relatively homogeneous subpopulations. The relevant dimensions which make these groups homogeneous are the dimensions or segmentation variables to which the marketer should direct his efforts.

Segmentation requires careful research and is often imprecise, but it has proved to be a very powerful tool for marketers in their attempt to serve consumers.

The Consumer Decision Process

In attempts to better serve consumers through segmenting markets, marketers and social scientists have accumulated a considerable body of theory and empirical research dealing with the thought processes and behavior of individuals in their role as consumers. Human behavior is varied, complex, and often obscure, and understanding it is no easy matter. Every individual approaches the marketplace with a highly personalized set of expectations, experiences, attitudes, opinions, beliefs, values, motives, perceptions, and environmental constraints. While marketing researchers cannot hope to understand all the factors affecting purchase decisions, we have learned that certain generalizations are appropriate in discussing consumer behavior.

Transaction:
- Benefit
- Energy and/or resources

Consumer behavior or buyer behavior is most appropriately viewed as a *transaction involving an ongoing decision process*. Like all transactions the consumer decision process is motivated out of anticipated benefit and requires a certain expenditure of energy and/or resources on the part of the individual. (We will have more to say about transactions in subsequent sections.) The consumer decision process involves a set of intra- and interpersonal interactions and a sequence of non-discrete stages through which the potential purchaser implicitly or explicitly progresses. The interactions include (see Figure 3.6):

Consumer ⟷ Environment

Consumer ⟷ Information sources

Consumer ⟷ Seller

Consumer ⟷ Other parties

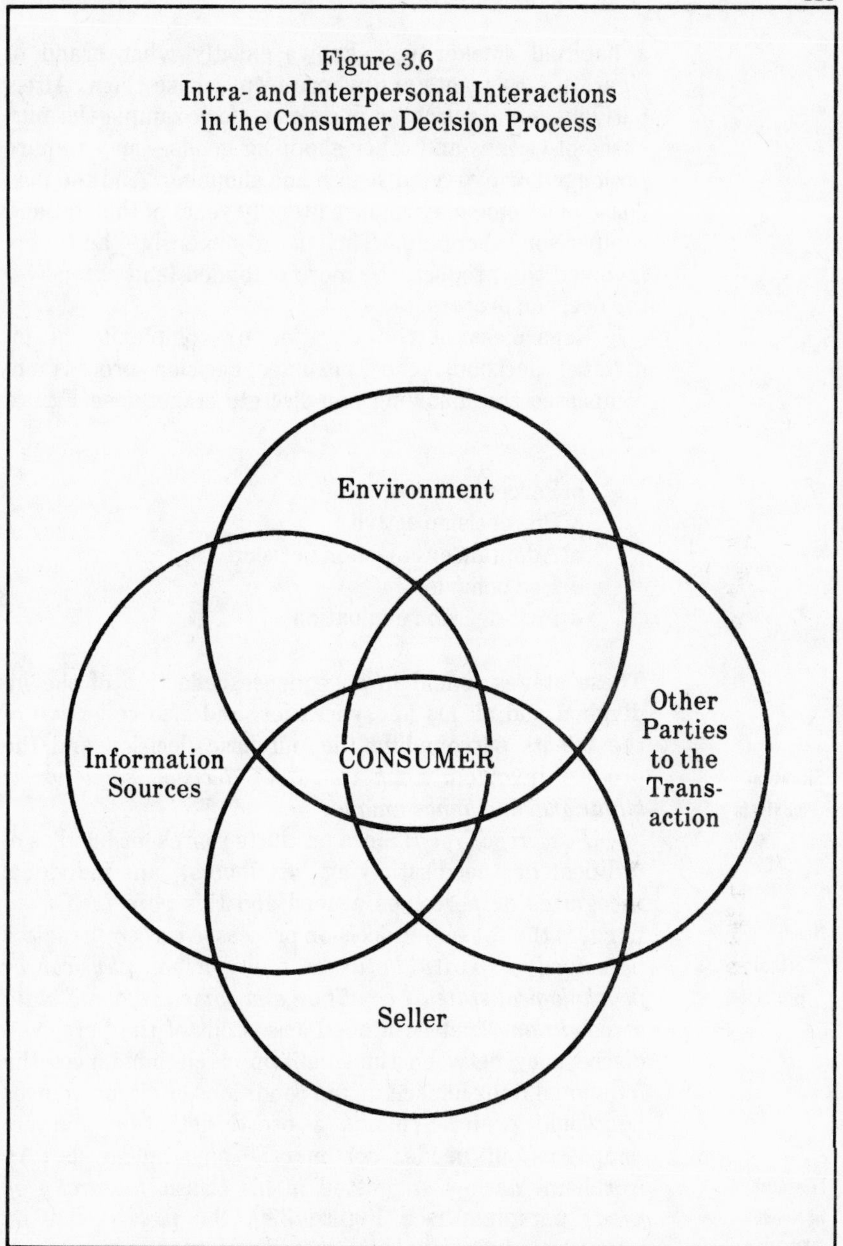

Figure 3.6
Intra- and Interpersonal Interactions in the Consumer Decision Process

The energy and/or resources which the potential purchaser is willing to expend – in terms of time, cost, effort, or risk – is a function of the *perceived satisfaction* he anticipates deriving from the product. For this reason, the decision process may unfold very rapidly, as in the case of a habitual smoker who knows exactly what brand of cigarettes he wants and where to purchase them. Alternatively, some purchase decisions—for example the purchase of clothes and other shopping goods—may require prolonged or extended search and shopping. And the purchase of a home may require literally years of thought and comparison shopping. The more expensive and ego-involved the product, the more extended (and extensive) the decision process.

Regardless of the duration or complexity of individual decisions, the consumer decision process encompasses the following non-discrete stages (see Figure 3.7):

- Perceived need
- Pre-decision activity
- Adoption or rejection decision
- Use behavior
- Post-decision evaluation

These stages unfold in a sequence reflective of the individual and all his idiosyncrasies, and also reflective of the events surrounding the purchase decision and the product involved. *Each consumer decision sequence is situational and hence unique.*

Situation analysis

Perceived Need. Since products represent bundles of utilities or need-satisfying attributes, an individual recognizes or perceives a need and this *perceived need* triggers the consumer decision process. *Needs represent a perceived disparity between some actual physical or psychological state or condition and some preferred state or condition.* That is, a need arises out of the perceived discrepancy between the condition or circumstances the individual finds himself in and conditions or circumstances he would prefer. This is a broad definition and encompasses all needs, not merely physical needs. As Abraham Maslow suggested in his classic *hierarchy of needs* paradigm (see Figure 3.8), the *psychogenic* or learned needs for love, esteem and self-actualization are as motivational as the so-called *biogenic* or inborn needs, particularly in a society in which needs for nourishment and safety are satisfied routinely. [61, pp. 80-92]

Need: actual vs. preferred

Hierarchy of Needs
- **Biogenic**
- **Psychogenic**

Intelligent marketing is very much a matter of recognizing the various needs that operate in a particular

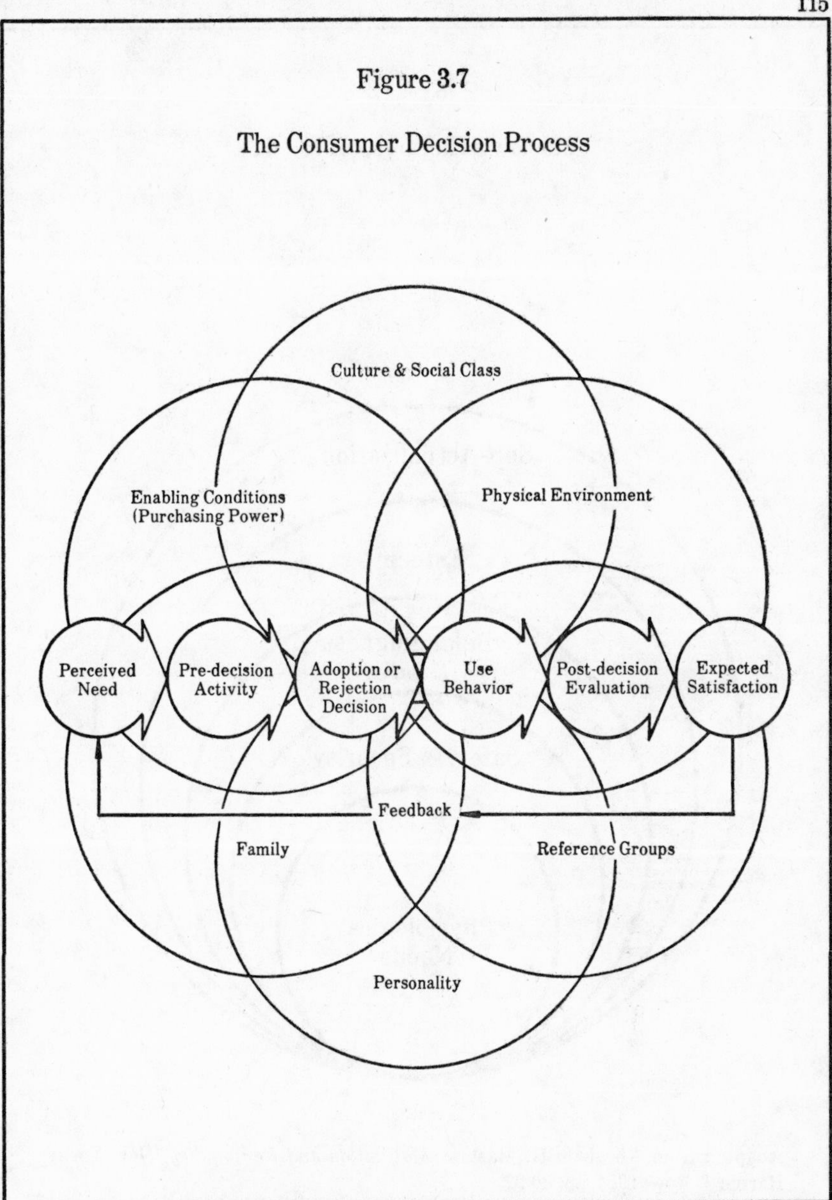

Figure 3.7

The Consumer Decision Process

product market and being the first to recognize which needs are insufficiently developed or satisfied through existing product alternatives. Intelligent marketing also requires continual recognition that products have symbolic utilities as well as physical ones, and that often a consumer purchases a product more for its ability to satisfy his higher order psychological needs than for its

Figure 3.8

Maslow's Hierarchy of Needs

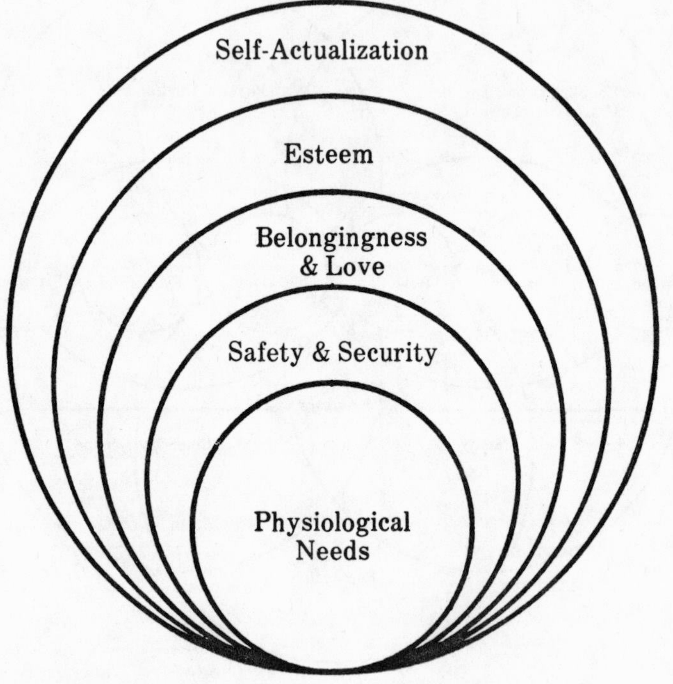

Adapted from Abraham H. Maslow, *Motivation and Personality*, New York: Harper & Row, 1954, pp. 80-92.

Utilities:
Physical
Symbolic

usefulness in satisfying a physical need. Charles Revson, President of Revlon, put it succinctly: "In the factory we make cosmetics . . . in the drugstore we sell hope."

Pre-decision Activity. After experiencing a need, the individual initiates *pre-decision activity* which includes both internal and external search for information about the various alternative solutions to his problem and then evaluation of these alternatives along dimensions that are personally relevant to him. The alternatives which the consumer considers and his relevant evaluative criteria are a function of many influences. Included among these intra- and interpersonal influences are attitudes, beliefs, opinions, values, experience, personality traits, motives, culture, social class, and reference groups. The length of pre-decision activity is a function of the amount of anticipated satisfaction – sociopsychological or physical – the individual perceives to be inherent in the purchase, and the expense of the product alternative in terms of time, effort, money, risk, etc. The length of the entire purchase decision process may vary considerably because the duration of pre-decision activity varies with the type of product and the personality of the buyer.

Industrial purchases

Pre-decision activity and in fact the entire purchase decision process *differs considerably between industrial products and consumer products*. Industrial purchasers, usually purchasing agents, buy for resale in the same form or for usage in business operations, whereas ultimate consumers buy for their own consumption. Industrial products are characterized by *derived* demand and include such items as raw materials, manufactured materials and parts, installations, equipment, operating and office supplies, and business services like maintenance and repair services. [49, p. 141] Moreover, industrial purchasers operate under a very different set of constraints from ultimate consumers in terms of product specifications, quantities, maximum prices and budgets, executive expectations, and quality requirements. Finally, industrial purchasers are often sought out by vendors or sellers of industrial products and are often courted on an interpersonal basis by sales representatives of vendors.

Derived demand

Consumer purchases

Ultimate consumers, on the other hand, normally perform the search function, actively seeking appropriate products and outlets in an attempt to cover the range of alternatives. It would be helpful if industrial goods were amenable to a classification based on the motives and search behavior of the purchaser, but the processes are only partially analogous. Figure 3.9 presents a classification of industrial goods by type of product and their marketing characteristics, while Figure 3.10 classifies consumer products into three categories based on consumer

Figure 3.9

Classes of Industrial Products: Some Characteristics and Marketing Considerations

Characteristics and marketing considerations	Type of Product				
	Raw materials	*Fabricating parts and materials*	*Installations*	*Accessory equipment*	*Operating supplies*
Characteristics:					
1. Unit price	Very low	Low	Very high	Medium	Low
2. Length of life	Very short	Depends on final product	Very long	Long	Short
3. Quantities purchased	Large	Large	Very small	Small	Small
4. Frequency of purchase	Frequent delivery; long-term purchase contract	Infrequent purchase but frequent delivery	Very infrequently	Medium	Frequent
5. Standardization of competitive products	Very high; grading is important	Very high	Very low; custom-made	Low	High
6. Limits on supply	Limited; cannot be increased quickly or at all	Usually no problem	No problem	Usually no problem	Usually no problem
Marketing considerations:					
1. Nature of channel	Short; no middlemen	Short; middlemen only for small buyers	Short; no middlemen	Middlemen used	Middlemen used
2. Negotiation period	Hard to generalize	Medium	Long	Medium	Short
3. Price competition	Important	Important	Not important	Not main factor	Important
4. Presale/postsale service	Not important	Not important	Very important	Important	Very little
5. Demand stimulation	Very little	Moderate	Salesmen very important	Important	Not too important
6. Brand preference	None	Generally unimportant, but some sellers try	High	High	Low
7. Advance buying contract	Important; use of long-term contracts	Important use of long-term contracts	Not usually	Not usually	Not usually

William J. Stanton, *Fundamentals of Marketing*, New York: McGraw-Hill, 1975, p. 140. Reprinted by permission of the publishers.

Figure 3.10

Classes of Consumer Products: Some Characteristics and Marketing Considerations

Characteristics and marketing considerations	Type of product		
	Convenience	*Shopping*	*Specialty*
Characteristics:			
1. Time and effort devoted by consumer to shopping	Very little	Considerable	Cannot generalize. May go to nearby store and exert minimum effort or may have to go to distant store and spend much time
2. Time spent planning the purchase	Very little	Considerable	Considerable
3. How soon want is satisfied after it arises	Immediately	Relatively long time	Relatively long time
4. Are price and quality compared?	No	Yes	No
5. Price	Low	High	High
6. Frequency of purchase	Usually frequent	Infrequent	Infrequent
7. Importance	Unimportant	Often very important	Cannot generalize
Marketing considerations:			
1. Length of channel	Long	Short	Short to very short
2. Importance of retailer	Any single store is relatively unimportant	Important	Very important
3. Number of outlets	As many as possible	Few	Few; often only one in a market
4. Stock turnover	High	Lower	Lower
5. Gross margin	Low	High	High
6. Responsibility for advertising	Manufacturer's	Retailer's	Joint responsibility
7. Importance of point-of-purchase display	Very important	Less important	Less important
8. Advertising used	Manufacturer's	Retailer's	Both
9. Brand or store name important	Brand name	Store name	Both
10. Importance of packaging	Very important	Less important	Less important

William J. Stanton, *Fundamentals of Marketing*, New York: McGraw-Hill 1975, p. 129. Reprinted by permission of the publisher.

motives and search behavior.

Consumer products are generally classified as *convenience*, *shopping*, and *specialty* goods. The category to which a given product belongs largely determines the range of desirable strategy options. Pricing, distribution, and communication decisions revolve around the consumer's willingness to expend effort and resources and undertake risk to obtain the product.

Convenience

- *Convenience goods* are products that consumers purchase with a minimum of search because the probable gain from a comparison of alternatives is slight. Convenience goods are mass distributed and have low unit price and hence there is little cost in terms of time, trouble or money involved.

Shopping

- *Shopping goods* are products from which the consumer hopes to derive relatively large potential gains by making price, quality or style comparisons. There tends to be greater ego-involvement and a sense of commitment in shopping goods, and hence the consumer perceives more risk in the purchase.

Specialty

- *Specialty goods* are those which have some particular appeal other than price which induces the customer to exert special effort to locate outlets handling them. Comparisons and search time for specialty goods may be extensive, and purchase may be postponed if an acceptable alternative is not available. The purchase of specialty goods is usually an extension of the individual's personality and value structure, and his use of the product is likely to be highly visible and involve greater risk.

Pre-decision activity unfolds in a *sequence of state-of-mind* changes which propel the consumer toward the adoption or rejection decision. This sequence of symbolic stages is called the *adoption or rejection process*, depending on its outcome (see Figure 3.11): [79, pp. 81 ff.]

Symbolic stages

- Awareness
- Interest
- Evaluation
- Trial
- Adoption or rejection

Figure 3.11

The Adoption or Rejection Process

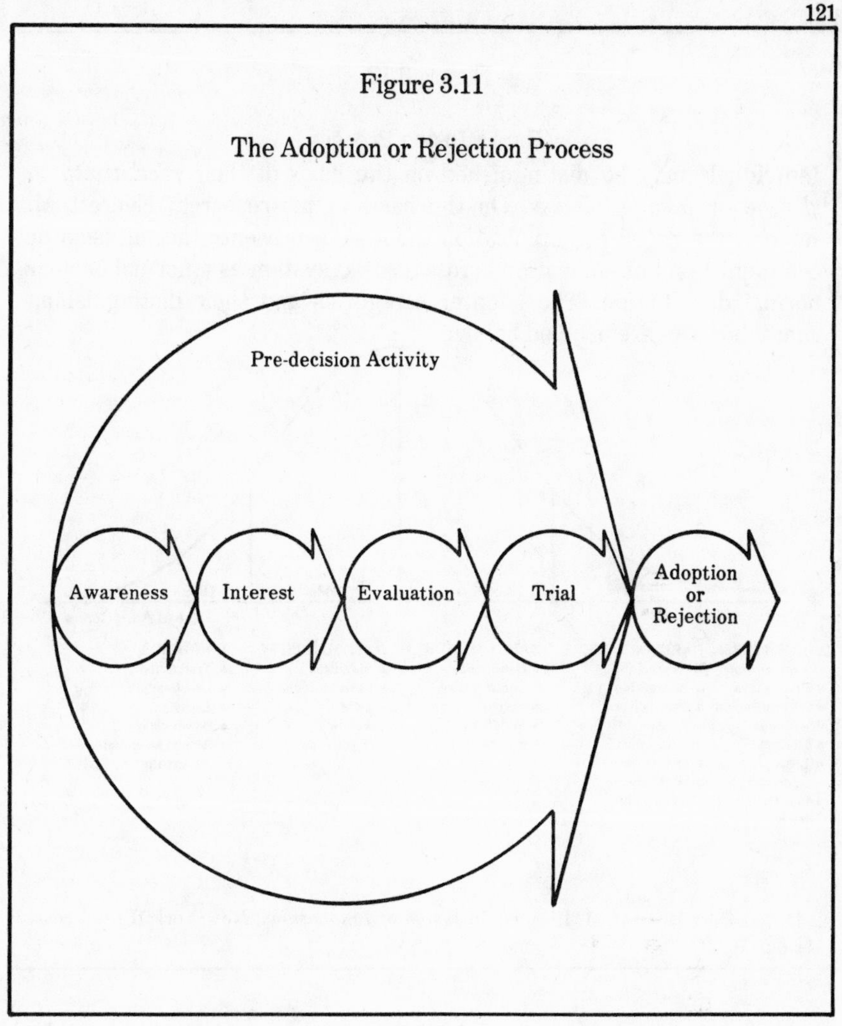

Receptivity to change = innovativeness

Progress to one stage in the sequence does not assure that the adoption process will continue to completion or purchase. Individuals differ markedly in their *receptivity to change.* This receptivity to change or willingness to adopt new ideas or products – *innovativeness* – also varies from one product category to another within the same individual. Consumers can be categorized according to their willingness to try or adopt innovations, whether the innovations are products or ideas. When these categories are plotted over time, they tend to normalize through the population in a longitudinal process commonly called the diffusion process (see Figure 3.12). [79, p. 162 ff.] The most relevant categories from a marketing strategy per-

Innovativeness: normally distributed

Figure 3.12

The Diffusion Process

Individuals may be distinguished on the basis of their *receptivity to change* or *innovativeness*. On the basis of his research, Everett M. Rogers, the noted communication theorist, represents the diffusion or communication of innovation across a social system as a normal or near normal distribution. The adopter categories and their distinguishing characteristics are profiled below:

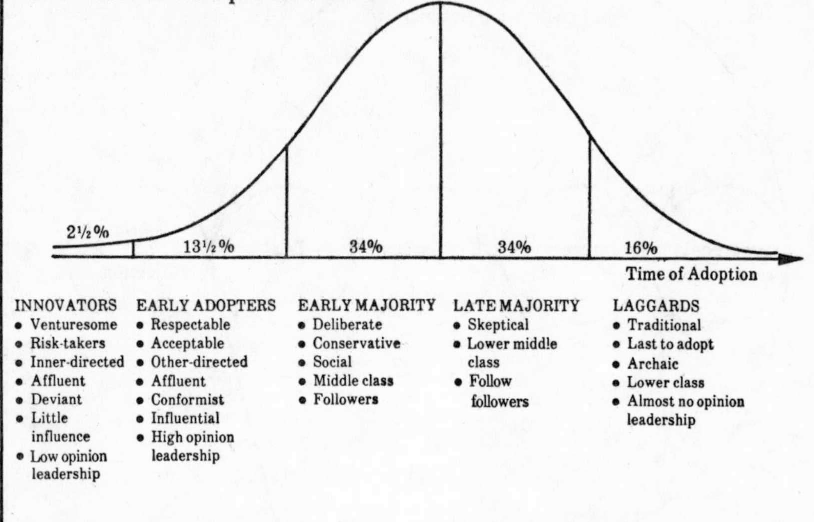

Adapted from Everett M. Rogers, *Diffusion of Innovations*, New York: Free Press, 1962, p. 162 ff.

Early adopters = opinion leaders

spective are the initial categories, particularly *early adopters*. Early adopters, for a variety of reasons, also tend to be *opinion leaders* and hence very powerful sources of nonmarketer-controlled information which may enhance or impede communication strategies of the firm. The significance of opinion leader influence will become more apparent when we discuss the communication mix.

During the adoption or rejection process the individual forms an attitude about a product alternative, translates that attitude into an intention, and intention into purchase or non-purchase behavior. The significance of pre-decision activity for the marketer is the awareness that needs incubate for a time before crystallizing in purchase action. During the pre-decision phase the potential buyer is most receptive to marketer- and non-marketer-controlled channels of information and stimulation concerning product values. He deliberately lowers many of his selective defenses and seeks communications with a relatively open mind. From a strategy point of view, the difficulty lies in identifying when the consumer is at the point of readiness, a task which may be impossible.

Culmination → decision

Adoption or Rejection Decision. Following predecision activity, the individual undertakes the actual decision to *adopt* or *reject* the product. The adoption or rejection decision is in reality a complex of interrelated decisions and at the very least may involve decisions concerning:

Complex of
• decisions
• parties

- product
- brand
- style
- quantity
- place
- dealer
- time
- price
- terms of purchase

The reconciliation of decisions on all these variables and more may or may not culminate in the act of purchase. In addition, several parties may be involved in the decision:

- buyer
- decider
- influencer
- user

For example, a mother may buy clothes for her children which her mother suggested she buy and which were determined by price limits set by her husband. The marketer must provide information appropriate to each of these dimensions or evaluative criteria, and to each party to the decision.

Use Behavior. The marketer should realize that a product is not purchased for its own sake but for its ability to satisfy a perceived need. Attention should therefore be directed to how the product is assimilated into the larger need and activity systems of the purchaser. The marketer should ask himself:

Assimilation into lifestyle

- Who uses the product?
- How is it used?
- Where is it used?
- When is it used?
- Why is it used?
- With what other products is it used?

Utilities

These questions point to the fact that utility is derived from *form, function, possession, time,* and *place*, and these utilities manifest themselves in many symbolic or socio-psychological dimensions of the product as well.

Adoption and initial use of a product do not assure repeat purchase. Far from it. Assuring repeat purchase or brand loyalty is a far more difficult challenge than eliciting an initial adoption. Repurchase and reuse of a product are indicators that the satisfactions the purchaser anticipated in the product actually materialized, and that the purchaser was willing to assimilate that product into his lifestyle. Purchasers, or in the aggregate, markets, can be categorized according to the degree of congruence between product expectations and perceived satisfaction derived from product consumption.

Market sectors

Any market can be usefully subdivided into three sectors: *core, fringe,* and *zone-of-indifference* (see Figure 3.13).

Core: extreme inelasticity

- *Core customers* are those whose product expectations are best approximated by the perceived characteristics of an available product alternative. As a consequence, core customers are highly brand loyal and very insensitive to price fluctuations. Hence the core of the market is characterized by *extreme inelasticity* of demand. Core customers are among the first to adopt a new product perceived to offer high levels of satisfaction, and the last to reject a product of proven potential.

Fringe: moderate elasticity

- The *fringe* of the market consists of those customers whose product expectations are to some degree approximated by the perceived characteristics of an available product alternative. Fringe customers are less brand loyal and more price sensitive than core customers. Thus the fringe is characterized by *moderate elasticity* of demand.

Figure 3.13

Market Sectors

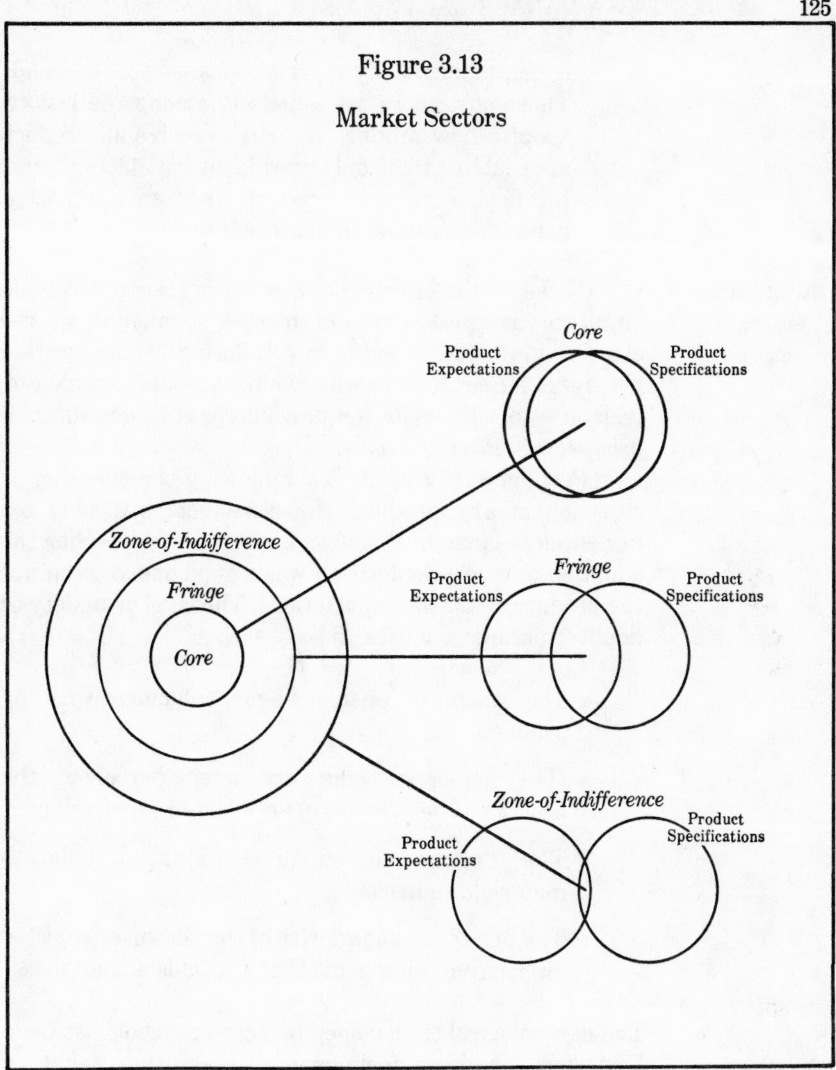

Fringe customers are cautious in adopting a new product, since few products are seen as offering high levels of satisfaction. They reject a product if its price increases or if an alternative perceived as superior appears.

Zone-of-indifference: extreme elasticity

- *Zone-of-indifference* customers are those whose product expectations are only marginally approximated by the perceived characteristics of available product alternatives. Consequently they are highly price sensitive and hence, prone to frequent brand-switching. The zone-of-indifference is characterized by *extreme elasticity* of demand. These customers are generally among the last to adopt a new product, as they perceive all product alternatives to be only marginally satisfactory, and the first to reject a product when an alternative perceived as superior is presented.

Market sectors: behavioral variable

These customer categories or market sectors provide an alternative perspective on market segmentation, and can provide useful insights into tailoring communication programs for consumers who exhibit a *behavioral* characteristic — a *willingness* or unwillingness *to assimilate a product into their lifestyles*.

Post-decision Evaluation. Following the adoption or rejection of any product, the consumer invariably experiences feelings of doubt or anxiety as to whether the adoption or rejection decision was a good one, or whether the product meets his expectations. The level of anxiety or doubt experienced varies directly with:

- The amount of consumer ego involvement with the product
- How important the consumer perceives the product to be in terms of anticipated satisfactions
- The degree to which anticipated benefits materialized in use
- The perceived superiority of the chosen or rejected alternative relative to other available alternatives

Cognitive dissonance = doubt

Consumers seek reinforcement

The psychological term coined by noted psychologist Leon Festinger for these feelings of post-decision doubt or discomfort is *cognitive dissonance*, [26] or in marketing terms, *post-decision doubt.* Consumers may go to great lengths to relieve feelings of post-decision anxiety. Normally they will seek out information about the product or the purchase which reinforces their decision, and avoid information discomfirming their choice. They may turn to nonmarketer-controlled channels like published research reports, or their friends, or they might turn to marketer-controlled channels like promotional messages.

Marketers can play an important role in dissonance reduction. It is critical that every effort be made to enable the consumer to reduce or resolve dissonance in order to assure positive word-of-mouth communication between potential purchasers, and to maximize the likelihood of repeat purchasing or brand loyalty. Many firms have begun to incorporate post-purchase promotional strategies which explicitly recognize the potentially powerful consequences of the process of dissonance reduction for reinforcing repeat purchases and building consumer loyalty.

The model of consumer behavior we have presented here is a general conceptualization that corroborates other more detailed models. One notable such model is that proposed by Engel, Kollat and Blackwell (see Figure 3.14). [23] The Engel *et al* model represents an expansion and elaboration of the model presented in the previous paragraphs. It incorporates many variables and subprocesses including perception or information processing, attitude formation, environmental press, reduction of risk through information search, and dissonance reduction. The Engel *et al* model is particularly useful because the authors have gone to great pains to assemble an eclectic array of empirical support for their conceptualization of consumer decision making.

Decision models generalizable

A corollary advantage of a number of models of consumer behavior is that they are *generalizable* to a variety of decision-making contexts or to decisions individuals make in other roles than that of consumer. Political or voter decisions, marriage and family decisions — in fact the adoption of any new idea — are processes which are better understood when interpreted in the framework of a decision model. In fact, much of the research on which the consumer decision models are based originated in arenas other than the marketplace.

Transactive model: Exchange of values

The advantage of the model presented in this text, which distinguishes it from others, is that it focuses on the transactive nature of the consumer decision process. Transactions pervade every aspect of human interaction. They require expenditures of energy and other resources, expenditures which are proportional to anticipated benefits resulting from the transaction. The consumer decision process, like any transaction, culminates in an *exchange of values*. If the exchange is mutually beneficial future transactions or exchanges will be facilitated and hence more efficient. Each consumer decision process is situational and unique, but many of the intrapersonal and

Figure 3.14

The Engel, Kollat and Blackwell Model of Consumer Behavior

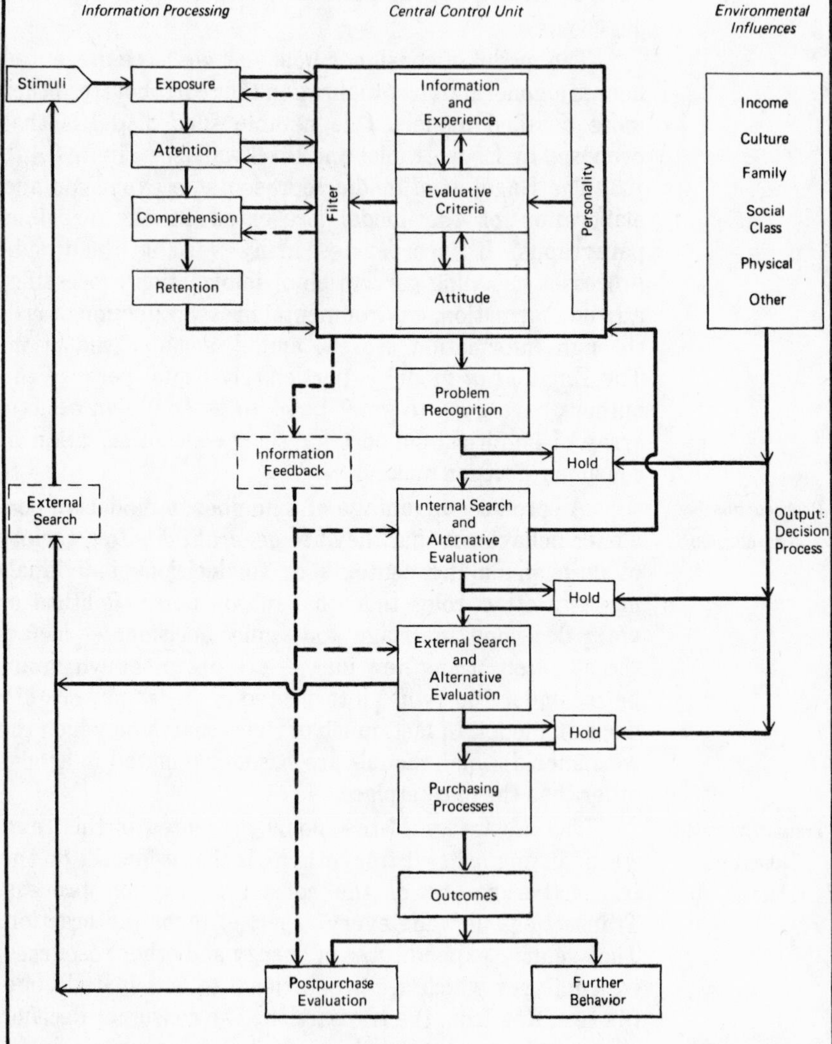

James F. Engel, David T. Kollat, and Roger D. Blackwell, *Consumer Behavior*, New York: Holt, Rinehart and Winston, 1968, 1973. Reprinted by permission of the publisher.

environmental influences which impinge on the purchase decision also pervade many other types of human transactions or interactions. *Hence, while other decision models are generalizable to other types of decision processes, a transactive approach permits generalization to all facets of social interaction.*

Individuals learn certain patterns of thought and behavior, and these patterns are repeated time and time again. Marketing research has contributed major insights to our understanding of how consumers function in a wide variety of purchase situations. The responsibility of marketers is to utilize their knowledge of consumer decision processes to better coordinate market offerings with consumer wants and needs.

The Marketing Research Process

Knowledge of consumer decision processes and appropriate segmentation axes is insufficient for the formulation of an entire marketing strategy. The firm must utilize a wide array of diverse sources and kinds of information in an attempt to reduce uncertainty and risk associated with rapid environmental change. Intelligence and information gathering and analysis are among the most important functions performed by a firm, and their widespread acceptance by management has been long in coming.

> *Marketing research, then, is the systematic gathering, recording, analyzing and interpreting of information concerning the process of enterprise anticipation and adaptation to the demands emanating from the relevant sectors of the firm's environment, including the communication, transfer, exchange, and sale of goods and services between producer and consumer.*

Actionable information

Marketing research provides *actionable information* pertaining to all the various aspects of the marketing process: analysis of market potential, product positioning, determination and evaluation of the elements of the communication mix, allocation of funds, consumer preferences and behavior, economic and competitive analysis, social and environmental impact evaluation, and a host of other diverse problems.

Conceptions of the scope and use of marketing research have historically been defined somewhat narrowly, paralleling narrow definitions of the scope and nature of the marketing process. Currently, however, marketing research is expanding to include:

- Definition of problem areas as well as provision of data for problem solution
- Analysis of intrafirm as well as extrafirm problems
- Analysis of information pertaining to the broader environment in which marketing management must make decisions, rather than merely focusing on the immediate competitive environment of the firm

Clearly the purpose of marketing research is not the gathering of data for data's sake, but for the purpose of improving marketing decision making and control.

Marketing research is one of the functions of a *marketing information system*. A marketing information system is

> *a continuously operating nondepartmentalized system for the gathering of marketing intelligence of all kinds.*

Feedback

In viewing the firm and the marketing process as systems the marketing information system can be regarded as the *feedback* function. There are two major distinctions between the marketing research process and a marketing information system:

Continuous versus Project-oriented

- The marketing information system is a continuous system encompassing many information flows, while marketing research is more task or project oriented

Intrafirm versus Extrafirm sources

- The marketing information system provides for the collection, processing, and dissemination of information to and from both intrafirm and extrafirm sources, whereas marketing research information normally is channeled to decision centers within the firm

Marketing research and marketing information systems have become a necessary adjunct to the marketing process as decision making has become more complex and managers are forced to make intelligent, high-stakes decisions in an atmosphere of rapid change and uncertainty. Information permits the firm to *anticipate* change, major and minor, rather than merely to *react* to it. *Innovation*, a major function of any firm, requires anticipating change and rapidly implementing solutions, so marketing research and the marketing information system permit the firm to innovate. Examples of changes in the environment for marketing which make innovation difficult and information critical include:

Innovation:
- **Anticipate**
- **Implement**

- The rapidly changing nature of the American domestic market – population growth and changing age composition, urban and suburban growth, affluence tempered by inflation, changing value structures, etc.
- Increased competition emanating from a variety of sources offering both similar and substitute products
- Expanding world markets offering considerable opportunities at considerable risk
- Fast-paced changes in technology which shorten product life cycles
- Extremely high costs of new ventures, including expansion and new product development
- Deteriorating and uncertain supplies of energy and other resources
- Deepening involvement of government in business operations

Information obsolescence

The list is potentially endless, as we have discussed earlier, but the implication is clear: environmental change leads to rapid obsolescence of existing information, which leads to the necessity for investing substantial sums in marketing information systems and marketing research.

Information is the firm's key to reducing the ratio of uncontrollables to controllables.

PROGRAMMING

The specification of enterprise goals and resources and the delineation of products and potential consumer segments determine the framework within which marketing management programs marketing effort. Conversely, decisions made at the programming or implementation level partially determine

- Which goals will be pursued and how
- Which physical, human, energy, and financial resources are required
- Which target markets will provide the focus for marketing effort

Readjustment

Programming is in a constant state of readjustment to the demands of altered goal requirements and resource restrictions imposed by the environment and the firm's manpower capabilities. It is through the marketing program that the firm interfaces with the environment and implements strategies of adaptation in response to demands emanating from various sectors in the firm's environment. Thus *the outcome of marketing programming is a set of integrated strategies and policies of adaptation which guide the process of enterprise adjustment to environmental forces.*

Interface with environment

In this section we will discuss the various elements or major decision areas involved in marketing programming (see Figure 3.15):

- Product/pricing strategy
- Distribution strategy
- Communication strategy

Competition for differential advantage

The firm seeks legitimacy and a competitive advantage through positive differentiation in these three major elements of the marketing program. The search for legitimacy, negotiation ability, and market power in the *product/pricing* arena compels the firm to undertake product innovation and to offer products in the marketplace at prices which consumers concur are reflective of

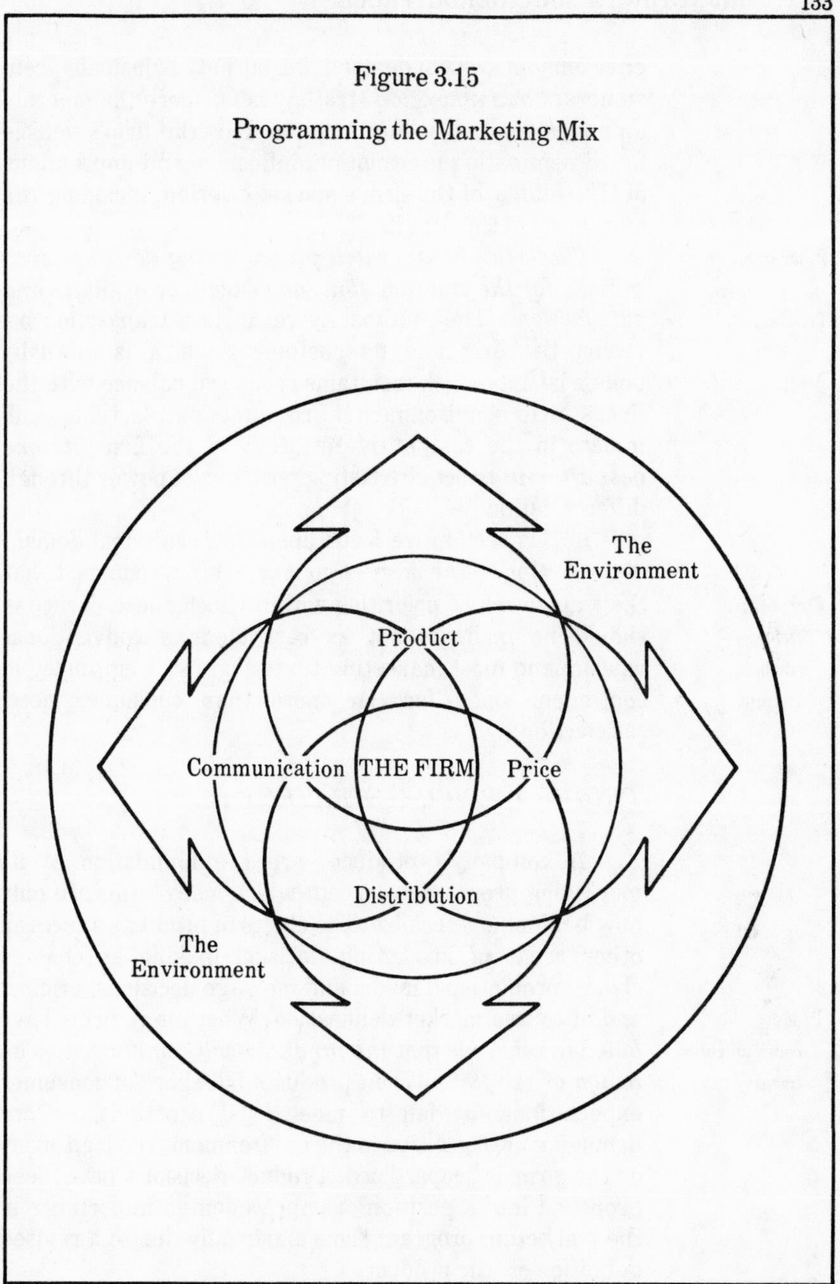

Figure 3.15

Programming the Marketing Mix

the anticipated value and utilities of the product. *Distribution* strategy decisions determine the efficiency with which the firm effects transfers of title or ownership, physical products, and services to those entities in the environment which demand its output, principally consumers. *Communication* strategy is far more than merely an advertising or selling function. It is the firm's vehicle for disseminating information, influence, and impressions of the totality of the firm's market offering, including the marketing of the firm itself.

Programming

Transaction

These three integrated programming decision areas provide for the creation, flow, and exchange of values and satisfactions. They ultimately result in a transaction between the firm and its customers which is mutually beneficial and which maintains ecological balance with the firm's macroenvironment. Programming decisions culminate in the competitive strategy of the firm, *its one best attempt* to acquire lasting positions of power through differentiation.

Competitive strategy = one best attempt

In this section we focus upon the traditional domain of marketing – *the marketing mix* – but we suggest that the framework of priorities within which these decisions should be made is not as restricted as conventional wisdom and most marketing texts suggest. Legitimacy is contingent upon far, far more than consumer need satisfaction.

PRODUCT/PRICING STRATEGY

Product communicates image

A company's products are the foundation of its marketing program, a concept which many firms are only now beginning to realize. The choice of products affects all other areas of marketing decision making – channel choice, promotional media and message decisions, pricing, and of course market delineation. What many firms have failed to realize is that *the product itself communicates an image of the firm.* When products fall short of consumer expectations, or fail to meet legal sanctions, or are damaging or disruptive in the environment, the legitimacy of the firm is jeopardized. Product decisions have been propelled into a position of unprecedented importance in the marketing program. This is partially due to a revised definition of "the product."

Product Strategy

Configuration of benefits
- **physical**
- **symbolic**

A product is a configuration of physical, functional, service and symbolic components expected to yield satisfactions or benefits to consumers. This focus on

Figure 3.16

Marketing Myopia

The railroads did not stop growing because the need for passenger and freight transportation declined . . . They let others take customers away from them because they assumed themselves to be in the railroad business rather than in the transportation business. The reason they defined their industry wrong was because they were railroad-oriented instead of customer-oriented . . .

Even after the advent of automobiles, trucks, and airplanes, the railroad tycoons remained imperturbably self-confident. If you had told them 60 years ago that in 30 years they would be flat on their backs, broke, and pleading for government subsidies, they would have thought you totally demented. Such a future was simply not considered possible. It was not even a discussable subject, or an askable question, or a matter which any sane person would consider worth speculating about. The very thought was insane. Yet a lot of insane notions now have matter-of-fact acceptance — for example, the idea of 100-ton tubes of metal moving smoothly through the air 20,000 feet above the earth, loaded with 100 sane and solid citizens casually drinking martinis — and they have dealt cruel blows to the railroads.

But memories are short. For example, it is hard for people who today confidently hail the twin messiahs of electronics and chemicals to see how things could possibly go wrong with these galloping industries. They probably also cannot see how a reasonably sensible businessman could have been as myopic as the famous Boston millionaire who 50 years ago unintentionally sentenced his heirs to poverty by stipulating that his entire estate be forever invested exclusively in electric streetcar securities. His posthumous declaration, "There will always be a big demand for efficient urban transportation," is no consolation to his heirs who sustain life by pumping gasoline at automobile filling stations.

And speaking of automobiles, in a sense Ford was both the most brilliant and the most senseless marketer in American history. He was senseless because he refused to give the customer anything but a black car. He was brilliant because he fashioned a production system designed to fit market needs. We habitually celebrate him for the wrong reason, his production genius. His real genius was marketing. We think he was able to cut his selling price and therefore sell millions of $500 cars because his invention of the assembly line had reduced the costs. Actually, he invented the assembly line because he had concluded that at $500 he could sell millions of cars. Mass production was the *result* not the cause of his low prices.

Excerpted from Theodore Levitt, "Marketing Myopia," *Harvard Business Review* (July-August, 1960), pp. 45-56. Reprinted by permission of the publisher.

anticipated utilities, satisfactions or benefits rather than physical or functional attributes of the product is the essence of the *marketing concept*. Also implicit in this definition is the recognition that higher-order needs — love, status, achievement — are equally legitimate with inborn biogenic needs, and marketers should therefore pursue their satisfaction as well as the satisfaction of the so-called lower-order needs. In a complex society such as the United States where biogenic needs are routinely met for virtually everybody, *it is foolish to assert that psychogenic needs are less legitimate*. A product, then, is a vehicle through which the firm communicates utilities or satisfactions to consumers, while conforming to other expectations and norms imposed by society, including laws and ecological imperatives. Therefore, product strategy should comprehend and affect *all* decisions regarding what the *consumer perceives* as the firm's marketing offering (see Figure 3.16). Through product strategy, a firm anticipates consumer needs and attempts to satisfy them.

Product = a vehicle

Product proliferation

Product proliferation is an artifact of the affluence which has characterized the post-World War II economy. Some major firms produce or handle as many as 250,000 different products, and the average supermarket often carries over 8,000 items. The proliferation of products within the typical firm implies that care must be exercised in developing a configuration of products which singly and collectively contribute to the legitimacy and power position of the firm and which respond to pressures and expectations emanating from non-consumer sectors of the firm's environment.

Product decisions
- **Item**
- **Line**
- **Mix**

Product Strategy Decisions. Product strategy decisions are formulated at three levels (see Figure 3.17): [49, p. 439]

- A *product item* is a specific version of a product that has a separate designation in the seller's list, for example, Levi's *Big Bells*.
- A *product line* is a group of products that are closely related either because they satisfy a class of need, are commonly used together, are sold to the same market segments, are marketed through the same channels, or fall within certain price ranges. Levi markets a varied line of sport pants, for example.

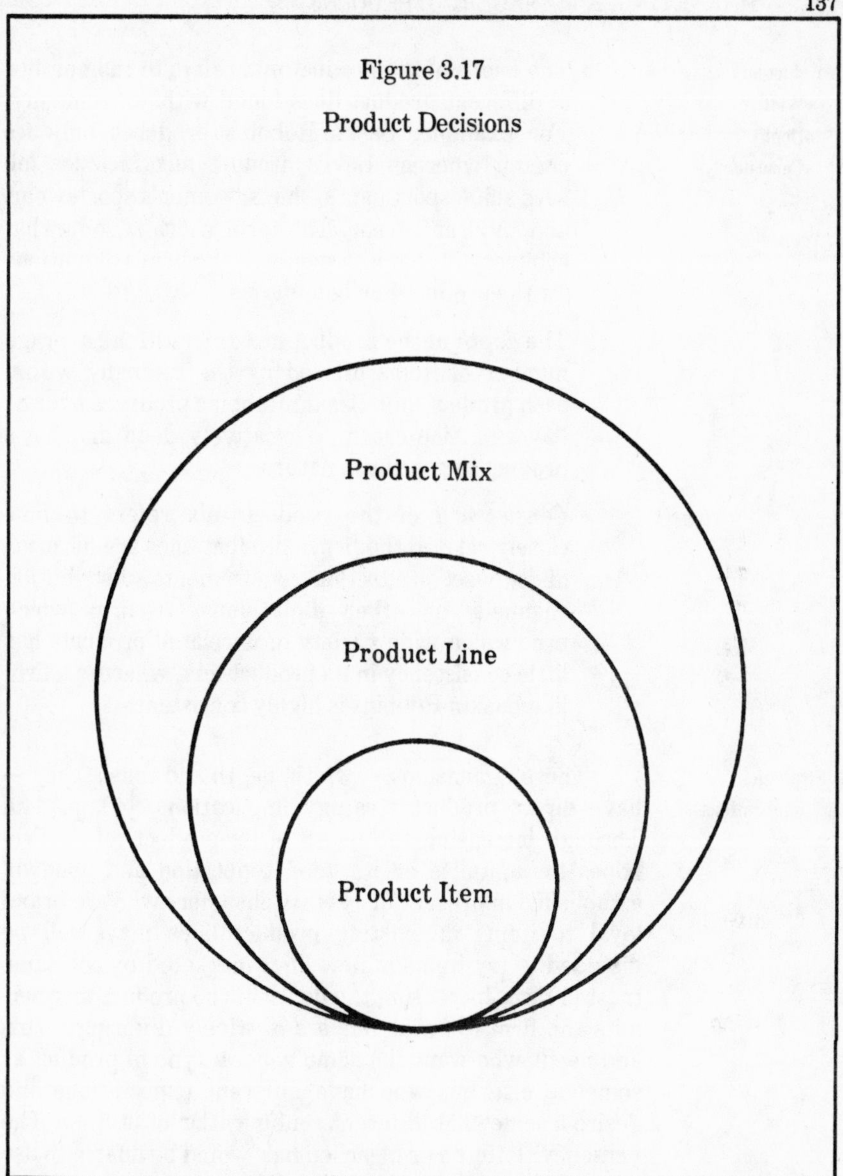

Figure 3.17
Product Decisions

- The *product mix* is the composite of products offered for sale by a firm, for example, all products carrying Levi's label.

The product mix exhibits the characteristics of *width, depth*, and *consistency*. [49, p. 439]

Product mix
- **Width**
- **Depth**
- **Consistency**

- The *width* of the product mix refers to the number of different product lines found within a company. For example, Baskin-Robbins produces only ice cream, whereas Levi's product mix includes leisure suits, sport pants, shirts, women's sportswear, and children's wear. The term width is somewhat arbitrary in that it depends on the firm's definitions for the product-line boundaries.
- The *depth* of the product mix refers to the average number of items offered by the company within each product line. Baskin-Robbins produces over 31 flavors of ice cream, a relatively deep line for a product so specific in nature.
- *Consistency* of the product mix refers to how closely related the firm's product lines are in terms of end-use, production requirements, distribution channels, or other dimensions. A firm which produces a wide variety of unrelated products has little consistency in its product mix, whereas a firm like Baskin-Robbins is highly consistent.

Strategic implications

These dimensions — width, depth and consistency — have direct product strategy implications. [49, p. 440] Through increasing the width of its product mix a firm hopes to capitalize on its good reputation and goodwill established in present markets. Consumers who are brand loyal to items in existing product lines may well be disposed to try items in new lines marketed by the same trusted firm. Increasing the depth of the product mix permits the firm to entice buyers of widely differing tastes and needs who want the same general type of product as someone else but who have different expectations and desire a somewhat different configuration of utilities. The person with tinted or bleached hair would be unable to use a *Toni* home permanent if *Toni* did not offer a special permanent for such people. Finally, by increasing the consistency of the product mix, the firm hopes to acquire a good reputation and skills in a particular product category. Such firms do not place a premium on being diversified, but rather on being very good at what they do. Kirby vacuum cleaners is an excellent example of a successful firm with a highly consistent product mix.

Company Objectives and the Product Mix. Product and marketing strategies are not solely contingent on product characteristics. Management's long-run objectives also are highly influential in determining the firm's product mix. These relationships again demonstrate the dynamic interactive nature of the marketing process in a very tangible way. If a firm is interested in improving its profit position, it can adjust its product strategy or its marketing strategy. Before making such adjustments, however, it is necessary to measure the profit and overhead contributions of the existing individual product items comprising the mix. Firms usually discover that a relatively small proportion of their products accounts for a disproportionately high percentage of its profits — a phenomenon referred to as the *iceberg principle*. An example might be a firm which produces 10 products, 4 of which contribute 80 percent of all profit and overhead. The strategy implications are that the firm should protect the top 4 products because the loss of one could be drastic. The company may be able to increase its average level of profits by dropping some of the bottom 6 products, especially those which absorb a disproportionate amount of time and resources relative to the profits they generate. Or, alternatively, the firm may wish to selectively allocate more support to less profitable products to strengthen sales, or selectively retain products which reinforce the sale of highly profitable products. This is a complex problem to assess, and a difficult and complicated decision to make.

Management objectives ↕ Product mix

• Profit position

• Stability

If one of the long-range goals of a firm is stability, marketing management might want to incorporate into its product mix product items which will stabilize sales and production. For example, producing seasonal products whose seasons are complementary will greatly improve the stability and efficiency of a firm. Many marketers of sporting equipment have adopted such a product strategy.

• Growth

If a company is committed to growth, four basic *product-market strategies* are available: [49, pp. 237-40]

- *Market penetration* is a strategy through which the firm seeks to increase sales for its present products in its present markets, by means of more aggressive promotion and distribution

- *Market development* is a strategy in which the firm attempts to increase sales by marketing its present products in new markets
- *Product development* implies increasing sales by developing improved products for present markets
- *Diversification* involves increasing sales by developing new products for sale in new markets

Lead from strength

These growth strategies should permit the firm to lead from the strength of product-market experience.

The Product Life Cycle. Whatever the goals and objectives of the enterprise, adjustments in product strategy and indeed adjustments in all other aspects of the marketing program are necessitated by a cycle of *perishable product distinctiveness* or obsolescence through which all products progress — the *product life cycle*. The number of stages in the product life cycle as well as their names is a somewhat arbitrary decision which varies from source to source. We suggest that the product life cycle is appropriately viewed as a *five-stage* sequence (see Figure 3.18): [87, Ch. 10]

Perishable distinctiveness

Five-stage cycle

- Pioneering
- Acceptance
- Turbulence
- Saturation
- Obsolescence

The product life cycle is a framework for analyzing the product in relation to its contribution to the firm's capacity for innovation. One source describes the product life cycle this way:

Framework of strategic choices

> The marketing concept known as the product life cycle . . . is the framework of strategic choices the marketer faces when his product is entering the market, when its sales are growing rapidly, and when those sales have matured or perhaps begun to decline. It is this [multiphase] cycle that makes marketing such a dynamic profession: A strategy that works beautifully in early stages of a product's life cycle can be disastrous in later stages. [30, pp. 265-66].

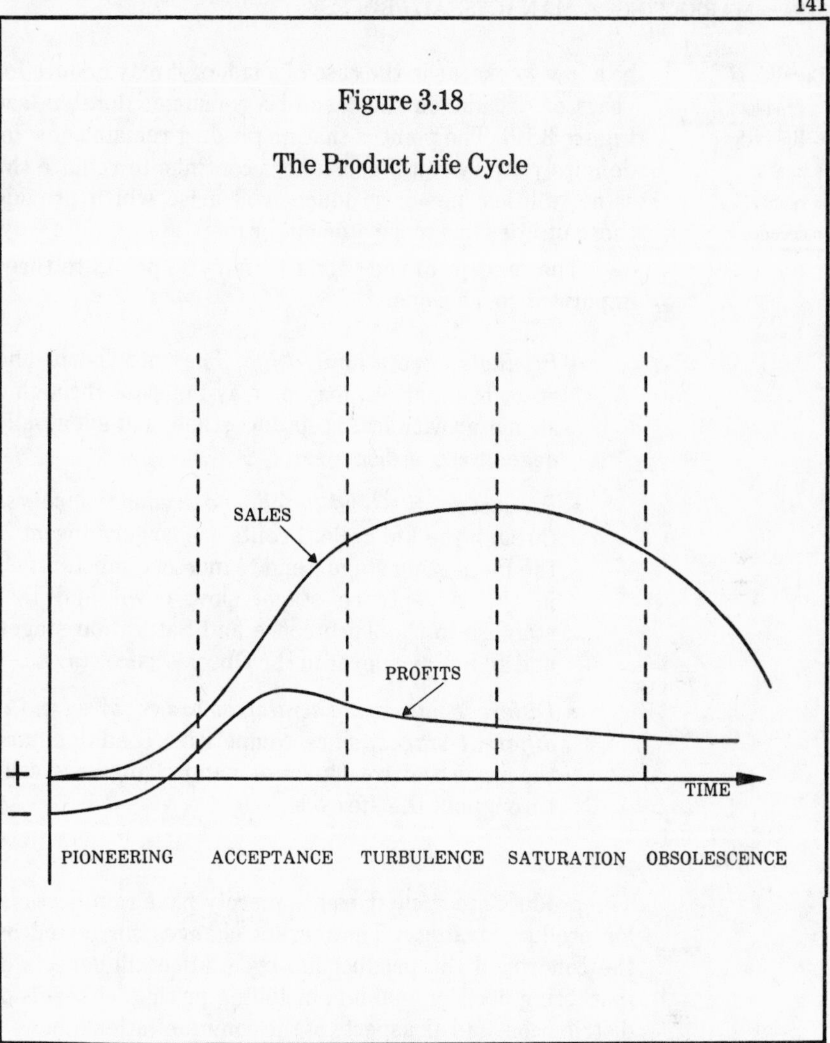

The product life cycle suggests that products are maximally innovative or distinctive when they are first introduced. As competitors enter the market in increasing numbers and have access to common sources of technological information, a given product diminishes in distinctiveness. Its contribution to the sales volume, profit margins, and market power of the enterprise increases to a peak at some point in time and then begins to deteriorate, becoming more of a burden than an asset as a vehicle for the firm to achieve and sustain positions of market power. The duration of the product life cycle may

Duration of product life cycle:
- **weeks**
- **years**
- **decades**

be a few weeks, as in the case of a fad, or it may endure for years or decades in the case of a consumer durable (see Figure 3.19). The point is that no product remains new indefinitely, and even if consumers continue to require the same utilities, newer products will arise which provide those utilities in a more efficient or more appropriate way.

The concept of the product life cycle points to three important conclusions:

- *Products have a limited life.* They are "born" and enter the market, may or may not pass through a strong growth or Acceptance stage, and eventually degenerate or disappear.
- Product *profits tend to follow a predictable course* through the life cycle. Profits are largely absent in the Pioneering stage, tend to increase substantially in the Acceptance stage, slow down and then stabilize in the Turbulence and Saturation stages, and all but disappear in the Obsolescence stage.
- *Different marketing strategies are required in the different stages*, since competitive conditions and the nature of consumer demand change radically throughout the life cycle.

The product life cycle does not merely have ramifications for product strategy. The market changes suggested by the concept of the product life cycle affect all aspects of marketing decision making, including pricing, channels of distribution, and all aspects of the communication mix.

The Product Life Cycle and adopter categories

The product life cycle is plotted in terms of sales volume and profit margins as they rise and fall over time. We stated earlier that individuals differ markedly in their receptivity to change, or in their willingness to adopt a new product. If we categorize people in terms of their receptivity to change — *the adopter categories* — we can plot a frequency distribution that approximates a normal curve and hence helps clarify the shape of the product life cycle (see Figure 3.20). What we find, then, is a close but not identical relationship between the adopter categories and the stages in the product life cycle. When the last adopter adopts a product it has achieved complete saturation.

Figure 3.19

Rate and Level of Adoption in Three Product Life Cycles: Fad, Fashion, Durable

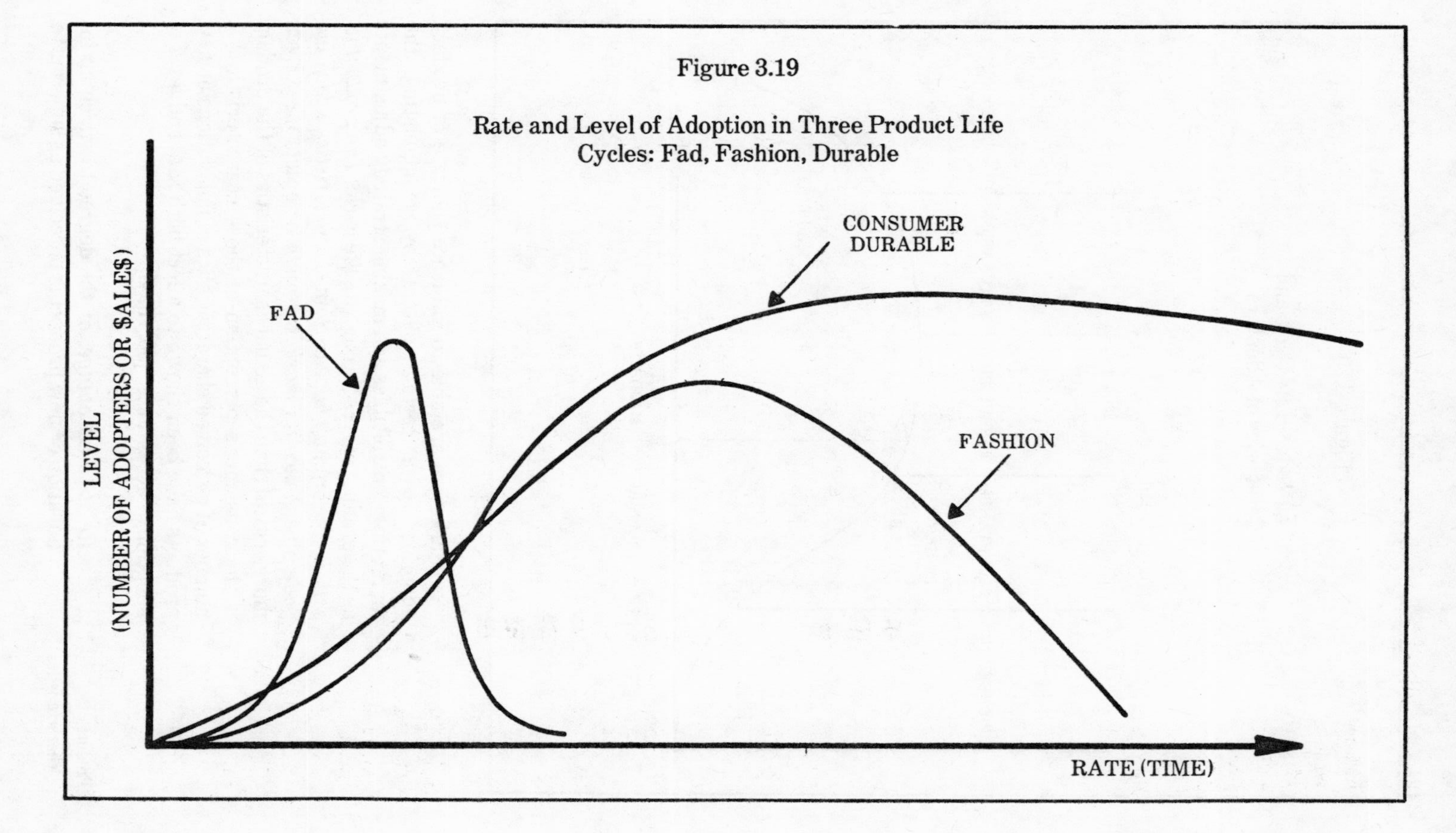

Figure 3.20

The Product Life Cycle and Categories of Adopters

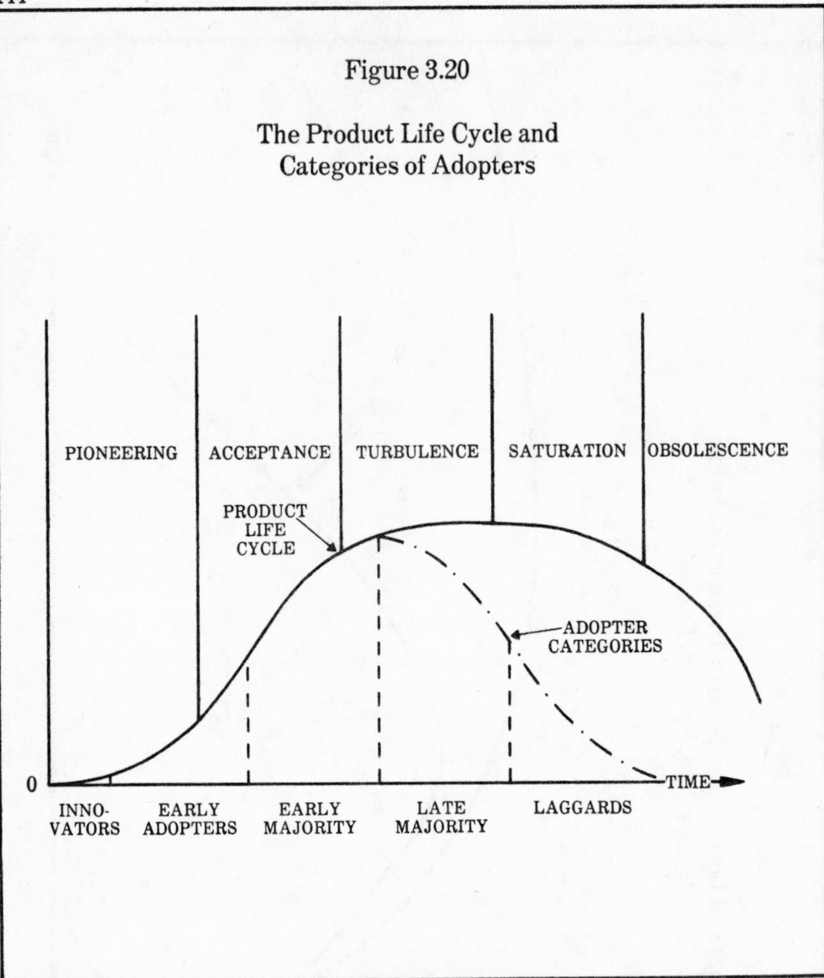

Marketers are able to influence the rate of product adoption to a certain extent by manipulating the marketing controllables and making strategy adjustments as the product moves through its life cycle. *The product itself, however, may have certain characteristics which impede or enhance its market growth* or acceptance. Even more critical than the actual characteristics of the product is the consumer's perception of those characteristics. A number of perceived characteristics of innovations or new products have been shown to affect both *rate* and *level* of adoption or acceptance: [80, Ch. 5]

Product characteristics

- *Relative advantage*, or the degree to which an innovation or new product is perceived as superior to

Rate and level of acceptance

the idea or product which it supercedes

- *Compatibility*, or the degree to which an innovation or new product is perceived as consistent with the existing values, past experiences, and lifestyle of the adopter
- *Complexity*, or the degree to which an innovation or new product is perceived as difficult to understand and use
- *Trialability*, or the degree to which an innovation or new product may be experimented with on a limited basis
- *Observability*, or the degree to which the results of adoption of an innovation or new product are visible to others

Marketing communications can greatly enhance the adoption rate and level of a new product by altering consumers' perceptions. For example, a product which is very complex can be explained or demonstrated in such a manner that it becomes much more comprehensible to potential purchasers. And, of course, most marketing communications are aimed at presenting the advantages of a product relative to the alternatives.

Product additions:
- **R & D**
- **merger**

Addition and Deletion Decisions: The Product Audit. Sometimes a modification in communication strategy is sufficient to revive a product which has entered the Obsolescence stage of the product life cycle. But *often drastic product modification or the addition or deletion of products is necessary if the enterprise is to maintain a competitive edge*. Firms can add products to their offering in order to add width or depth to the product mix or to pursue a policy of innovation or diversification. New products can be added either through research and development and production, or through merger. In either case, careful attention should be paid to the product addition decision.

- **complementary**
- **unrelated**

Often a firm elects to market a product which is new to the firm but well established in the product life cycle. When a firm researches and develops an innovation, however, tremendous expense is involved and the new product runs an extremely high risk of failure in spite of the firm's best efforts. Addition of new products, whether they complement existing lines or are totally unrelated, can enhance the market strength of a firm along dimensions of reputation, diversification, growth and many others. Product additions can be very costly, however, both in terms of money and in terms of positions of power in the marketplace.

• money costs
• power

Marketing management often encounters the difficult decision of whether to eliminate certain products altogether. Businessmen are wont to neglect the subject of product elimination in comparison with the attention they give to product modification and new product development. But *weak products are costly*, and many of the hidden costs associated with weak products are hard to isolate or evaluate. Weak products consume time, attention and resources since they require frequent adjustments of production, inventory, price, advertising, and personal selling. They can also undermine the reputation of the firm. One bad product may give the firm a bad name and erode sales of its other strong products. Determining if this is indeed the case and making the decision to alter the product mix, requires careful observation and *periodic product audits*. Firms are only now beginning to realize the importance of product audits, particularly when resources are scarce and must be allocated among an array of products in the firm's offering. Product audits, however, permit the firm to upgrade its product offering in response to the changing strength and nature of demand, legal requirements, technological innovations, and limited material and energy resources.

Hidden costs

Periodic product audit

Product decisions are an integral component of all other marketing decisions. The legitimacy of the firm might be jeopardized if product decisions are not made in response to both short- and long-term constraints, demand, and objectives of the firm. Positive product differentiation, like differentiation in other components of the marketing mix, leads to market power. Product differentiation represents innovation, or constant adaptation to a changing environment, and innovation leads to lasting legitimacy. A strong product offering permits the firm to negotiate more successfully in the marketplace. The product mix should be viewed as a dynamic, balanced constellation of items and lines, constantly being reviewed, upgraded and adjusted, with an eye to its critical importance in the market offering.

Product mix = constellation of items and lines

Pricing Strategy

Price:
• communicated value
• perceived value

An inseparable attribute of a product is its price. Price is often a critical feature of a consumer's perception of the satisfactions embodied in a product. A firm communicates its assessment of the worth and cost of the product through its pricing policy and the consumer articulates his assessment of the product's value by his adoption or rejection decision. An established demand for a product in part reflects a meeting of the minds between the firm and the consumer regarding the perceived value of the product. In fact, price is often used by the consumer as a surrogate indicator of the value of the product in the absence of an objective standard of comparison or complete information concerning the product. Hence, pricing strategy is an integral component of the product mix.

Administered pricing

Controllable versus Uncontrollable. Pricing strategy, unlike other aspects of the marketing mix, is usually severely circumscribed by the firm's environment. Six factors combine to determine the discretionary latitude of marketing management in *administering* or setting prices:

- Total costs of production and marketing
- Stage in the product life cycle
- Industrial or consumer product classification
- Governmental regulation
- Market sector (core, fringe, or zone-of-indifference)
- Market structure (monopoly, oligopoly, or monopolistic competition)

The interaction of these six factors, however, places pricing somewhere *between* controllable and uncontrollable in terms of marketing management's ability to administer prices autonomously.

Costs

Most firms utilize some variation of cost-plus pricing, but even if cost-plus is not used, *costs* will have to be carefully analyzed and reflected in pricing strategies or the firm will eventually face severe financial problems. Costs change over time, among other things as a function of stage in the product life cycle and continual inflationary pressure and economic fluctuations. Assessing production and marketing costs may be extremely difficult and inexact, but the firm clearly cannot afford to ignore costs even when pricing competitively. *The fact that a price reflects the cost of a product is not relevant at the point of purchase*. Consumers will only pay prices which they *perceive* to reflect the value of the product's utilities.

Position in the Product Life Cycle

The product's *position in the product life cycle* determines not only costs but also the degree of differentiation of the product and the ability of the firm to realize economies of scale. Production and marketing costs are generally quite high in the Pioneering phase of the product life cycle, as the product is essentially a prototype requiring labor-intensive production and marketing. However, the product is also unique, which permits the firm to recover high initial costs of new product introduction quickly by implementing a policy of *price skimming*, should the product gain rapid and widespread acceptance. Later the product relinquishes its uniqueness as competitors enter the market but economies of scale derived from mass production and distribution drive costs down. Prices are usually lowered as a result of cost efficiencies and competitive pressures, but net profits tend to be higher in the Acceptance stage than at any other phase in the product life cycle. Costs and prices both tend to rise in the Obsolescence phase.

Product classification
- **Industrial**
- **Consumer**

We have suggested that price is an integral attribute of a product, so it follows that the *product classification* is a major determinant of an appropriate price range. The unit price range for categories of *industrial* products is from very low in the case of raw materials to extremely high in the case of installations and special equipment. In an era of resource scarcity, however, prices for certain raw materials have skyrocketed, while many electronic instruments have experienced significant price declines as a result of improved technology. In general, industrial purchases are characterized by rationality and deliberation, large quantity purchases, and price and credit negotiation, so the purchaser is in a good position to reject untenably high prices. In the *consumer* goods category, we find three general price ranges corresponding to the three conventional product classifications — convenience, shopping, and specialty. Convenience goods are purchased often and mass distributed, so their unit price must be low and very competitive. Shopping goods can carry a much higher price and margin, since consumers are generally willing to spend more money and effort to find exactly what they want and there are a finite number of outlets offering product alternatives. Specialty goods offer unique utility and carry very high margins and very high prices compared to their counterparts which provide many of the same functional utilities in a more ordinary way. Gourmet foods and custom-tailored clothes are excellent examples.

Legal constraints

Government regulation of pricing manifests itself in many ways. In general pricing legislation is designed to protect competition from unfair pricing practices like price discrimination and price-fixing. Horizontal price-fixing is illegal *per se* according to the Sherman Act, and the Clayton Act and Robinson-Patman Act closely regulate price discrimination. The only legal price-fixing is resale price maintenance, which permits manufacturers to protect their branded items from price-cutting by distributors. In recent times, we have seen the institution of price controls by the federal government in an attempt to contain inflation, and requirements that price increases be cost or competition justified in some industries. Finally, federal law protects consumers from deceptive pricing practices such as the advertising of sales reductions from artificially inflated list prices. Such activities are regulated by the Federal Trade Commission. Such restrictions have severely circumscribed the autonomy of the firm in setting its prices.

Market sectors

The characteristics of the firm's *target markets* may enhance or impede the ability of marketing management to administer prices. You will recall that core customers, those who perceive that the product's specifications approximate their expectations, are largely insensitive to price fluctuations and will continue to purchase a product even in the face of price increases. Fringe customers constitute a somewhat more price elastic market sector, and zone-of-indifference customers are highly sensitive to price changes since they perceive all product alternatives as being only marginally satisfactory. A firm may temporarily attract zone-of-indifference customers via an effective communication program or price competition, and then drive them away with price increases. Pricing strategies clearly need to reflect a sensitivity to the relative elasticity of demand of different market sectors.

Market structure

Finally, pricing decisions are subject to the *nature and extent of competition* faced by the firm in similar or

Figure 3.21

Pricing and Price-Related Policies

PRICING POLICIES

- *Odd pricing* refers to two types of pricing policies: a price ending in an odd number and a price just below a round number. The presumption is that odd pricing policies will result in substantially greater sales than conventional pricing policies.

- *Psychological pricing* means pricing within ranges which are psychologically significant to the prospective purchaser. Such prices need not necessarily be tied to any round number, but are idiosyncratic to the type of product and outlet.

- *Customary pricing* means pricing at levels which are conventional or traditional for the product type.

- *Pricing at the market* means adopting the prevailing market price on the assumption that a price higher than that of competitors would result in sharply curtailed sales, while a price lower than market would result in reduced profits. Pricing at the market is based on the assumption of a "kinked" demand curve.

- *Prestige pricing* assumes that high prices connote high quality to the prospective consumer. By implication, the higher the price, within a range of acceptability, the higher the connotation of quality.

- *Price lining* means adhering to customary or established price levels for given classes or lines of products and adjusting merchandise quality to meet altered market conditions.

- *Uniform pricing* means quoting prices at specified levels for all customers purchasing the product under substantially similar conditions.

- *Varying pricing* means granting price concessions to favored customers or to customers with superior bargaining position in a competitive market. Varying pricing policy must meet the justifications for price discrimination outlined in the Robinson-Patman Act of 1936.

- *Stable pricing* refers to the maintenance of one or a limited number of prices over a considerable period of time.

Fig. 3.21 Continued

- *Guaranteed pricing* means insuring against price declines over a specified period of time in order to secure orders sufficiently in advance of manufacture to facilitate production and distribution scheduling.

- *Price skimming* refers to a policy of pricing high initially to test the demand potential for a product and to yield quick cost recovery, and subsequently reducing the price gradually to attract more price-elastic market segments. Price skimming is price discrimination over time.

- *Penetration pricing* means pricing a product at a relatively low price initially in order to stimulate market growth, capture a sizeable market share, and insulate the product from competitive inroads.

PRICE-RELATED POLICIES

- *Trade (functional) discounts* involve quoting list prices subject to reductions if the purchaser is buying for resale. Trade discounts enable the manufacturer or supplier to compensate distributors for the performance of essential marketing functions which would otherwise have to be performed by the manufacturer or supplier.

- *Quantity discounts* are granted by suppliers or distributors to customers purchasing in quantities sufficiently large to pass along cost savings realized through economies of scale.

LEGALIZED PRICE-FIXING

- *Delivered pricing systems*, including basing point systems, are arrangements under which different firms in the same industry charge the same delivered price for their products at prescribed destinations. Delivered pricing arrangements have typically evolved in industries characterized by highly standardized products and high logistics costs relative to the value of manufactured products.

- *Resale price maintenance*, including that protected under state and federal "fair trade" laws, generally involves the determination by the manufacturer of prices below which his branded product cannot be sold by wholesale distributors or retailers. Resale price maintenance policy is formulated to prevent predatory retail price cutting by distributors of standard branded merchandise and thereby to protect the manufacturer's goodwill associated with branded products.

substitute product markets. You will recall from the continuum of market structure in Figure 3.2 that price discretion is maximized for monopolists, since they are the unique supplier, and minimized for firms engaged in intense competition with many firms selling essentially the same product. Most industries, however, are characterized by monopolistic competition or oligopoly. In an industry characterized by monopolistic competition, there are many substitutes for the product so the consumer responds (at least in theory) to price changes, although he also exhibits promotional elasticity. Oligopolists exercise a fair amount of price discretion because there are few substitutes for their product. However, if an oligopolist raises his price his competitors probably will *not* follow suit, and his sales will likely fall. If he lowers his price, his competitors *will* follow suit and his demand will not expand by much. Hence, oligopolists, and to some extent those engaged in monopolistic competition, rely heavily on nonprice competition to maintain market power. Even though the tenets of pure competition are a myth, a firm and its competitors are inextricably linked where pricing strategy is concerned. *Price is far and away the most vulnerable component of the marketing mix to competitive retaliation and governmental regulation.* The firm ignores these relationships at its peril, even in instances when competitors are few and far between.

Internally Determined Prices. Although a wide range of pricing strategies are potentially available to the firm (see Figure 3.21), *pricing usually falls into one of two general categories – internally determined or externally determined.* Internally determined prices are those which were formulated by some variation of a cost-plus formula.

Cost-plus
Incremental cost
ROI

Conventional *cost-plus* pricing, *incremental cost* pricing, and *return-on-investment* pricing are examples. Cost-plus methods require that the per unit price cover fixed costs, or variable costs, or both, and/or provide for an absolute or percentage margin on each unit sold. The various forms of cost-plus pricing share a common disadvantage, however. They are absolutely unresponsive to changes in the competitive environment, either in terms of changing levels of consumer demand or in terms of competitive actions in the marketplace. Cost-plus ignores, for example, increases in consumer demand or decreases in the price elasticity of demand which would permit the firm to raise prices without forfeiting sales. Conversely, if the level of demand falls off or demand becomes more elastic, the firm which fails to lower price accordingly may discover that its market share has been eroded by competition.

Externally Determined Price. Externally determined pricing, on the other hand, reflects the firm's attempt to respond to changes in the competitive environment. This does not mean that the firm should shelve its goals and objectives in an ill-conceived attempt to match competitors price for price. Not only is such a practice illegal, it is counter-productive to the legitimacy of the firm. Competition, legal requirements, level and elasticity of demand, consumer preferences, margin requirements of intermediaries, future availability of resources, and stage in the product life cycle are but a few of the additional considerations which make externally determined pricing preferable. Furthermore, since price invariably communicates something to the consumer about the product and the firm, it becomes even more critical that pricing strategies be flexible and responsive to changing environmental conditions. Price and quantity sold do not always move in opposite directions. Sometimes the consumer is willing to pay a high price if he feels that high price correlates with high quality or connotes prestige. Gone are the days when consumer reactions to prices were viewed as strictly "rational" and predictable.

Price levels are extremely vulnerable to the dynamics of competition and the marketplace and in this era of shortages, vulnerable to legislation and national and international politics as well. The ability to differentiate the firm from its competition in terms of price leads to competitive advantage and positions of power. Pricing strategy is critical to product strategy and to the entire marketing program. Differentiating through price, however, may be the most difficult challenge confronting marketing management. Price levels must be determined with a strong sense of awareness of environmental circumstances.

DISTRIBUTION STRATEGY

Exchange

In the marketing of almost any product, effecting *exchange of title* through performance of the buying and selling functions is paramount. The task of adjusting

Profitable opportunities for exchange of title

product supply to demand and the performance of logistic and communication functions is contingent upon profitable opportunities for exchange of title or ownership. Because of the importance of title transfer, we view

> *the channel of distribution as the course taken by the direct and indirect flow of title in the transfer of ownership to a product, including origin, intermediaries, and destination.* [6, p. 230]

Flow of ownership: legal problem

Flow of product: logistics problem

This definition focuses on the exchange or flow of ownership rather than on the exchange or flow of the physical product. The exchange channel may be identical with the logistics channel or it may follow a different path. The flow of title does not always parallel the movement of the product. Clearly, the exchange of ownership is a *legal* problem, while the physical transfer of the product is a *logistics* problem. While both flows are critical, exchange of ownership is prerequisite to enterprise legitimacy and power. Hence the design of logistic systems is contingent upon prior decisions concerning flows of title.

Channel of Distribution

The various individuals, establishments, and other agencies engaged in the marketing of goods and services comprise the channel of distribution or institutional structure for marketing. According to some authorities, the channel of distribution begins with extractors of raw materials and ends with the ultimate consumer. Others contend that the channel begins with the manufacturer and ends with the ultimate consumer. Still others view the channel as beginning somewhere after manufacture and ending at the retail level. Whatever the conceptualization, each institutional channel member performs specific functions which require interactions with many other members in the trade channel to permit flows of ownership or title and of physical commodities.

Functional approach: series of flows

Much of the conventional channel literature views the channel from one of two frames of reference. One approach is the *functional* approach, which views the channel as a series of flows (physical, title, payment, information, promotion) both forward and backward, which facilitate the movement of products and title. [27] Elements in the

Institutional approach: series of firms

channel are broken down into functional groups. The *institutional* approach, on the other hand, views the channel in terms of the various firms or institutions which comprise it. We have discussed the limitations of a strictly functional approach to marketing systems. The institutional approach is equally limited in its failure to deal with the dynamic nature of the channel of distribution. Many analysts, however, have begun to apply systems concepts to the conceptualization of the channel of distribution and the result has been greater understanding of the processes and interactions operating in a channel.

Vertical Marketing System

Channel: An interactive system

It is vital to understand and conceptualize the marketing channel as an *interactive system*, one in which channel structures are interdependent with marketing functions and with other structures. There is not and has never been a one-to-one relationship between a given market structure or institution and specific marketing functions. Structure and function are closely tied and interdependent, however, as is the case in all systems, and are also involved in an interactive relationship with their relevant environment.

The systems concepts presented in Chapter 1 are highly relevant in evaluating and understanding the channel of distribution. Each firm or business entity operating in the channel is engaged in legitimacy seeking, and through its business operations seeks to entrench itself in sustained positions of legitimacy and power relative to its horizontal competitors and counterparts throughout the channel. It is necessary to understand the relationships operating within a channel in order to determine:

- Which member firms have in fact achieved legitimacy
- How power is distributed among member firms
- Where the locus of control is centered
- Which alternative channel alignments realize maximal efficiency in responding to fluctuating consumer preferences and tastes

Members of the channel of distribution together comprise a complex system of organizations existing in order

Figure 3.22

A Conventional Channel versus the Vertical Marketing System

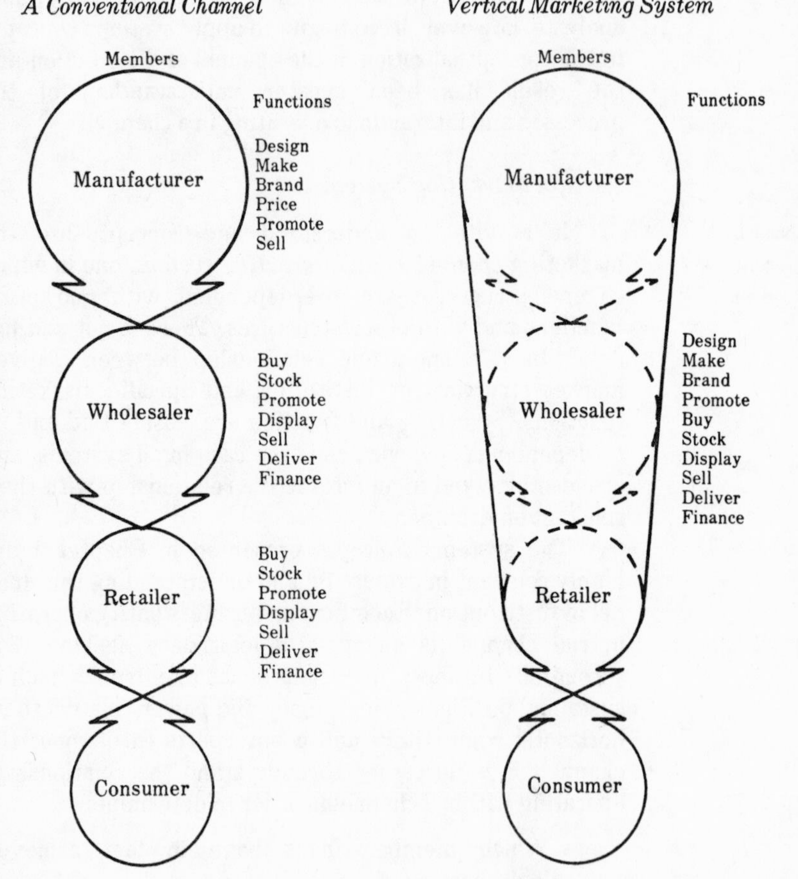

Adapted from David T. Kollat, Roger D. Blackwell and James F. Robeson, *Strategic Marketing*, New York: Holt, Rinehart and Winston, 1972, p. 289.

to satisfy the demands of consumers. Thus channel members form an integrated, goal-oriented *vertical marketing system* (see Figure 3.22). The concept of a vertical marketing system implies that:

- Channels are *integrated systems* oriented toward the common goal of *consumer satisfaction*

- *Consumers* dictate channel alignments
- Marketing functions are *shiftable* among firms operating within the channel, and even shiftable to the consumer, and in the absence of artificial constraints
- Marketing functions tend ultimately to *gravitate* to those channel members who perform them most effectively and who contribute most to consumer satisfaction
- Member firms which demonstrate the highest degree of *responsiveness* to the demands of consumers will dominate and control the channel of distribution, simultaneously establishing legitimacy and power

Interpreting the channel of distribution as a vertical marketing system is essential because it underscores the fact that enterprise legitimacy is contingent upon integration and coordination with other firms operating within the same vertical marketing system (see Figure 3.23). Thus the conventional view that firms compete horizontally with similar firms offering substitute products to the same market targets is only partially correct.

Competing systems

In reality firms compete as integral component elements of competing vertical marketing systems oriented toward the common goal of consumer satisfaction. This is especially evident among firms offering competitive products in the Saturation stage of the product life cycle when efficiency of distribution is a major determinant of product profitability.

Vertical marketing systems may be implemented in any of three ways:

- Informally through the process of *negotiation* and *conflict resolution*
- Through *vertical* or *horizontal integration*, where successive stages of production and distribution or distributors on the same plane of distribution are combined under single ownership
- Through *contractual arrangements* among independent firms, most notable of which are *franchise systems*

Figure 3.23

Characteristics of Contrasting Distribution Networks

	Type of Network	
Network Characteristics	*Vertical Marketing System*	*Conventional Marketing Channel*
Composition of network	Network composed of isolated and autonomous units, each of which performs a conventionally defined set of marketing functions. Coordination primarily achieved through bargaining and negotiation.	Network composed of interconnected units, each of which performs an optimum combination of marketing functions. Coordination achieved through the use of detailed plans and comprehensive programs.
Economic capability of member units	Operating units frequently unable to achieve systemic economies.	Operating units *programmed* to achieve systemic economies.
Organizational stability	Open network with low index of member loyalty and relative ease of entry. Network therefore tends to be unstable.	Open network but entry rigorously controlled by the system's requirements and by market conditions. Membership loyalty assured through the use of ownership or contractual agreements. As a result, network tends to be relatively stable.
Analytical focus of strategic decision makers	Strategists preoccupied with cost, volume, and investment relationships at a *single* stage of the marketing process.	Strategists preoccupied with cost, volume, and investment relationships at *all* stages of the marketing process. Corresponding emphasis on the "total cost" concept accompanied by a continuous search for favorable economic trade-offs.
Underlying decision-making process	Heavy reliance on judgmental decisions made by generalists.	Heavy reliance on "scientific" decisions made by specialists or committees of specialists.
Institutional loyalties of decision makers	Decision makers emotionally committed to traditional forms of distribution.	Decision makers *analytically* committed to marketing concept and viable institutions.

Excerpted from Bert C. McCammon, Jr., "Perspectives for Distribution Programming," in *Vertical Marketing Systems* by Louis P. Bucklin (ed.), Glenview, Illinois: Scott, Foresman, 1970, pp. 32-51. Reprinted by permission of the publisher.

Negotiation and Conflict Resolution. Much channel behavior can be explained by power relationships and negotiation, and particularly by the diffusion of influence from the locus of control within the channel. Objectives of member firms are only attainable through channel interaction. However, intra-channel and inter-channel conflict are inherent in the process of channel operation. Each member firm tries to maximize its position of power by acquiring a significant competitive advantage. In the process of jockeying for competitive advantage, firms comprising the vertical marketing system invariably come into conflict with each other and with firms external to the system (see Figure 3.24). Since conflict is inevitable, and since not all firm are equal in their resources and ability to achieve competitive advantage, *we usually find the emergence of a locus of control — a channel leader* or *captain.* Often control derives from the ability to better serve other channel members and ultimate consumers. The channel captain occupies a strong negotiating position and is often able to resolve channel conflict in his own favor. This in turn generates more power and greater negotiating ability.

Conflict resolution ↕ Locus of control

Vertical and Horizontal Integration. Often channel leadership is an informal system of power and influence, but increasingly we are seeing the institutionalization or legalization of relationships among channel members. Since channel is a vertical concept, and since channel leaders often accrue power by merging with or subsuming other firms above or below them in the channel, this phenomenon of institutionalized captaincy or leadership is called *vertical integration.* A firm which is vertically integrated has maximum control over both its environment and its counterparts in the channel. Firms can integrate forward or backward through the channel but the result is much the same — increased power and decreased channel conflict.

Formal power relationships
- **Vertical integration**
- **Horizontal integration**

Horizontal or interchannel *integration* to achieve economies of scale and efficiencies of complementary operations also occurs on a large scale, particularly among chain store systems of the department, supermarket or discount variety. Many firms represent both forms of integration and as such are highly subject to legal scrutiny. The argument for integration — and in many instances a justifiable one — is that products and services are

Figure 3.24

Potential Channel Conflict: Differing Expectations of Channel Members

	MANUFACTURER EXPECTS OF:		WHOLESALER
	WHOLESALER	RETAILER	MANUFACTURER
Product	Know mfgr's products Not carry competing brands Relay customer ideas, complaints	Know mfgr's products Honor warranties Provide adequate shelf space Not develop private brands, relay ideas, complaints Offer services (delivery, installation, etc.)	Quality products Secure packaging Wide, deep line Not to sell to retailer
Price	Sell at low margins Pass on discounts Pay promptly	Keep prices low Pass on discounts	Low prices and price concessions
Distribution	Serve many retailers Meet shipping schedules Maintain adequate inventories	Serve many customers Maintain adequate stocks Keep convenient hours Open branch locations, deliver, etc.	Liberal returns policy Exclusive distribution rights
Communication	Aggressively push mfgr's products Grant credit to retailers	Advertise mfgr's products Maintain quality image	Extensive consumer advertising/ Liberal credit terms

Fig. 3.24 Continued

EXPECTS OF:	RETAILER EXPECTS OF:	
RETAILER	MANUFACTURER	WHOLESALER
Accept wholesaler's assortment Provide adequate shelf space	Quality Products Wide, deep line New products Mfgr-honored warranties Attractive packaging	Wide assortment Product knowledge
Keep prices low Pass on discounts Prompt payment	Suggested price that permits large margins	Low prices and price concessions
Stable ordering pattern Orders on large lots	Adequate supplies of popular items Fast on-time shipments	Fast delivery in small lots Liberal returns policy
Promote wholesaler's lines	Missionary work—displays, product, advice, etc. Extensive customer advertising	Helpful, not aggressive salesmen Cooperative advertising Liberal credit

Ben Enis, *Marketing Principles: The Management Process*, Pacific Palisades, California: Goodyear, 1974, pp. 460-461. Reprinted by permission of the publisher.

marketed more efficiently through integrated systems and that therefore the consumer derives more time, place, and possession utility from the product. Nonetheless, because of the power derived from such arrangements, many integrated channel arrangements border on monopoly and other forms of anticompetitiveness.

Contractual Arrangements. Contractual arrangements among independent firms operating at different levels of production and distribution in order to achieve economies and efficiency in responding to consumer demand take a variety of forms. Franchise systems in particular have shown explosive growth in recent years.

Franchises = Formalized exclusive dealing

Franchise arrangements, currently popular in the fast-food business, represent the ultimate in exclusive dealing and integrated channel systems. They normally formalize the power relationships in the channel and eliminate conflict to a large extent by means of contractual arrangements binding the franchisee to the franchisor's products, themes, and equipment. Like other exclusive dealing and integrated relationships, franchises are subject to close legal scrutiny.

Channel Alignments

Distribution management
- **Select alignments**
- **Allocate functions**
- **Satisfy consumers**
- **Control costs**

The firm must evaluate alternative channel arrangements to develop an alignment which is appropriate to its product, target market, and overall marketing strategy. Channels of distribution vary in length, width and complexity. *Distribution policies of the firm represent management's attempt to formulate rules of action for selecting among alternative channel alignments and allocating marketing functions among channel members in accordance with the structure of consumer demand, and with geographic, legal, and cost constraints.*

Channel alignments and member relationships hinge upon several interrelated factors:

- *Intensity of distribution* required
- Degree of *market control* desired
- Relative *cost* of alternative channel alignments

The marketing enterprise may elect *intensive, selective,* or *exclusive* distribution, depending upon the desired level of product exposure, given the nature of the product and the competitive or market conditions (see Figure 3.25).

Figure 3.25

Alternative Channel Alignments for Consumer Products Manufacturers

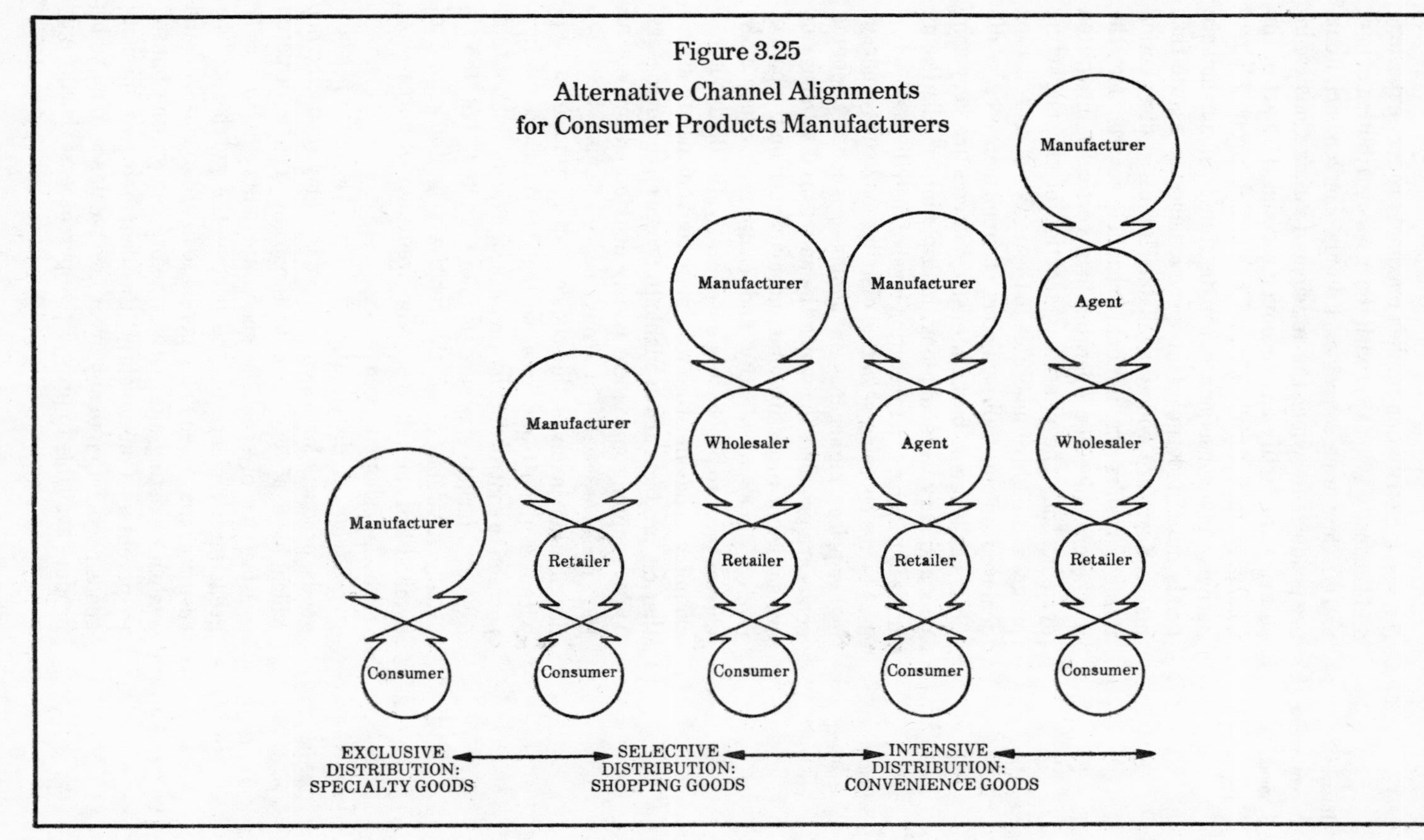

Intensive: convenience goods

Intensive distribution implies maximal product exposure, and is usually associated with the mass distribution of low-margin, low-price *convenience* items. Convenience items are products for which the anticipated satisfactions are insufficient to justify any inconvenience on the part of the consumer in determining and evaluating product alternatives. As a consequence, the distributor of convenience goods must undergo great inconvenience to assure that his products are widely available. Intensive distribution usually results in minimal channel control for the marketer, unless he operates in a vertically integrated system. Thus the effective execution of the marketing program is highly vulnerable to the degree of coordination achieved among multitudinous channel members, a difficult challenge at best. Intensive systems are very complex and very wide and long. Multiple intermediaries are utilized to achieve a saturation level of distribution.

Selective: shopping goods

Firms choosing *selective* distribution usually market higher-price, higher-margin *shopping* goods. Shopping goods are products for which the anticipated satisfactions are sufficient to justify some inconvenience on the part of the consumer to identify and compare product alternatives prior to purchase. Consequently, the distributor of shopping goods must go to some inconvenience to assure that his products are available to prospective purchasers. Thus, shopping goods are widely distributed but not on the massive scale of convenience items. Selective distribution involves the choice of a pattern of outlets within a given trade area, so that the marketer is in a position to control distribution to a significant but not total extent. Market exposure is more limited, but this is usually desirable given the relatively limited extent of demand and the relatively slow frequency of purchase or turnover of shopping goods.

Exclusive: specialty goods

Exclusive distribution is desirable for *specialty* goods, products for which demand is highly restricted but which have a very high unit margin. The anticipated satisfactions of specialty goods are sufficient to justify great inconvenience on the part of the purchaser. The customer may even delay purchase in order to isolate and evaluate existing alternatives before committing himself to purchase. Consequently, the distributor of specialty goods need not go to any great inconvenience to make his product available to prospective purchasers. Usually only a single distributor within a given trade area will carry the product. Furthermore, there is a prestige factor operating in exclusive dealing arrangements, which operates for the marketer, the retail outlet, and the consumer. Exclusive distribution arrangements permit all parties to exercise power in the channel, since each has leverage relative to the others.

Channels of distribution for industrial products, like channels for consumer goods, vary in width, length, and complexity (see Figure 3.26). Normally channels are very short and direct for products like raw materials, installations, and expensive, custom-made pieces of equipment. The purchaser prefers to communicate and deal directly with the manufacturer since each purchase involves large sums of money. Channels for operating supplies and small parts, on the other hand, tend to be long and complex, since these items are mass distributed and carry low prices and low unit margins analogous to convenience items in the consumer market.

Channel Structures

In the absence of integration, channels are characterized by a system of independent or agent middlemen. Middlemen perform a wide and varied array of marketing functions and are categorized by the types of functions they perform and the nature of their relationship with business entities above and below them in the channel of distribution. *Merchant* middlemen are those who assume ownership or title to the goods in which they deal, regardless of whether they assume control over physical distribution. *Agent* middlemen do not assume title. They operate under an agency relationship with their principal, operating on his behalf.

Categories:
- **Function**
- **Relationship**

Merchant middlemen can be categorized as *wholesalers* or *retailers* on the basis of the *status or motive* of their respective customers. Establishments engaged in *wholesaling* sell for *resale in the same form*, or for *business*, *industrial*, or *institutional use*. Firms in *retailing* sell items destined for *personal*, *family*, or *household consumption*. Wholesalers and retailers perform services or functions for each other, for manufacturers, and for ultimate consumers and industrial purchasers. The wider the array of functions performed, the greater the entrepreneurial return on investment.

Merchant middlemen:
- **wholesalers**
- **retailers**

Figure 3.26

Alternative Channel Alignments
for Industrial Products Manufacturers

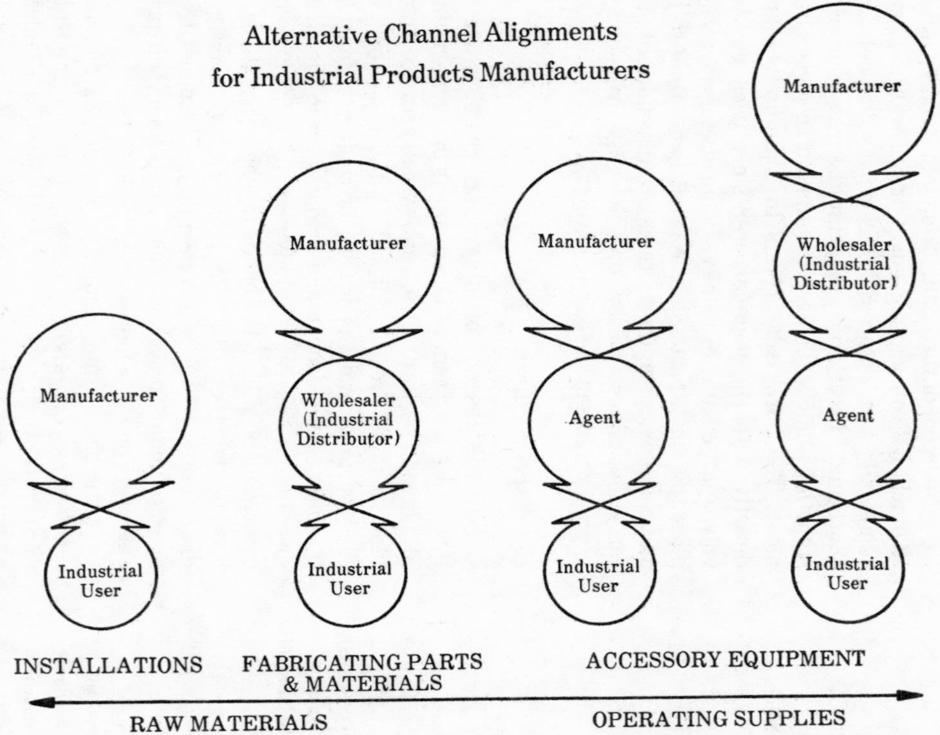

Sometimes legal, contractual arrangements like franchises or chains exist between middlemen, and sometimes informal but nonetheless stable relationships emerge. The most stable and effective channels are those in which conflict is minimized. Manufacturers, wholesalers and retailers may be separate and disparate in function, but they are closely interrelated by mutual interdependency in promoting consumer satisfaction, while competing with other vertical marketing systems seeking to serve the same markets with similar products.

Innovations in Retailing

Adaptation

Innovation

We noted earlier that channel structures have shown a relatively high degree of adaptation to the environment, especially to the shifting needs of consumers in terms of time, place, and possession utility (see Figure 3.27). One underlying trend has been a shift toward integration, both vertical and horizontal. This trend has been manifested in a proliferation of *chain* stores, or organizations consisting of two or more centrally owned and operated units offering substantially similar lines of merchandise on the same plane of distribution. [6, p. 284] Integration of the vertical type is also characteristic of most of the leading firms in most industries.

There have been five profoundly important developments in retailing which have had reverberations for wholesaling as well (see Figure 3.28):

- *Supermarket merchandising method*
- *Planned shopping centers*
- *Automated merchandising*
- *Convenience stores*
- *Boutiques*

Supermarket Merchandising. The supermarket emerged as a unique institutional development in the 1930's in response to the fractured economy of the Great Depression, revolutionizing food distribution and initiating profound changes in the marketing of all classes of consumer goods. Supermarket merchandising, however, *has emerged as the dominant form of mass distribution of consumer goods*, including non-food items, usually of the convenience or shopping classifications. Supermarket merchandising is characterized by a

Figure 3.27

The Wheel of Retailing

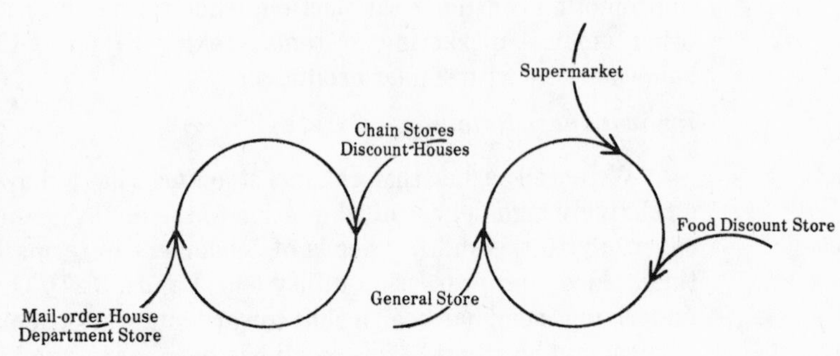

Professor Malcolm T. McNair coined the phrase "wheel of retailing" to explain the evolution of retail institutions. His hypothesis was that new retailing institutions enter the market at the "low-status" end of the wheel: low prices, low margins, reduced services, inconvenient locations, low overhead, and little or no store image or promotion. Gradually, these establishments "trade up" and undertake more elaborate operations: higher quality goods, wider variety, attractive atmosphere, locational convenience, more services, and more emphasis on promotion. Investment and operating costs rise, and the result is a high-cost, high-price operation which becomes more vulnerable to the next entry on the wheel. Discount stores, supermarkets, and chain stores are the classic prototypes of the wheel of retailing, while department stores exhibit the phenomenon to some extent. Vending machines and department store branches in shopping centers do not support the hypothesis, however, being high-cost, high-margin, high-convenience establishments. The wheel of retailing concept does not appear to be transferable to other cultures, and in fact McNair acknowledges that the pattern is most common in "industrialized, expanding economies" such as that in the United States.

Stanley C. Hollander, "The Wheel of Retailing," *Journal of Marketing* (July, 1960), pp. 37-42.

persistent emphasis upon low prices, self-service operations, broad merchandise assortments, and convenience in location, hours of operation and parking facilities. Overhead is usually low as are other operating costs. Margins are also low, however, and supermarket merchandisers owe their survival to rapid merchandise turnover and high average dollar sales of many low-margin items. The extensive application of supermarket merchandising techniques beyond their origin in food merchandising gave rise to the discount store and fueled growth of department stores. Moreover, in recent years the traditional boundaries between retailing institutions have tended to break down, as supermarkets have expanded into non-food items, discount and department stores into grocery products, and department stores into discount operations. This phenomenon is termed *scrambled merchandising.* [49, p. 67] The outstanding advantage of the supermarket merchandising form of distribution from the point of view of the consumer is that it offers a vast array of products at moderate prices at convenient times and places.

Scrambled merchandising

Planned Shopping Center. The planned shopping center *emerged in response to rapid growth in suburban areas* following World War II. Their development was further fueled by spreading ownership and use of automobiles and the associated congestion and parking problems in the central business district. Access to mass media communication facilities and the universality of supermarket merchandising methods also accelerated growth of planned shopping centers.

Planned shopping centers consist of spatial arrangements of retail stores offering a balanced concentrated shopping attraction in suburban locations. They may offer a full spectrum of convenience, shopping and specialty products and services, and an array of extensive, selective, and exclusive distributors oriented toward a broad target market. Shopping centers project a distinctive image that rests, but is not wholly dependent upon the stores which comprise the center. Thus the whole image is greater than the sum of its parts. Hence, shopping center shopping is frequently an end in itself or an alternative mode of entertainment or social contact often

Figure 3.28

Defining Characteristics of Five Major Innovations in Retailing

SUPER MARKET MERCHANDISING

Emphasis on low prices
Self-service operations
Broad merchandise assortments
Limited customer services
Exposition-like atmosphere
Emphasis on national brands
Broad target market
Low operating costs
Inexpensive buildings and fixtures
High traffic locations
Long hours of operation
Rapid merchandise turnover
Spacious parking
High average dollar sale
Scrambled merchandising

PLANNED SHOPPING CENTERS

Balanced concentrated shopping attraction
Spatial arrangement of retail stores
One-stop shopping
Shared spacious parking facilities and shopping mall
Convenience, shopping, and specialty goods
Extensive, selective, and exclusive distributors
Scrambled merchandising
Suburban high traffic locations
Ease of access
Exposition-like atmosphere
Broad merchandise and service assortments
Shopping center with a personality
Broad target market
Shopping an end in itself
Alternative modes of entertainment
Family participation

Figure 3.28 Continued

AUTOMATED MERCHANDISING	CONVENIENCE STORES
Vending machines Self-service Emphasis on time and place convenience Extensive distribution Impersonal High prices Average margins Broad target market Emphasis on national brands Convenience goods Food and novelty items Demand widespread and well established Impulse purchases Small quantity purchases High unit packaging costs Pilferage low Less damaged merchandise	Emphasis on time and place convenience Self-service Urban and suburban locations Emphasis on national brands Broad target market Impulse purchases Convenience goods High price High margins High rent locations Inexpensive buildings and fixtures Rapid merchandise turnover Long hours of operation Low average dollar sale Scrambled merchandising Average operating costs Limited customer services Limited parking

BOUTIQUES

Store with a personality
Charged atmosphere
Ego-involving
Personal service
Shopping or specialty goods and services
Exclusive distribution
High margins
High prices
Narrow target market
Store and brand loyalty
Private and national brands
High psychological component
High operating costs
Emphasis on decor
Slow merchandise turnover
Shopping an end in itself

involving entire families. The rise of the planned shopping center has accompanied and accelerated the demise of the central business district.

Automated Merchandising. A more recent retailing trend has been the development of automated merchandising, or selling through the use of vending machines. Automated merchandising is a *response to the consumer's demand for convenience or immediate gratification* or satisfaction of needs for certain convenience items. Vending machines are highly impersonal. The products they offer generally carry higher prices than other grocery or novelty items because they are sold in small quantities with high unit packaging costs and hence depend upon rapid merchandise turnover. Moreover, some vending machines require substantial investment, particularly those dealing in food items.

From a marketer's point of view vending machines offer the advantages of twenty-four hour selling without a salesman, less pilferage, less damaged merchandise, [49, p. 67] and location in a wide variety of settings other than conventional retail stores. Most products sold in vending machines are cigarettes, soft drinks, and candy, although a wide assortment of other food and nonfood items are today marketed through automated means. Only items for which demand is widespread and well established are amenable for sale through vending machines.

Convenience Stores. Convenience stores, like vending machines, *represent the ultimate in provision of time and place utility*, or convenience. Convenience stores abound in urban and suburban areas. A consumer is usually only a short walk or drive from such a store. They offer items similar to those found in a supermarket, except that the emphasis is on convenience items like soft drinks, snacks and alcoholic beverages that people are likely to want on a moment's notice or on an emergency basis at all hours of the day or night. Convenience stores offer a wide assortment of brands in these popular impulse items, and usually a single brand of items with slower turnover. Prices are usually significantly higher than those in the supermarket, but, as in the case of vending machines, consumers are willing to pay the price for speed and ease of purchase.

Boutiques. Whereas automated merchandising represents an extreme of impersonality, boutiques are *stores with a personality.* Boutiques in fact emerged in *response to impersonality* and affluence. They respond to the need of consumers to consume or use products specifically geared to their unique personal style and needs, and sold to them by personal salesmen rather than through impersonal communication. Boutiques normally carry shopping or specialty goods focused on a narrow target market, which are not readily available elsewhere, and which tend to be priced higher than their mass-produced counterparts. *They symbolize the consumer's climb up the hierarchy of needs in response to accelerating affluence.* Shoppers tend to exhibit patronage or store loyalty as well as brand loyalty, and in fact boutiques often carry their own lines under private labels. They are characterized by a very high psychological component or charged atmosphere, which enhances the ego-involved nature of the products they carry.

Response to consumers

These five significant trends in retailing along with the significant trend toward integration, represent dramatic examples of environmental responsiveness on the part of marketing structures. Other distribution trends have also emerged in recent years, including *fast-food franchises, private branding, computer-assisted transactions, scrambled merchandising,* and *the reverse channel of distribution* designed to recycle products and packaging. Such trends emerge and gradually evolve into new channel structures and methods of merchandising in response to shifting consumer preferences and lifestyles and pressures from other sectors of the marketing environment. Franchise setups, for example, are evolving in response to more stringent legal regulations. Supermarkets are undergoing integration and utilizing computers to increase their distributive efficiency and cut costs.

Channels of distribution, perhaps more than any other consideration in the marketing program, lend themselves to systems thinking and systems jargon. The interrelationships and conflicts characteristic of channel alignments, their structural response to functional needs and their continual evolution into improved methods provide excellent examples for comprehending the operation of systems. Channel strategy, of course, requires that the firm achieve optimum channel arrangements which facilitate customer satisfaction. Channel differentiation and efficiency are vital sources and manifestations of competitive advantage and, hence, legitimacy and market power.

COMMUNICATION STRATEGY

Marketing communication constitutes by far the most controversial component of the marketing mix both in terms of its impact on the individual consumer and its impact on society-at-large. Marketing communications are variously accused of manipulating consumers, limiting their range of product and priority choices, arousing artificial wants and needs, and creating an imbalance between private and public goods. The controversial Harvard economist John Kenneth Galbraith presents an eloquent case for "the dependence effect," as he has termed the contention that wants are contrived by the process by which they are satisfied – production and marketing. Figure 3.29 presents the Galbraithian point of view, and the opposing view of another prominent economist, Frederick von Hayek.

The communication controversy

The dependence effect

Galbraith carries the argument further, claiming that not only has advertising produced a skewed distribution of wealth in "the affluent society," but that the orientation of advertising toward stimulating demand for consumer goods has resulted in an imbalance between private goods and services designed to satisfy individual wants and needs and public goods designed to meet societal needs, such as public housing, mass transportation, environmental rehabilitation, and education. [32, p. 223]

Private goods versus Public goods

Noise

Proponents of advertising stress the fact that the individual is bombarded with literally thousands of communication messages daily, of which advertising messages constitute but a small portion. Individuals rapidly develop selective defenses which filter out much advertising and tend to create an immunity from influence. Moreover, whatever influence advertising does have is mediated by the influence of a host of additional factors, including peer and reference groups, opinion leaders and personal observation and experience, which are frequently more important determinants of product purchasing behavior. In the past, both sides of the debate have tended to rest their cases on speculation rather than on scientific fact.

Selective defenses

Reference groups
Opinion leaders
Observation

The Role of Marketing Communication in Society

Controversy aside, advertising, or more broadly marketing communication, *clearly performs a number of social functions*: [97, Ch. 1]

Demand

- Marketing communication acts to *stimulate demand*, a function which is essential to society's long-term goal of economic growth and the associated goal of rising standards of material welfare. Consumption is the impetus to production. The maintenance and growth of mass production technology requires stimulation of mass consumption. Whether this orientation should be blunted is a value judgment which we will explore in Chapter 5.

Ascribe meaning

- Marketing communication helps *ascribe and clarify the meaning* of products and services. Products or services assume meaning only in the context of the individual's lifestyle on the basis of how, when and where they are used. Much as costumes and props help give meaning to an actor's roles, products give meaning to an individual's roles. The matching of products with appropriate role contexts is facilitated through marketing communication. Thus marketing communication helps define material standards of living associated with divergent lifestyle patterns.

Impetus to competition

- Marketing communication provides a constant *impetus to industrial competition*, benefiting the consumer by providing exposure to a broad array of product options at competitive prices. Competition extends not simply forward to the consumer in ever finer product differentiation and distributive efficiency, but backward to product planning and development as well. Competition promotes higher levels of enterprise efficiency in serving consumer interests, both within and across industries.

Mass media

- Marketing communication provides the major source of *financial support for the mass media.* Television, radio, newspapers, and magazines per-

Figure 3.29

The Dependence Effect

Pro

John Kenneth Galbraith

"... The notion that wants do not become less urgent the more amply the individual is supplied is broadly repugnant to common sense ... if the individual's wants are to be urgent they must be original with himself. They cannot be urgent if they must be contrived for him. And above all they must not be contrived by the process of production, by which they are satisfied ... The fact that wants can be synthesized by advertising, catalyzed by salesmanship, and shaped by the discrete manipulations of the persuaders shows that they are not very urgent. A man who is hungry need never be told of his need for food. If he is influenced by his appetite, he is immune to the influence of Messrs. Batten, Barton, Durstine & Osborn. The latter are effective only with those who are so removed from physical want that they do not already know what they want. In this state alone, men are open to persuasion. ... One must imagine a humanitarian who was long ago persuaded of the grievous shortage of hospital facilities in the town. He continues to importune the passers-by for money for more beds and refuses to notice that the town doctor is deftly knocking over pedestrians with his car to keep up the occupancy.

"... As a society becomes increasingly affluent, wants are increasingly created by the process by which they are satisfied ... want thus comes to depend on output."

Excerpted from John Kenneth Galbraith, *The Affluent Society,* Boston: Houghton Mifflin, 1971, pp. 146-154.

Figure 3.29 Continued

Con

Frederick A. von Hayek

Individuals . . . "would not desire any of the amenities of civilization – or even of the most primitive culture – if we did not live in a society in which others provide them. Innate wants are probably confined to food, shelter, and sex. All the rest we learn to desire because we see others enjoying various things. To say that a desire is not important because it is not innate is to say that the whole cultural achievement of man is not important . . . most needs which make us act are needs for things which only civilization teaches us exist at all, and these things are wanted by us because they produce feelings or emotions which we would not know if it were not for our cultural inheritance.

"How complete a *non sequitur* Professor Galbraith's conclusion represents is seen most clearly if we apply the argument to any product of the arts, be it music, painting, or literature . . . the argument could easily be employed without any change of the essential terms, to demonstrate the worthlessness of literature or any other form of art. Surely an individual's want for literature is not original with himself in the sense that he would experience it if literature were not produced. Does this mean that the production of literature cannot be defended as satisfying a want because it is only the production which provokes the demand?"

Excerpted from Frederick A. von Hayek, "The *Non Sequitur* of the Dependence Effect," *Southern Economic Journal* (April, 1961), pp. 346-358.

form vital informational and entertainment roles in society, and their survival is contingent upon their continued ability to solicit financial support from marketing communication. The alternatives would be governmentally supported media or direct control of media editorial content by marketing firms, either option undermining the independence and objectivity of print and broadcast media.

Support to causes

- Marketing communication also has been extensively relied upon to provide creative, managerial, and financial *support to numerous causes* in the public interest, such as aid to higher education, equal opportunity employment, highway safety, environmental rehabilitation, and conservation. Clearly, whether one assumes a positive or a negative view of marketing communication, it is a pervasive feature in our lives and it is critical to understand the role marketing communication plays in society.

The Role of Marketing Communication in the Firm

Decisions converge in communication

Decisions as to which product will be offered for sale, at what prices, and through which distribution systems represent marketing management's best judgment as to the precise combination of differentiating actions required to establish and sustain positions of legitimacy and power in the environment. *The strategies of adjustment to the unique demands posed by the various systems that comprise the firm's environment are reflected in the elements of the marketing program as communicated through the components of its communications mix.* Hence, decisions concerning product, pricing, and distribution strategies required to sustain positions of legitimacy and power all converge in communication strategy decisions. Viewed in this framework, the role of effective communication in effective marketing comes sharply into focus:

> If communications is not *the* critical element in competitive consumer marketing today, it is very nearly so. For almost everything the marketer *does*, as well as what he *says*, communicates something to the consumer about the product or the company behind the product. Communications, in this sense, involves far more than the substantive content of the written or spoken word. It involves all of those elements about the product, package, price, channel of distribution, and other factors which shape the consumer's awareness and buying behavior. The realization of this simple fact has been one of the more important developments in consumer marketing in recent years. [70, p. 263]

Effective communication

Legitimacy

Marketing communication is concerned with establishing and maintaining positions of legitimacy and power in relevant sectors of the firm's environment. This requires precise coordination of communication strategy decisions with other decision areas under marketing management's direct control. More precisely, the effectiveness of marketing communication is contingent upon:

- The focus and relative emphasis among components of the communication mix (advertising, personal selling, publicity, public relations, and sales promotion) designed to carry out communication strategy (see Figure 3.30)
- The precision with which communication strategy is integrated and coordinated with product, pricing, and distribution strategies to yield relatively invulnerable positions of legitimacy and power

Essential to the design of effective marketing communication, however, is a thorough understanding of the communication process and the process of social influence, as well as the potential persuasive impact of alternative components of the communication program.

Figure 3.30

Components of Communication Programs

- *Advertising* is any paid, nonpersonal public presentation of products, services, or ideas by an identified sponsor. Advertising may involve such diversified media as television and radio commercials, newspaper and magazine advertisements, outdoor advertisements such as billboards, signs, and posters, catalogs, circulars and leaflets, and directories. The distinctive qualities of advertising are its public nature, pervasiveness, impersonality, and potential for dramatizing both producer and products through creative combinations of visual and sound elements.

  Advertising may be classified as *product* or *institutional*, depending upon whether it is directed toward developing or reinforcing demand for specific products or establishing and maintaining legitimacy for its sponsor. Alternatively, advertising may be distinguished according to its intended audience as *consumer*, *industrial*, *trade*, or *professional*, or according to its sponsor as *manufacturers'*, *wholesalers'*, *retailers'*, or *cooperative*.

  The design and execution of an advertising campaign may involve the services of an advertising agency. Agencies provide the principal services of planning, preparing, and placing advertising for their clients. They offer the advantages of experience and expertise, independence and objectivity, cost savings through media commissions and economies of scale, and a means of transferring responsibility to a replaceable external agency.

- *Personal selling* involves personally persuading or aiding a prospective customer in purchasing a product or service or accepting or acting on an idea. The distinguishing features of personal selling are face-to-face interaction, and therefore greater personal participation, flexibility of presentation, and the potential to persuade or prompt attitude formation or change. Personal selling, too, takes a number of forms, including field selling, retail selling, and industrial selling, and may be used to create product awareness, focus interest, channel preference, close a sale, and provide post-purchase reinforcement.

  Personal selling encompasses *service selling* and *creative salesmanship*. Service selling involves supplying a customer who is predis-

Fig. 3.30 Continued

posed to buy and knows approximately what he wants with sufficient information to make the purchase decision. Service selling is characteristic of retailing where the prospective purchaser typically initiates the sales contact, motivated by a specific want or need and with an approximate idea as to the means of satisfying it. Thus selling to ultimate customers is characterized by less knowledge and skill than is required by alternative types of selling.

Creative salesmanship involves stimulating demand for new products or brands, or inducing customers to switch from one brand to another. Creative salesmanship is prominent in selling to wholesalers, retailers, industrial users and other marketing intermediaries. Salesmen specializing in sales to wholesalers or retailers face the problem of convincing the prospective customer that sufficient consumer demand exists for the product to justify its inclusion in the firm's product line. Knowledge of the distribution system of the prospect's firm, profit margins, and mark-ups is essential. Selling to industrial users may be distinguished from other selling situations by the relatively high degree of technical competence and product and industry information required of successful industrial salesmen.

- *Public relations* encompasses those activities employed by the firm to establish and maintain favorable relationships with relevant sectors in the firm's environment, such as customers, stockholders, employees, governmental agencies, the academic community, and the public at large. Public relations may include (1) creating or extending public knowledge or awareness of the firm and the nature of its activities with the objective of improved sales over the long run, (2) correcting or compensating for erroneous or incomplete impressions or information about the company and its activities, (3) cultivating interest in the firm among members of the financial community or others, and (4) attracting qualified personnel into company employment [97, p. 618].

- *Publicity* is any news item or editorial comment concerning products, services, business activities, or marketing institutions communicated publicly through the mass media that is *not* paid for by the benefited firm. Although their importance is often overlooked or undervalued, public relations and publicity contribute significantly to the general atmosphere of public acceptance or indifference within which the firm attempts to induce consumer response to specific promotional appeals.

Fig. 3.30 Continued

Public relations and publicity are not customarily perceived as commercially sponsored messages. The source is generally perceived to be the communications medium rather than the manufacturer or marketer and public relations and publicity are therefore freed from the bias which attaches to commercial sponsors whose communication motives are transparent.

- *Sales promotion* includes all supplementary or coordinative activities which promote greater effectiveness and efficiency of marketing communication. Among the more common sales promotion tools are prizes, premiums, contests, coupons, samples, store demonstrations, point-of-purchase displays, discounts and trading stamps, refunds, special offers, and services. Common techniques for soliciting retailer and wholesaler support of selling effort are point-of-purchase advertising and display, dealer merchandising aids, such as cooperative advertising and training programs, and incentive travel plans for salesmen, agents, distributors, or dealers. While sales promotion activities typically absorb only a minor proportion of the marketing communication budget, they frequently play a pivotal role in focusing consumer attention toward specific brands or dealers.

- *Reseller support* is any form of communication undertaken by a wholesale or retail middleman with the intent of persuading a prospective customer to act favorably toward the goods and services offered by a manufacturer or other seller. [24, p. 3] Reseller support also includes promotional assistance provided by a manufacturer for his distributors. Reseller support may take the form of displays, contests, advertising, incentive payments, in-store promotions, selling aids, and packaging. From the manufacturer's point of view reseller support is critical to assure continued acceptance by resellers of a manufacturer's products. From a reseller's point of view reseller support facilitates the speed and ease with which goods move through the channel. Wholesalers engage in promotional activities to cultivate relationships with retailers, and retailers to cultivate store patronage by ultimate consumers. Reseller support is a critical component of a communication campaign, but one whose importance is often underestimated by manufacturers and distributors.

Figure 3.31

The Communication Process:
"Who .. says what .. why .. how .. and when .. to whom .. with what effect?"*

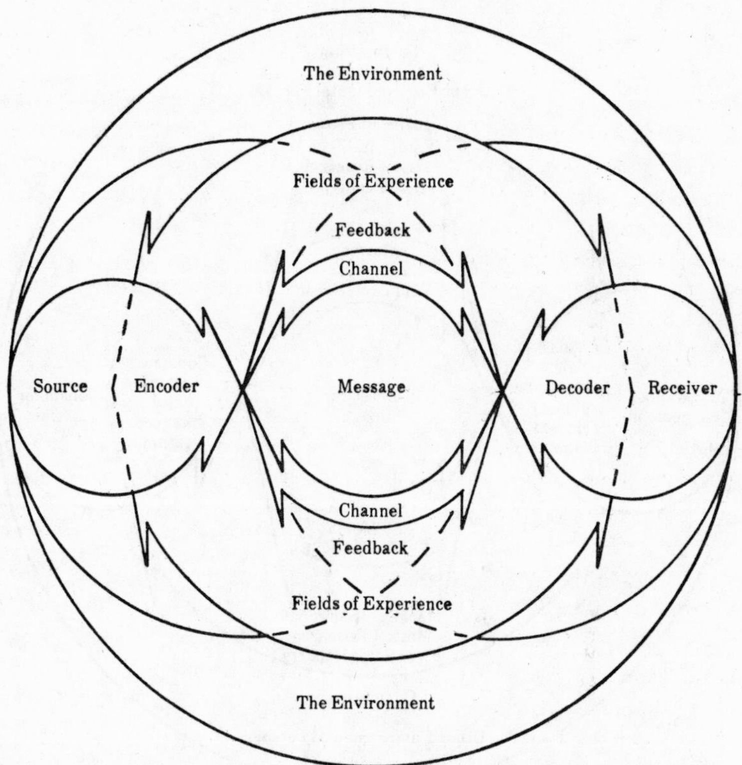

Adapted from Wilbur Schramm (ed.) *The Process and Effects of Mass Communication.* Urbana, Illinois: University of Illinois Press, 1965, p. 6.

*Based on the discussion in H. D. Lasswell, *Power and Personality*, New York: Norton, 1948, pp. 37-51.

The Communication Process

Communication: A transaction

Communication, including marketing communication, is most appropriately viewed as a transactional process involving (see Figures 3.31 & 3.32): [10, Ch. 2]

- a communicator or *source*
- an *encoder* which translates communicator purposes or intentions into

Figure 3.32

The Process of Marketing Communication

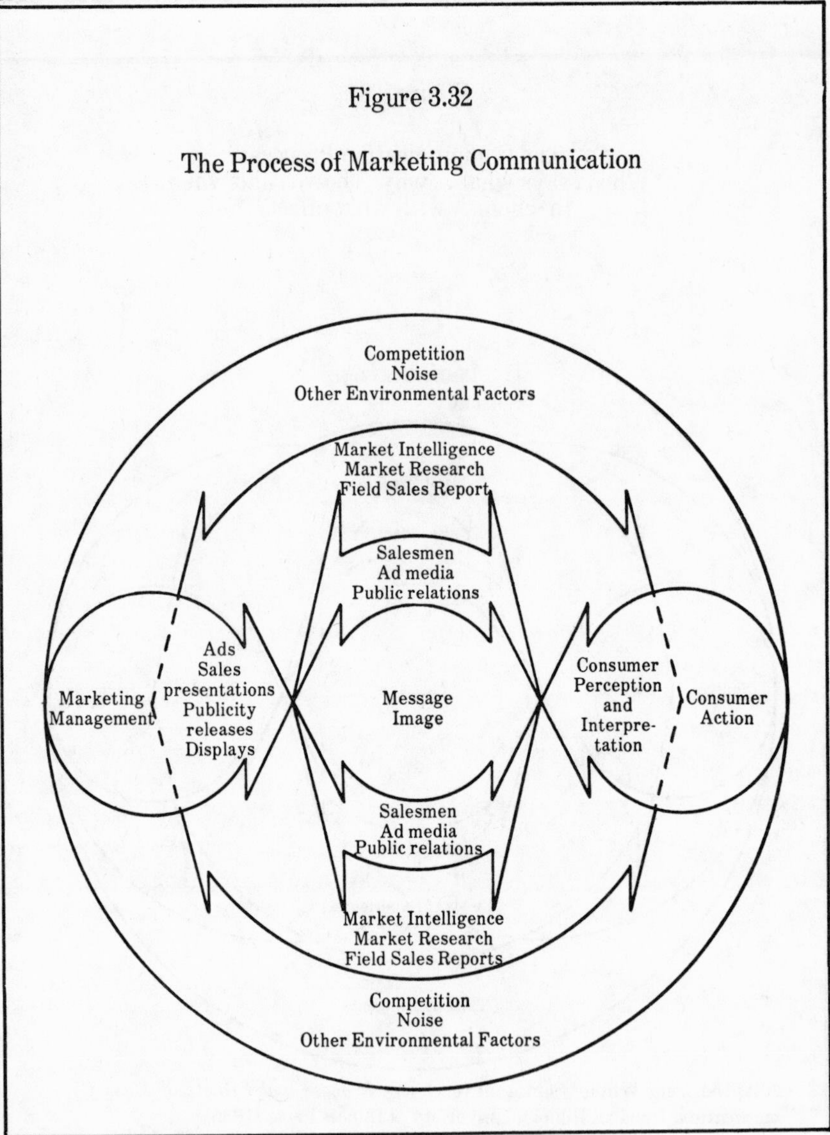

- *messages* consisting of systematic sets of symbols representing ideas, intentions and purposes which are transmitted across
- a *channel* or medium to
- a *decoder* which retranslates messages into forms which are useful to
- an audience or *receiver*

In the case of interpersonal or face-to-face communication, source and encoder usually coincide, as do receiver and decoder. Credibility, empathy, attraction, and ultimately the effectiveness of communication hinge upon the relationship between the source and the receiver.

Communication System. Sources and receivers do not communicate in isolation from communication interactions in the surrounding social environment. Both frequently maintain a complex array of communication interactions with others in their social setting, requiring simultaneous encoding and decoding of a variety of messages. Thus, communication skills encompass both the encoding and decoding abilities required to perform the roles of communicator and receiver.

Array of interactions

This complex array of communication interactions branching out in all directions through the social system and spanning organizational boundaries and hierarchies, forms an elaborate communication network or system integrating both mass media and interpersonal, formal and informal, marketer- and non-marketer controlled channels. Thus the individual, performing multiple source and receiver roles, is linked in an intricate communication web interwoven through the social system, sometimes spanning great geographical and social distances.

Web

The communication system literally submerges the individual in a torrent of information from both commercial and non-commercial sources. It has been estimated that

> some 560 advertising messages of one sort or another . . . assault the average American each day. There are so many, in fact, that he mentally blots out most of them – a feat that gains him time to read newspapers, listen to radios, watch television, and otherwise fill his day. Through it all, the average individual ingests between 10,000 and 20,000 words of printed matter daily; TV and radio add 20,000 words more. [2, pp. 132-137]

The barrage of information diffusing through the communication system is so great that marketing firms are as bewildered in trying to communicate effectively with prospective purchasers as are consumers in attempting to discriminate relevant from irrelevant information

Noise

or "noise" in making product selections. *Noise is information which is extraneous and therefore dysfunctional to effective communication.* Yet noise is inherent in the cross-currents of communication traffic colliding throughout the social system. Regardless of its source, however, noise always undermines communication effectiveness.

Both interpersonal and mass media sources compete for the attention of specific audiences or receivers in this highly cluttered communication system. The individual's attention to messages emanating from competing communication sources is significantly conditioned by the repertoire of roles he performs. Occupation-prescribed roles, for example, including supervisory, advisory, subordinate, and informal group membership roles, will influence

Roles dictate:
- **who**
- **what**
- **how**
- **when**
- **why**
- **effect**

- *who* the individual communicates with, and who communicates with him
- *what* an individual communicates, and what is communicated to him
- *how* he communicates, and how others communicate with him
- *when* he communicates, and when others communicate with him
- *why* he communicates, and why others communicate with him
- the persuasive *effect*

In addition, the individual will don a distinctly different array of roles off the job: family roles, friendship roles, consumer roles, and many others. Each role set will dictate appropriate communication behavior and define sources, media, and messages to which the individual will attend.

Endless influences

The list of factors influencing the communication process is virtually endless. To outline and explain the variety and nature of such influences is beyond the scope of this section. What is significant to note is the relatively limited capacity of the individual to absorb and cope with the virtually boundless volume of information diffusing through the formal and informal communication systems of which he is himself a part.

The systems perspective of communication is indicative of the complexity of communication in the social system, both inside and outside the business organization, and suggestive of the magnitude of management's task of communicating effectively to a specified audience of consumers. The goal of effective marketing communication is thus complicated by:

- The increasingly cluttered nature of the communication system, and
- The selectivity of individual attention, perception, and retention of messages from competing sources

The selective nature of individual information processing suggests that messages need to conform in some measure with existing knowledge, previous experience, or preferences, or to stand out sufficiently to be perceived. The perception of a message is clearly prerequisite to communication realizing any effect.

Prerequisites to Communication. It is instructive to examine other prerequisites to communication because one or another is so frequently absent in marketing communication. The result is substantial waste and inefficiency.

Communication: free choice

From the foregoing discussion we can readily see that in order for communication to occur a source, encoder, message, channel, decoder and receiver must be present. In addition, however, communication in a free choice situation, where source and receiver have the option of participating, must be motivated out of anticipated benefits on the part of the communication participants. Both source and receiver must *anticipate* some *benefit* in participation for communication to occur.

Anticipated benefits

Overlapping experience

Communication also requires *overlapping fields of relevant experience* on the part of the communicators. Unless both source and receiver share at least some prior direct or indirect familiarity with issues or ideas being communicated, as well as common language or codes used to communicate such issues or ideas, attempts to communicate will be futile.

Energy

Communication also requires the *expenditure of energy* on the part of both source and receiver, as well as other parties to the communication, such as channel members, encoders, decoders, advertising copywriters, speechwriters, and others. Communication, in other words requires *active* participation. This fact is seemingly overlooked by many advertisers who behave as if they think television viewers will passively absorb and respond positively to commercial messages.

The mere presence of the prerequisites to communication reveals nothing about the effectiveness of communication effort. Communication is perhaps the most important, yet least understood facet of human behavior. Three key concepts are essential to understand the nature of communication: *effectiveness, fidelity, efficiency*. They are frequently confused.

Effectiveness
Fidelity
Efficiency

Communication Effectiveness. The purpose of *all* communication is to *persuade*; that is, all communication seeks to elicit from a specified audience or receiver a pattern of responses which conforms to the intentions of the communicator or source. Thus all communication is triggered by *intent to influence* on the part of a communicator. [10, Ch. 1]

Persuasion

Intent to influence

Marketing communication is no exception to this rule. The purpose of advertising, personal selling, and sales promotion is to persuade present or potential customers to purchase the firm's products, or to perceive the firm, its methods of operation, and its output in a favorable light. Accordingly, the criterion by which the effectiveness of the firm's marketing communication should be gauged is the extent to which the firm is successful in soliciting customers, shifting public opinion in a favorable direction, or achieving another predefined communication objective.

Responses match intentions

The standard by which the effectiveness of any communication should be evaluated is the extent to which the responses of a receiver or audience match the intentions of the communicator or source.

Responses activated in a receiver or audience may involve modifications in behavior, additions to knowledge, or shifts in attitude, opinion, or belief. The goal of maximizing the effectiveness of communication effort suggests the necessity of the source anticipating how the audience or receiver will:

- Interpret messages encoded by the source
- Respond on the basis of those interpretations

The fact that all communication is an attempt to persuade may not be intuitively clear. One may speculate, for example, that frequently we communicate informally on insignificant issues, or simply exchange ritualized greetings, not really caring that the audience or receiver respond in a specified manner. The point is, however, that even in such trivial communication situations as these we do have expectations as to patterns of response (or *non*response) on the part of the audience or receiver which are appropriate in the context of our messages. To confirm this we need merely recall situations in which people with whom we have communicated have responded in unexpected or surprising ways, ways that failed to meet our expectations. In such instances we are aware that our communication efforts have been less than effective.

Expectations of response (or *non*response)

If the responses elicited from an audience or receiver correspond to our expectations, our intentions concerning appropriate reactions (or inactions) to our messages are realized, and *we have effectively communicated* our intentions. Thus intent to influence or persuade is present in even the most elementary communication act.

Communication Fidelity. A frequent source of confusion in trying to bring about more effective communication entails the transfer of meaning from one individual to another. The fact that perceptions of words, gestures, expressions and symbols are subjective, or interpreted in the context of the individual's internalized conception of reality, implies that meanings cannot be transferred unchanged between individuals. "*Meanings are in people*," [10, p. 188] not in words, gestures, expressions, or symbols. The critical question in determining the effectiveness of communication effort is "What

Transfer of meaning

"Meanings are in people"

meanings does the receiver derive from the messages of the source?"

To the extent that a source is able to anticipate the meanings his messages will arouse in an audience or receiver, he can more fully gauge their probable responses. Thus, the task of achieving effective communication is facilitated by the source's ability to empathize with his receiver or audience.

Empathy

> *We term the correspondence between meanings which the source anticipates the receiver will ascribe to his messages, and the meanings which the receiver actually ascribes to such messages, communication fidelity.*

Fidelity

Effectiveness

High fidelity, or correspondence of meanings between those which the source anticipates and those the receiver actually ascribes to the source's messages, facilitates effective communication. Thus *high fidelity promotes effective communication.* Low fidelity undermines communication effectiveness.

Trade-off: energy versus benefits

Communication Efficiency. Effective communication requires the expenditure of energy and the active participation of source and receiver. Marshalling sufficient energy for communication may entail significant commitments of time, effort and money. Hence, motivation to participate in communication is determined by one's subjective evaluation of the trade-off between the energy required and the anticipated benefits to be derived from communication.

The potential effectiveness of communication rises as energy required for communication declines and as anticipated benefit rises. Source and receiver will differ as to their assessment of the energy/anticipated benefit trade-off and therefore differ in their motivation to communicate.

> *Communication is efficient to the extent that the source is able to motivate intended responses with a minimum expenditure of energy.*

The potential effectiveness of communication is directly related to the efficiency of communication. For example, personal selling may prove highly effective in

Figure 3.33

Mass Media versus Interpersonal Communication

	Interpersonal Communication	*Mass Media Communication*
Access to a Large Audience		
Speed	slow	fast
Ability to select receivers	high	low
Cost per individual reached	high	low
Feedback		
Direction of message flow	2-way	1-way
Message distortion	high	low
Speed of feedback	fast	slow
Amount of feedback	high	low
Accuracy of feedback	high	low
Influence on the Individual		
Ability to attract attention	high	low
Ability to overcome receiver selectivity processes	high	low
Number of receiver senses activated	2 or more	2 or less
Possible effects	persuasion, attitude formation or or change	creates awareness, focuses interest, knowledge, reinforcement
Efficiency	low	high
Fidelity	high	low
Effectiveness	high	low

Adapted from James F. Engel, Hugh G. Wales, and Martin R. Warshaw, *Promotional Strategy*. Homewood, Illinois: Irwin, 1971, p. 27; and Everett M. Rogers and F. Floyd Shoemaker, *Communication of Innovations*. New York: Free Press, 1971, p. 253.

stimulating sales, but prohibitively costly or inefficient in dollars and manhours. Continued or frequent communication between a source and receiver will facilitate effective communication, not only because of the increased fidelity of communication, but because of the increased efficiency of communication effort as participants learn to gauge how others will interpret and act upon their messages.

Mass Media versus Interpersonal Communication. In Figure 3.33 we present some basic differences between mass media, such as television, radio, newspapers, or magazines, and interpersonal or face-to-face communication. These differences are equally valid for mediated marketing communication, including advertising and sales promotion on the one hand, and personal selling, or interpersonal communication, on the other. A sound knowledge of these differences is essential in designing a marketing communication strategy which capitalizes upon the strengths and minimizes the weaknesses of advertising, personal selling, sales promotion, publicity, and public relations. The marketing communication strategy which the firm ultimately develops will in all likelihood involve a balanced combination of mass media and interpersonal channels to elicit the most favorable response from a market segment. The proportions of each, however, will depend upon the communication goals of the marketing firm, the characteristics of the product, the distinguishing characteristics of consumers comprising markets of interest, the product's position in the product life cycle, and other factors (see Figure 3.34).

Communication mix: Balanced Combination

Interpersonal:
- **Persuasion**

The strengths of mass media communication are the weaknesses of interpersonal communication and vice versa. The principal difference between mass media and interpersonal communication, however, lies in their persuasive effect. *Interpersonal communication offers the potential for persuasion. In general, mass media channels do not.* Face-to-face communication permits the source to make numerous adjustments based on immediate feedback from the receiver. The source can more effectively persuade the receiver, altering his message on the basis of the receiver's reactions. The source can therefore be more effective in creating attitudes where none previously existed, adding to the receiver's level of knowledge, or shaping his behavior.

Figure 3.34

Advertising versus Personal Selling

Advertising represents the principal tool available to marketing management for communicating an undistorted message quickly to a large audience of potential customers. Advertising is likely to be most effective:

- When the product is in the Pioneering or Market Acceptance stages of its life cycle
- When primary demand for the product type has not been fully exploited
- When product awareness is minimal or interest unfocused
- When the consumer is engaged in post-decision evaluation
- When the product is technically simple
- When a product is significantly differentiated from products serving the same need
- When product attributes are not readily apparent to the prospective customer
- When the basis for purchasing is strongly emotional

Personal selling offers the potential to persuade consumers to purchase the firm's products. Personal selling is likely to be most effective:

- When the product is in the Turbulence, Saturation, or Obsolescence stages of its life cycle
- When the marketing communication problem is one of creating selective demand for a given brand of product
- When product awareness is high and interest focused
- When the consumer is engaged in comparative product evaluations and limited experimentation with product alternatives
- When differentiating features of the product are apparent to the prospective customer
- When the product is technically complex
- When the basis for purchase is relatively unemotional

Because mass media communication disallows immediate and substantial feedback, mediated communication generally does not offer the potential of persuasion. Mass media communication instead provides a vehicle for creating *awareness*, focusing *interest* or for *reinforcing* existing attitudes, knowledge, or behavior. Contrary to popular misconception, except in rare instances, advertising and sales promotion cannot by themselves create favorable attitudes toward products or producers where none previously exist. Nor can advertising or sales promotion persuade consumers to purchase products they otherwise would not. The principal contributions of advertising and sales promotion to the firm's marketing communication strategy are threefold:

Mass media:
- **Awareness**
- **Interest**
- **Reinforcement**

- Creating *awareness* of the firm, its products, and methods of operation
- Focusing *interest* on the firm, its products, and methods of operation
- *Reinforcing* existing consumption behavior or favorable consumer perceptions of the firm's products or methods of operation

Multi-stage flow

The Process of Social Influence. Influence diffuses in a multi-stage flow through a social system. [79, Ch. 6] Information from mass media sources is translated into influence by opinion leaders to their followers, some of whom are opinion leaders, and so forth (see Figure 3.35). Thus influence diffuses in a web of word-of-mouth interactions.

Imputed

The term opinion leader is more than a little misleading. Opinion leadership is earned or imputed by one's followers, rather than assumed. Opinion leaders possess high source credibility, since they are usually perceived as trustworthy, competent, and objective or independent. However, *followers are not "passive patsies" pushed around by opinion leaders.* Communication is a transaction, a two-way street. Followers are *active* agents in the process of social influence, seeking new information and corroborating previously held opinions.

Followers active

In comparison with their followers, opinion leaders are generally:

- more technically competent
- more socially central

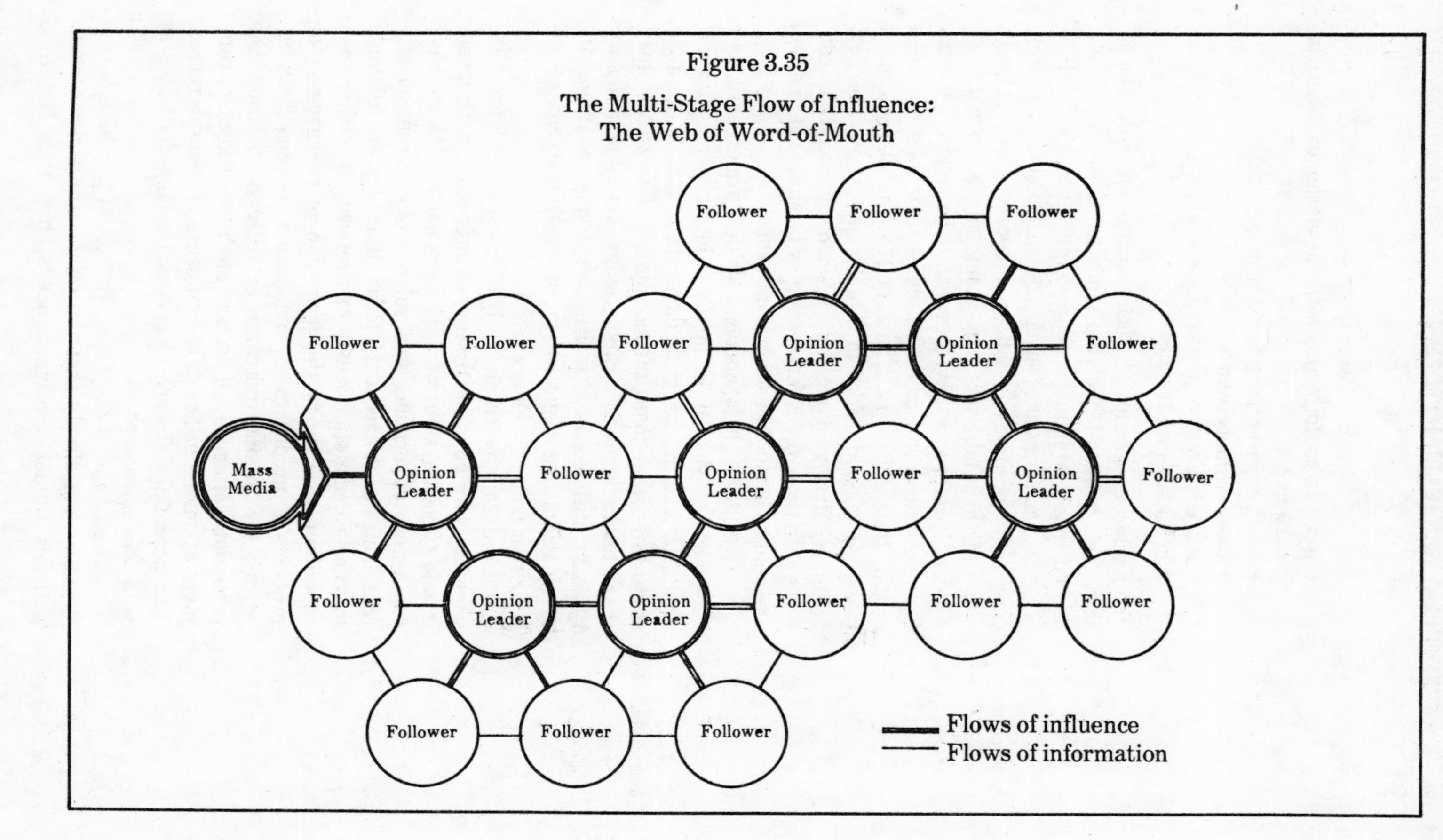

Figure 3.35

The Multi-Stage Flow of Influence: The Web of Word-of-Mouth

- more in conformance with the norms of the social system
- more exposed to all forms of communication
- more cosmopolitan
- more innovative, or receptive to change
- of higher social status

Opinion leaders occupy all social strata, but in developed economies opinion leadership tends to be restricted to a limited sphere of influence since competence is difficult to achieve in many areas of specialization. Opinion leaders occupy their positions of influence because they embody many of their followers' important beliefs, opinions, attitudes, preferences, values, and behavioral norms. Opinion leaders are more like *all* of their followers than *any* of their followers. The requirements of conformity place the opinion leader in a highly precarious position, however. Merely advocating a belief or opinion which conflicts with those of his followers may be sufficient to erode the opinion leader's position of influence.

Opinion leader: conforms to norms

Attitudes, beliefs, opinions, values, preferences, and behavior are shaped in multiple interactions with individuals who are very similar, rather than in a single stage flow from mass media sources. *Information* may reach an audience in a single stage flow, but *influence* typically diffuses in a multi-stage sequence among individuals drawn together in informal patterns of interpersonal interaction.

Information versus influence

Product preferences, like most attitudes, are generally formed in the process of interacting with others in one's social system who are very similar. As we have suggested, advertising and sales promotion frequently contribute to awareness, focus interest, or reinforce existing consumption habits or preferences, rather than contribute directly to the formation of preferences for products or producers. By implication, as consumers approach the product purchase or rejection decision, the potential influence of mass media marketing communication diminishes as the influence of peers increases. The potential influence of personal selling decreases as well but not as much.

Total package satisfactory

The Image of the Firm. The act of purchase is confirmation not simply that the product in some measure satisfies unmet consumer needs, but that the total package of appeals communicated by the firm through the components of the communication mix — advertising, personal selling, public relations, publicity, and sales promotion — conforms to the consumer's anticipated level of satisfaction. Programmed as well as nonprogrammed communications emanating from the firm determine its image. It is in response to a perceived image, identity, or reputation of a firm that the various environmental sectors confer legitimacy on that firm. *Thus a central concept in the design of marketing communication strategy is the image of the firm.* Image ranges across and is founded upon all points of contact between the firm and its external environment: products, packaging, brands, advertising, salesmen, sales promotion, distributors, and employees, to name a few.

Image = perceived personality

Image is essentially the *perceived personality* of the firm. As perceptions are subjective, the image of the firm will vary among the various groups and individuals from which it seeks legitimacy. These differences may be important in determining the responses specific sectors are likely to make to the communication package of the firm. Such differences must be accommodated in designing communication strategies, since communication effectiveness is contingent upon the communication source's ability to anticipate the receiver's expectations and state of mind, and tailor messages accordingly. In the final analysis, "all marketing communications both contribute to and are interpreted in the context of the firm's image." [97, p. 605] Hence the design of communication strategy cannot be considered independently of the goal of creating and enhancing the firm's image.

Image = source credibility

The concept of image has its parallel in the notion of source credibility. Attempts to enhance the firm's image are essentially efforts to convey an impression of technical capability and consistent quality and associated levels of consumer satisfaction, which combine to yield source credibility.

> Source credibility is an important determinant of response to communication because it provides the *context* within which all marketing communications are interpreted . . . In Gestalt terms, the [firm's] image is the background against which the potential customer evaluates informational cues received from

advertising, sales personnel, the package, and other elements of the communication program. [97, p. 607]

Credibility ↓ Effectiveness

A credible image can augment the effectiveness of all components of the firm's marketing communications program and reinforce the sales effectiveness of distributors and dealers. A weak or negative image can undermine or even offset the effectiveness of advertising, personal selling, publicity, public relations, and sales promotion, and can retard reseller support.

Legitimacy-seeking: focuses in communication

The legitimacy-seeking efforts of the firm all come into focus in the marketing communication function. The effectiveness of marketing management's prior decisions concerning which products will be offered for sale, at what prices, through which distribution channels, all hinge upon the effectiveness with which advertising, sales promotion, publicity, public relations and personal selling are carried out. The components of the firm's marketing programs are combined into a balanced array of appeals designed to carry out communication strategy and, hopefully, to facilitate the establishment of positions of legitimacy and power. Effective marketing communication is essential to effective marketing. Indeed, effective marketing communication can partially offset poor product, pricing, or distribution decisions, *but only in the short run.*

TRANSACTION

Transactions universal

All of the relationships within any system can be viewed as interactions or transactions. *Transactions involve an exchange of values.* Individuals, institutions and other groups engage in transactions because they perceive that the potential benefits to be derived from the transaction outweigh the effort and cost. In examining the transactive nature of communication, we noted that individuals engage in communication because they anticipate certain benefits in the responses of the receiver. Transactions manifest themselves in many ways other than through verbal communication. *They pervade every facet of human interaction; they make society work.* Citizens give up time for a political candidate in anticipation that the candidate's political posture will in some way benefit them. They may give up a certain lifestyle in return for spiritual edification or sensory gratification. They commit themselves to certain

Figure 3.36

Convergence of The Marketing Process and The Consumer Decision Process

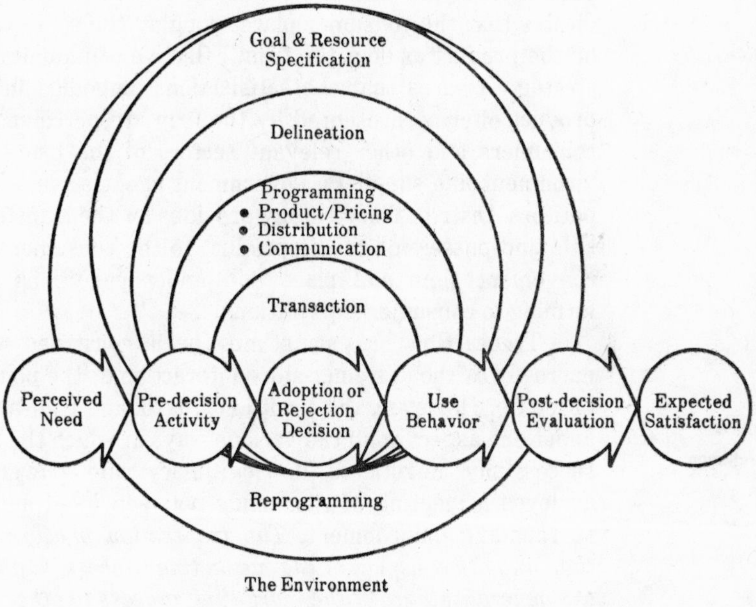

responsibilities and ways of living in return for a secure family life. Economic transactions are just another extension of a universal human phenomenon in which parties exchange something of value, in this case, usually money for a product or service.

> *The transaction phase of the marketing process is the consummatory phase, the point at which the marketing process converges with the consumer decision process and culminates in a purchase act or exchange of values* [see Figure 3.36].

Each component of the marketing program or mix contributes to the consummation of the transaction. The product embodies benefits sought and anticipated by consumers, and communicates the firm's willingness and ability to recognize and respond to consumer needs. The price of the product is the result of negotiations with the environment, particularly consumers, which have resulted in a meeting of minds and a willingness on the part of the purchaser to pay the market price. This willingness indicates that the consumer places roughly the same value on the product as does the firm. Effective communication strategy assures that the satisfactions embodied in the product offering presented by the firm are perceived by consumers and other relevant sectors of the firm's environment like suppliers, government agencies, and competitors. Distribution strategy provides for the transfer of title and possession of the product to the consumer at a convenient time and place and under conditions conforming to consumer expectations.

Parity of value

Transaction has sometimes been construed very narrowly as the customer-store interaction at the point of purchase. However, the traditional exchange transaction is but one aspect of all the various ways in which the firm successfully negotiates its legitimacy and power or achieves a meeting of the minds between itself and its surrounding environment. *The transaction phase, more than any other aspect of the marketing process, suggests the generalizability of the marketing process to other contexts and interactions*. All transactions have an implicit or explicit cost and involve a subjective evaluation of benefits versus efforts. Transactions are a two-way street. They are the very essence of the interactive, interdependent and dynamic nature of systems and systems concepts.

Response to change

REPROGRAMMING

Reprogramming is the process of adjusting or fine-tuning the marketing program in response to shifts in environmental demands and constraints.

It involves tactical adjustments in the market offering, as opposed to strategic adjustments which would require major re-evaluations of enterprise goals and priorities. Reprogramming is a response to shifts in consumer preferences and characteristics; technological innovation and the spread of innovation through the culture; perceived shortcomings in product or pricing policies; altered economic conditions; new laws and trade regulations; internationalization; and political upheavals, to name a few.

Reprogramming and the Product Life Cycle

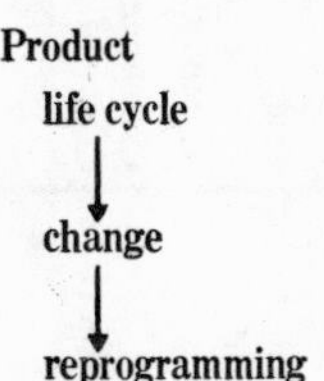

We have suggested that marketers are able to influence both the rate of new product adoption and the longevity of a product by continually monitoring the product's progress and making tactical adjustments in the marketing program. Every aspect of the environment in which the product is marketed changes as the product moves through the stages of its product life cycle. The nature and extent of consumer demand, the strength and extent of competitors marketing essentially the same product, new technological developments and the willingness and ability of channel intermediaries to distribute the product are but a few of the environmental changes affecting the success of a product as it progresses through its life cycle. Costs, sales volume and profits provide barometers for gauging the effectiveness of a given marketing program, but other feedback like buyer behavior research and knowledge of what competitors are doing is necessary as well. Figure 3.37 illustrates the various ways in which adjustments may be necessitated by the changes occurring throughout the product life cycle in the macro- and microenvironment of the firm.

Understanding the changes that are occurring in the life cycle of a specific product and the implications for marketing strategy contributes a great deal to the efficiency of reprogramming. Communication strategy, for example, varies drastically from the Pioneering stage when the product is new and has virtually no competitors, to the Saturation stage when competitors may number in the hundreds. The entire marketing mix may need to be overhauled to prolong the usefulness of a product and to perpetuate its contribution to the market power of the firm.

Anticipation and Adaptation. Firms have traditionally been very lax in their attempts to adjust their marketing programs in response to changes in the environment.[48] Most firms fail to anticipate change, so they have little in the way of contingency plans when an

Figure 3.37

Programming Implications of the Product Life Cycle

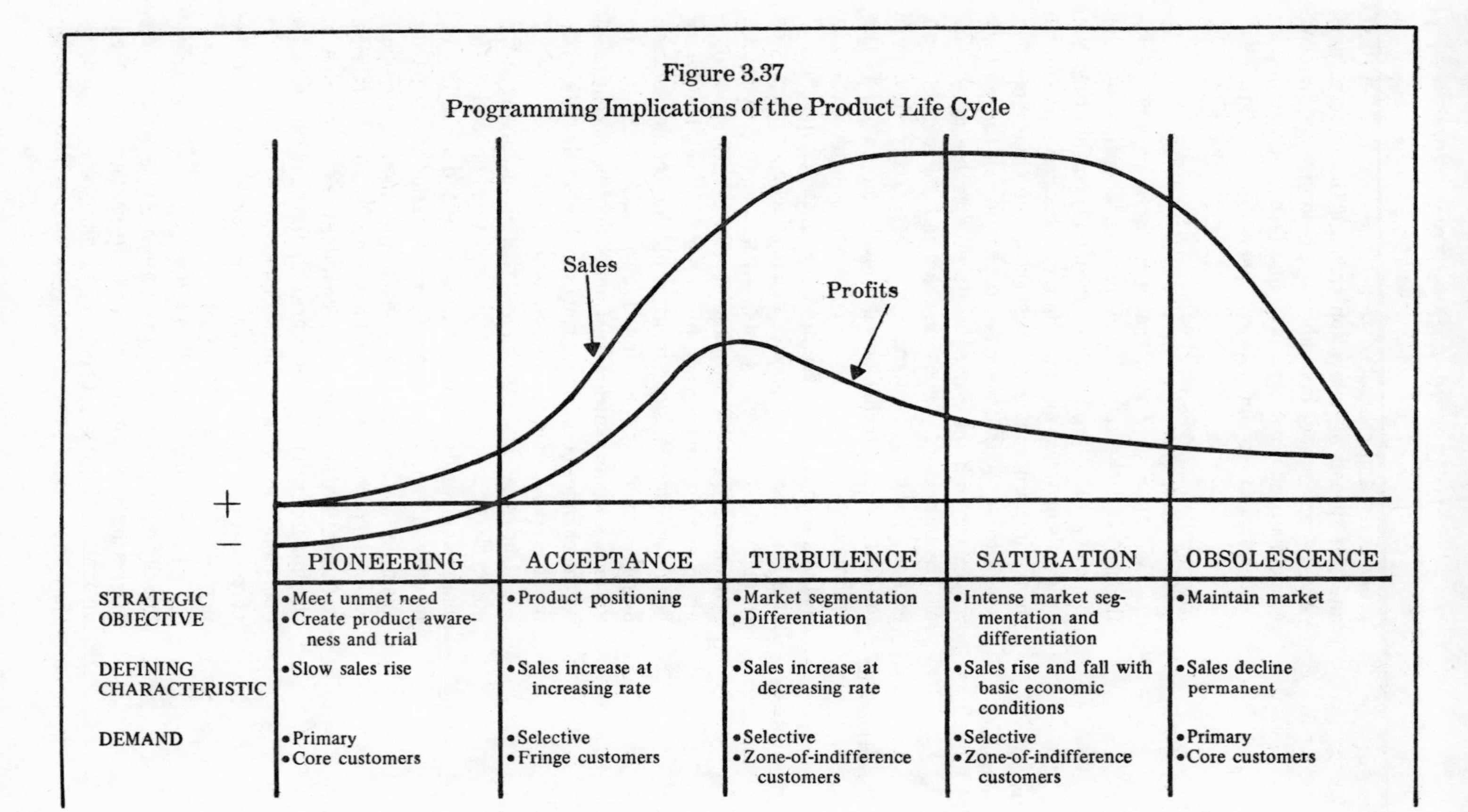

	PIONEERING	ACCEPTANCE	TURBULENCE	SATURATION	OBSOLESCENCE
STRATEGIC OBJECTIVE	• Meet unmet need • Create product awareness and trial	• Product positioning	• Market segmentation • Differentiation	• Intense market segmentation and differentiation	• Maintain market
DEFINING CHARACTERISTIC	• Slow sales rise	• Sales increase at increasing rate	• Sales increase at decreasing rate	• Sales rise and fall with basic economic conditions	• Sales decline permanent
DEMAND	• Primary • Core customers	• Selective • Fringe customers	• Selective • Zone-of-indifference customers	• Selective • Zone-of-indifference customers	• Primary • Core customers

COMPETITION	• None of importance	• Explosion in number of competitors	• Competition of desperation • Marginal firms fail	• Number of competitors stabilizes	• Number of competitors declines Survivors specialize
PRODUCT	• Frequent modifications • Experimental production methods • Product differentiation • Limited lines	• First major improvements • Line production methods • Multiple lines	• Annual models appear • Emphasis on style • Trade-ins appear • Parts and service requirements increase • Institutional brand loyalty	• Trade-ins dominate • Annual models • Emphasis on style • Parts and service requirements • Institutional brand loyalty	• Product lines simplified
PRICE	• High • Price skimming	• Prices soften • Penetration pricing • Price lining	• Intense price competition	• Intense price competition	• Prices soften, stabilize. increase
DISTRIBUTION	• Exclusive or selective	• Scramble for outlets • Intensive • Multiple lines carried	• Dealer margins shrink • Intensive • Simplify lines	• Dealer strength critical • Intensive • Logistics complex and costly	• Exclusive or selective • Market exposure not critical
COMMUNICATION	• Create product awareness and trial • Personal selling and informative advertising	• Create brand preference • Heavy competitive advertising	• Maintain consumer franchise • Heavy competitive advertising • Reseller support	• Reinforce institutional loyalty • Heavy competitive advertising • Reseller support	• Create product awareness • Reinforce demand for product • Market exposure not critical
COST STRUCTURE	• High production costs • High marketing costs	• Costs decrease	• Costs stabilize	• Cost control essential for survival	• High production costs • Moderate or low marketing costs
PROFITS	• Negative profits	• Healthy profits	• Profits peak	• Profits decline	• Profits decline • Profit opportunities may be good

Adapted from Thomas A. Staudt and Donald A. Taylor, *A Managerial Introduction to Marketing*, Englewood Cliffs, New Jersey: Prentice-Hall, Chapter 10.

unexpected situation occurs. The recent energy crisis provides a dramatic case in point. The domestic automobile manufacturers failed to plan for the impact of the energy crisis, even when all indications were that petroleum products would soon be in short supply. Instead of attempting to gauge all possible effects of a possible energy crisis, including changes in gasoline consumption habits and the resulting demand for small and economical automoiles, Detroit executives continued a policy of predominantly large car production. They were then faced with a tremendous backlog of large automobiles and a burgeoning demand for small cars which they were unable to supply. Economic conditions were worsening at the same time the energy crisis was deepening, and the automobile manufacturers were faced with their worst marketing crisis in years. Deciding that a reactionary policy was better than none, they unloaded as many of the larger cars as possible at reduced prices and began producing small cars as rapidly as possible. In an astonishing display of market insensitivity, Detroit attempted to recoup lost profits by pricing the small cars very near the high levels of the large cars. Many customers who would have been in the market for a small car as soon as it rolled off the assembly line revolted at the untenably high prices and refused to buy a car at all. The continued ill health of the domestic automobile industry brought on by such shortsighted thinking has had negative reverberations throughout the economy.

Automobile crisis: failure to anticipate and adapt

Anticipation, not reaction

The case of the automobile crisis points out three critical facts:

Information

Effective reprogramming

- The inescapable interaction between managerial policies and events in the firm and environmental factors external to the firm
- The vital importance of providing for adjustments in marketing programs through contingency planning and reprogramming
- The necessity of adequate market information if programming and reprogramming are to succeed at all

We have discussed at length the need for knowledge of consumer attitudes and behavior in making marketing decisions, but clearly consumer behavior research alone is insufficient. The other sectors of the environment must be monitored as well, and on a continual rather than on an *ad hoc* basis. Marketing under conditions of constant and rapid change requires tremendous banks of data concerning the environment, not only in terms of past and present conditions but also in terms of future projections. As we have suggested, *the vehicle for continual environmental surveillance is the marketing information system.*

CONCLUSIONS

The task of marketing management under conditions of rapid and constant environmental change clearly extends beyond traditional functional definitions of the marketing process. Functional definitions fail to account for the dynamic, interactive *transactive* nature of the firm's quest for legitimacy. The firm must communicate with and transact with all sectors in the environment from whom legitimacy is sought. Systems thinking and concepts infuse an awareness of the interactive nature of the marketing process into an analysis of that process.

As the firm attempts to maximize control over its environment, management must manipulate its finite array of tools — the marketing controllables — in such a way that legitimacy is assured even in the face of uncertainty and change. The marketing process must unfold in a logical and recursive chain of activities which should include:

- Goal and resource specification
- Delineation
- Programming
- Transaction
- Reprogramming

The programming phase encompasses the conventional focus of marketing efforts. All phases converge to produce a total market offering which establishes the legitimacy and power of the firm and assures that the enterprise engages in a mutually beneficial transaction with the environment over time.

In Chapter 4 we will examine the social systems context within which marketing activity unfolds, with particular emphasis on the interdependent social institutions which form the fabric of American society, and the role of the economic system and of marketing in facilitating the attainment of social goals and perpetuating a constellation of cultural values. It is the societal context for business and marketing activity which is most frequently overlooked in the intense preoccupation with marketing functions. But an assessment of the role of the economic system in American society, and the role of marketing within the economic system, is essential in evaluating the efficiency and effectiveness of the economic system and marketing activity. Moreover, an understanding of cultural values, institutions, interrelationships, integration, and change is critical in isolating severe malfunctions in American society which imply a radical redefinition, reorientation, and reorganization of the economic system and the marketing process.

CHAPTER 3: REVIEW QUESTIONS

1. What is entrepreneurship and how does it enhance the firm's ability to establish legitimacy and market power?

2. How does the position of the firm on the competitive continuum we have called the field of competition enhance or undermine the market power of the firm?

3. Do traditional business incentives promote free or pure competition? Why or why not?

4. What is wrong with traditional functional definitions of marketing, like that of the marketing staff of The Ohio State University?

5. What is the sequence of stages in the marketing process suggested in this text? Are they really stages? Why or why not?

6. What is the relationship between goal and resource specification?

7. Why are conventional measures of enterprise performance short-sighted at best and destructive at worst?

8. What is the significance of social auditing?

9. What are the two functions of market delineation (briefly)?

10. What should be considered in defining or delineating a product market?

11. What is a market segment?

12. What determines if a given segmentation axis is useful?

13. What are the advantages of segmentation?

14. Why is the consumer decision process appropriately viewed as an ongoing transaction?

15. What is the general sequence of stages in the consumer decision process?

16. Discuss the three categories of consumer goods in terms of effort.

17. What are adoption categories and the diffusion process?

18. Discuss market sectors in terms of repeat purchasing behavior. Why is the core of the market more likely to engage in brand loyal behavior?

19. What is the implication of cognitive dissonance for the marketer?

20. Are consumer decision processes generalizable to other contexts? Why is this particularly true for a transactional model of the consumer decision process?

21. What is the difference in marketing research and a marketing information system?

22. How does programming relate to and interact with decisions made in the goal and resource specification and delineation phases of the marketing process?

23. Why does a broad conceptualization of "needs" require a broad definition of "product?"

24. Define: product item
    product line
    product mix
    width
    depth
    consistency

25. What are the major stages in the product life cycle and why is it important that the product life cycle be considered in marketing decision making?

26. What is the advantage of a periodic product audit?

27. Is pricing controllable or uncontrollable? Why?

28. What sorts of factors impinge on the autonomy of the firm in setting prices?

29. What are the two broad categories of price policies? Which is preferable and why?

30. What are the important implications of the concept of vertical marketing systems?

31. What are the three general ways that a vertical marketing system may be implemented?

32. What is meant by intensity of distribution and how does this relate to the three categories of consumer goods?

33. What are the five major innovations in retailing? Give four major characteristics of each innovation.

34. What social functions, if any, are performed by marketing communications?

35. What are the six major components of the communication mix?

36. Discuss the "communication system."

37. What are the prerequisites to communication?

38. Define communication effectiveness, efficiency, and fidelity.

39. Does mass communication have the potential to persuade?

40. Why are opinion leaders able to translate information into influence?

41. What is "image" of the firm and why is its cultivation so important?

42. What is meant by the "transaction" phase of the marketing process?

43. What is reprogramming and why is it necessary?

44. What are some programming implications of the product life cycle?

MARKETING: A SOCIETAL ROLE

CULTURE AND SOCIAL INSTITUTIONS

- Culture
- Goals and Means
- Social Institutions and Norms
- The Economic System

A CONSTELLATION OF VALUES IN AMERICAN SOCIETY

- Individualism
- Equality
- Activity and Work
- Achievement-Success
- Materialism
- Morality

INSTITUTIONAL INTERRELATIONSHIPS

SOCIAL INTEGRATION

SOCIAL CHANGE

- Causes of Illusory Change
- Causes of Real Change
- Shifting Value Orientations
  - Instrumental toward Consummatory
  - Achievement toward Expressionism
  - Competitive Individualism toward Cooperation
- And the Future?
  - Commitment and Consensus
- Alternative Value Orientations

THE AMERICAN ECONOMIC SYSTEM

- Values and Economic Organization
- Cultural Norms and Economic Activity
- Principal Structural Features

THE ROLE OF MARKETING

INTERRELATIONSHIPS, INTEGRATION AND CHANGE

- Economic and Political Institutions
- Economic, Educational and Scientific Institutions
- Kinship, Stratification and Economic Institutions

CONCLUSIONS

Marketing: A Societal Role

In the preceding chapter we underscored the fact that marketing is far more than a process of identifying and satisfying consumer wants and needs. Legitimacy seeking is a process of anticipating as well as adapting to pressures emanating from a vast spectrum of environmental forces, of which consumers comprise but one. In short, marketing is a process of securing and sustaining the firm's legitimacy by identifying significant social or individual needs which may be met by the firm's output or methods of operation. We stressed the importance of systems thinking in understanding the formative and adaptive nature of the firm; in understanding the nature of environmental impacts on the firm's output and methods of operation; and in organizing for marketing activity.

In the present chapter we will examine marketing from a societal perspective. We will explore the nature of American society, its interdependent social institutions, the role of the economic system in American society, and the role of marketing within the economic system. Our discussion will focus on five key concepts:

- Institutions
- Values
- Interrelationships
- Integration
- Change

These five critical concepts are essential to understanding the social context within which marketing activity unfolds and the role of marketing in social integration and change. By examining the major components and functions of society, marketers gain valuable insight into what is expected of the firm by various elements of society. Responding to these expectations is the essence of legitimacy.

The economic system, the firm, and marketing are all components of a complex social system. To focus too narrowly on legitimizing efforts in one sector of the social system risks loss of legitimacy from other parts of the system. Loss of legitimacy in turn produces pressure upon the firm to change. The marketer ignores this pressure at his peril. In this chapter we will examine the various structures which comprise the social system within which the firm operates: *social institutions;* their rules for behavior — *norms*; and the likely consequences of failure to respond to pressure for change — *sanctions*. First we must examine how societies work.

Social institutions
Norms
Sanctions

CULTURE AND SOCIAL INSTITUTIONS

Structure = patterns

Underlying each of the concepts we will discuss is the idea of *social structure*. Human behavior is not random, unpredictable, or wholly individualistic. Instead, behavior is organized into *patterns*. Without these patterns, there could be no expectations and no predictability in interpersonal relationships. The result would be chaos. Instead, there is a pervasive set of behavioral expectations that attach to all aspects of our lives. These expectations shape us and form us into unique individuals. No two individuals are subjected to the same set of expectations and pressures. Nonetheless it is possible to derive generalizations concerning the social expectations which bind individuals together into cultures and subcultures. At the most refined levels, these expectations become ritualized. We speak when spoken to; nod to those we meet. The point is that human interactions show structure. They are to some extent recurrent and predictable. At its most general level, this structure is culture.

Culture

Behavioral prescriptions

Culture, essentially, *consists of a set of fairly standardized prescriptions concerning what must be done, should be done, may be done, and must not be done.* These prescriptions are handed down from generation to generation and remain more or less stable over time. Prescriptions prescribe not only how we should *behave* but also what our *goals* should be. These cultural goals are largely insatiable and are generally pursued throughout our lives with consistency and intensity. In the United States youthfulness – a cultural goal – is prized and is manifested, among other ways, in grandmothers wearing bikinis, grandfathers in toupees, and both in tennis shorts on the tennis court.

Goals

Goals and Means

Goals vary from culture to culture, and where different cultures share the same goals the relative importance or priority of goals may vary. Education, for example, is more highly valued in Germany than in the United States. Even within a single culture, the importance of goals may shift with shifting environmental conditions or social priorities. Military careers and martial talent, for example, count for little in peacetime, but for much in war.

Even where the goals of different cultures are the same, the means of achieving cultural goals is likely to vary. Americans, for example, have a vast array of socially prescribed ways to find excitement – sports, movies, books, sex. Most Americans, however, do not turn to dueling, bear baiting, Russian roulette or bullfighting for excitement. Undeniably these diversions are exciting, but they are not currently part of the American culture.

Culture
- Orientation
- Goals
- Means
- Perspective

What culture gives us then is an overall *orientation*. It provides a set of *goals* and a variety of *means* for attaining these goals. Too, it rules out certain behavior as antisocial and provides a unique *perspective* of the world. It provides, in other words, a cultural binding which can have severe dysfunctional consequences, particularly in dealing with individuals of different cultural or subcultural background. [65, pp. 132-9]

Social Institutions and Norms

Culture also provides a set of behaviors or *social institutions* for dealing with society's major recurring problems (see Figure 4.1): [21, Part IV]

- Reproduction (kinship institution)
- Education and knowledge (educational and scientific institutions)
- Distribution of power (political/governmental institution)
- Ranking (stratification institution)
- Survival (economic institution)
- Death (religious institution)

Social institutions
- Expected behaviors
- Solutions to society's problems

In other words, *social institutions consisting of clusters of expected behaviors arise in any culture to provide solutions to society's recurrent problems.* The regular performance of these behaviors is vital to the continued existence of society. As a consequence, these behaviors tend to be obligatory for the members of society.

By levying *sanctions* society encourages its members to conform to the behaviors expected by its social institutions. Sanctions take many forms including humor or ridicule, ostracism, and physical punishment. The most common and possibly most effective sanction is the withdrawal of affection by others.

Conceptions of conduct mirror value structure

Social institutions guide or shape individual behavior by *conceiving of the individual in a particular way and encouraging him to conform to that conception.* [77, p. 176] The conceptions of proper and improper conduct reflected in the social institutions emerging in any culture mirror the fundamental *value structure* of the culture. Religious and philanthropic institutions conceive of the individual as an immortal soul. To protect the individual's

Figure 4.1

Institutional Structure of Society

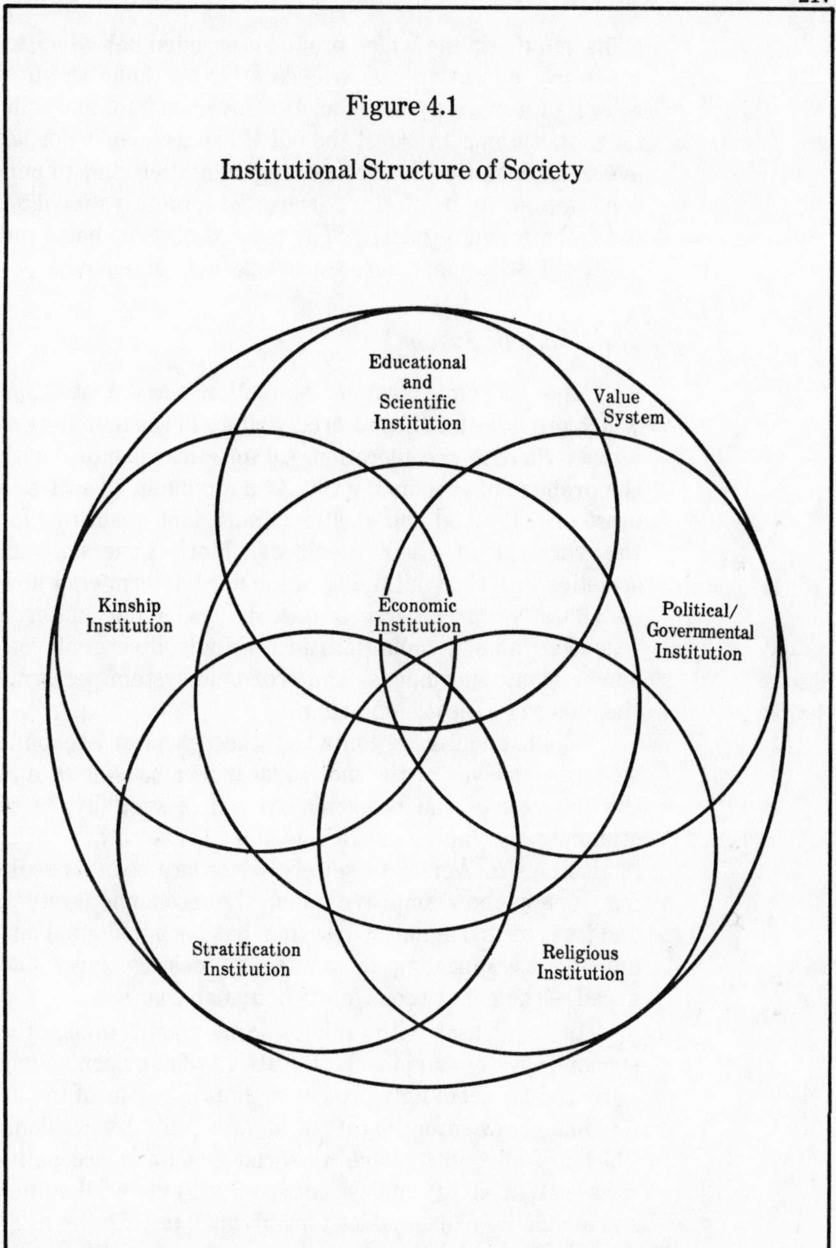

soul, religious and philanthropic institutions attempt to inculcate virtue and consideration for the rights and privileges of others. The reward they offer is salvation. Schools, universities, and scientific organizations view the individual as guided by reason and seek to develop the skills and discipline which produce reasoned behavior. As a reward, education and science offer the hope through reason of a more perfect society. Governmental and military institutions interpret the individual as favoring order over chaos and seek through regimentation and impersonalization to inculcate a sense of order, rationality, consistency and regularity. The reward governmental and military institutions afford is predictability of behavior.

The Economic System

The economic system is itself a social institution which provides for the material welfare of the members of society via resource allocation. All societies must deal with the problem of economic want. At a minimum all societies must provide food and shelter in sufficient quantities for the survival of their members. More generally, all societies face the continuing problem of determining how to allocate scarce, and frequently dwindling material resources among unlimited, increasingly divergent consumer wants and needs. The economic system performs the resource allocation function.

Resource allocation

The particular way in which the American economic system conceives of the individual is as a *consumer*, and the purpose of the economic system, essentially, is to stimulate the individual to consume. Unlike other social institutions in American society which are seen as seeking to somehow improve man, the economic system, and its principal agent, marketing, has been maligned and indicted as appealing to wants and desires, envy and greed — the nonvirtuous facets of human character.

In contrast with other social institutions, the economic system and marketing activity have been widely criticized for seemingly promoting improvement of the individual or accentuation of social value only by accident. They are alleged to have no social goals and accept no social responsibility, unless conformity to material values and avoidance of overt deceit qualify. [17, p. 415]

These criticisms of the economic institution stem from the fact that different social institutions place different weights on cultural values, although all social institutions subscribe to the same basic set of values. Religious institutions obviously don't encourage absolute material abstinence, but do stress morality over materialism. In seeking legitimacy, the marketer must try to account for the relative priority of these cultural values among different social institutions.

Paradox of purpose

Despite their alleged historical lack of social sensitivity or responsibility, the economic system and marketing perform a definite function: to match supply of material goods with demand. The economic system, then, may be viewed as a partial or attempted solution to the paradox of preserving a materially-oriented society under conditions of spreading material affluence and resource scarcity and splintering social priorities and goals. We will have a great deal more to say about this in Chapter 5.

A CONSTELLATION OF VALUES IN AMERICAN SOCIETY

Expected behaviors → Values

The essence of any culture is the constellation of values and associated norms that are considered mandatory for the members of society. Social institutions form a sort of blueprint of expected and obligatory behavior by individuals in any society, clustering around the various value vectors that comprise the constellation of cultural values. Institutions are in fact sets of norms or expectations governing individual role performance in different role contexts. Thus institutions provide not only *externally imposed sanctions* shaping individual behavior, but are *internalized* as *values* which have a binding and directing impact on personality and behavior. We internalize obligations as our own, rather than as arbitrary externally imposed rules. We accept behavioral standards and goals which are held by our parents, peers, and others whom we may wish to emulate, as valuable and right for us, independent of their presence.

External

Internal

> Thus, institutions . . . are both "facts of the external world" that the individual must take into account and value patterns within the personality. Every act, or failure to act, in the interdependent web of sociocultural life has consequences; institutions and the values they represent are continually being reinforced, maintained, changed, or destroyed by the

> shifting patterns of human thought and action. "Stability" of culture is, therefore, a dynamic process in which a delicately balanced system of values is maintained. [98, p. 439]

Conflict

Further, *conflict in society is largely the result of the differing behavioral expectations of different social institutions*. By conforming to the expectations of one social institution, an individual may violate the expectations of another. In our society, requirements to satisfy the expectations of the economic and religious institutions are often highly divergent. The governmental and religious institutions are sometimes marked by more vivid conflict: the soldier who kills an enemy. Hence conflict in society is frequently a consequence of colliding role expectations.

Much is often made of the heterogeneous nature of American society. This implies that the concept of a common constellation of values and associated norms applies very loosely, if at all, to the United States. This is, at least in part, an empirical question and the evidence is mixed. But as one observer put it,

> It seems preferable to opt for simplicity. To take a simple point: income is such a crucial mechanism for transfer of goods and services in a contemporary society that a genuine rejection of income aspirations cannot be interpreted as a preference for a different set of cultural values; it is simply insane. [68, p. 313]

Pervasive values and norms

American society, despite its obvious heterogeneity, can be characterized by a constellation of pervasive values and norms which have shown slow transformation but persistent influence.

The constellation of values which lies behind the institutional structure of society is not easily disentangled. Value systems are not simply distributed at random across the fabric of society but are instead patterned in a mosaic of reciprocal dependence. It is difficult to caricature a national character or typical American values or a national personality profile because of the enormous diversity of values within the American culture. However, the major constellations of values which have had a binding and directing influence on the evolution of American society and which are mirrored in varying degrees in all our social institutions are sixfold (see Figure 4.2):

- Individualism
- Equality
- Activity and work
- Achievement-success
- Materialism
- Morality

Individualism

Freedom

Freedom from arbitrary, externally imposed restraints on behavior and thought has been a major thread through American history, traceable to this country's Western European heritage. While all social life is constrained in some degree, the desire for freedom from religious, political, and economic restraints or oppressions was a fundamental motivation binding together founders of the American colonies.

Rights & duties

Checks & balances

Precarious premise

The desire for freedom from actual or perceived constraints has had a major impact on patterns of thought and evaluation in American culture. Americans have a deep-seated aversion to centralized authority and coercive restraint through regulation and regimentation. We think first of *rights*, second of *duty*. The origins and organization of both the political and economic systems emerged from a pernicious fear of centralized power and control. The checks and balances built into both systems were intended to restrict collectivized or centralized governmental and economic action to prescribed areas of authority. The particular interpretation of freedom mirrored in both political and economic systems of organization was predicated on the *precarious premise that individuals were competent to make individual decisions which benefited themselves alone, infringed minimally on the rights of others, yet simultaneously benefited society-at-large*. The insufficiency of this article of faith is evidenced in the mushrooming trend toward socialism and centralized power and authority in the last half-century. America's Asian Drama rapidly drawing to a close is testimony to this assertion. [71] Still, however, individualism remains a value of central priority in American culture.

Figure 4.2

A Constellation of American Values

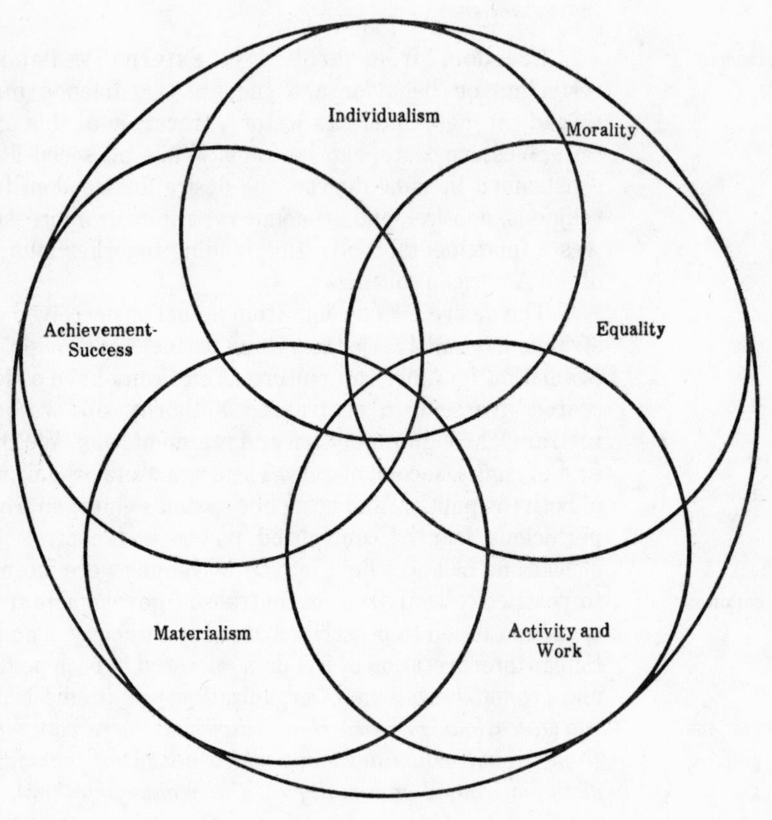

Equality

Individualism versus Equality

The countervailing value in the American constellation of values to the principal of individual determinism is equality. Nowhere is this apparent contradiction more evident than in the contemporary economic organization which in many ways epitomizes *inequality*, yet emphasizes *equality of opportunity*. It has long been believed that such economic virtues as hard work, frugality, and prudence should receive proportionate rewards. This axiom has been closely linked with the premise that everyone, at least everyone who resembles me, should have equal access to opportunity. However, this entire principle is undergoing severe strain and radical redefinition.

Charter value

Equality is a "charter value" in America along with individualism, and was implicit in the initial political organization of society. The break with the hierarchical tradition of Western Europe was favored by a complex of factors: middle- and lower-class origins in European society; mass access to material resources; Protestant emphasis on individualism and hard work; a shared aversion to abusive authority. It was not until the aftermath of the Industrial Revolution in the Eighteenth Century that American society confronted the inevitable and widespread collision of the principle of equality and the principles of achievement and individualism. Different levels of achievement naturally produced inequality. The Industrial Revolution radically altered the basis for status and status mobility, resulting in inequalities of wealth, power, and prestige and in access to opportunity to acquire these things. Just as individuals are not in fact equal in specific abilities or capacities, in a highly complex, increasingly specialized interdependent society, access to opportunity is likely to be unevenly distributed across society. And yet, and more essential, is the fact that equality is manifested in the manner in which individuals interact with others in ordinary interpersonal activity. Historically, American society has been characterized by extraordinary informality, directness and relative immunity from status differences in interpersonal interactions. *Openness in interpersonal relationships can only operate continuously in a culture in which intrinsic personal value is assumed.*

Inequality of
- **wealth**
- **power**
- **prestige**
- **access to opportunity**

Equality manifested in interaction

Historically the principles of economic freedom and individualistic achievement have dominated the principle of equality. Where reward has been the consequence of achievement — in business, governmental, or military service — inequality of reward has been widely accepted as legitimate. Thus the operating principle of business has long been equality of opportunity rather than equality of reward or outcome. Equality in America means a dual emphasis on *individual rights* and *equality of opportunity*. All of this, of course, has been violated or ignored in the case of minority Americans, an irony which in recent years has resulted in intensifying social tension and pressure toward reform and change. [8, pp. 98-9]

Equality
- **Individual rights**
- **Opportunity**

Activity and Work

Americans have historically placed tremendous importance on activity, on "doing something." The stereotype of the American character is an individual who seeks to dominate, shape, and exploit his natural environment. This pattern forms the *leitmotif* throughout American history and emerged out of a combination of religious tradition (the Puritan ethic), frontier experience, ceaseless change, unexploited opportunity, and fluid social structure. [98, pp. 458-9]

The emphasis upon discipline and productivity is a thread traceable all the way back to the origins of American society. Work was a prerequisite for survival along the moving frontier: he who did not work did not eat. As one observer put it:

> Americans are good at getting things done. In any task calling for organization, power, and mass production, they equal the best and excel most . . . Americans or any frontier people are not much given to introspection and contemplation. Work was what the frontier [American] first went for. [95, p. 50]

Achievement-Success

Activity and work are closely linked to achievement-success, the achievement motive providing the impetus for productive effort or work. The Horatio Alger story of personal achievement and the esteem accorded the self-made man are distinctly American. The ideal of personal excellence is a thread of continuity running through Western culture, *but a striking feature of American culture is the interpretation of personal excellence in terms of competitive occupational achievement.* Indeed, the values of the business executive have slowly assumed a position of dominance in American society and have permeated national character. In recent years how one spends his income, rather than what he did to earn it, has also materialized as a barometer of achievement. Yet it is not simply sufficient that one be successful. One must be successful within a prescribed ethical framework. Americans prefer the illusion that virtue triumphs over vice. In American culture failure is still more likely to be attributed to a defect of character than to bad luck, impersonal social or economic forces, or blind fate.

Occupational achievement

Virtue & Vice

Materialism

The particular end toward which the work-achievement value complex has historically been oriented is materialism. Moreover, in a society of relatively high social mobility, in which position within the social hierarchy depends principally upon occupational achievement, material wealth is one of the few obvious signs of one's place on the ladder. Standard of living in America has its undertones and overtones of meaning, from national identification to symbol of achievement, competence, and power, and from a triumph of personal virtue to something approximating the ultimate level of need satisfaction.

Standard of living

> A case can be made that business leaders have been the real energizers of this materialistic society. Turning its back on Europe's luxuries and privileges, America from the beginning set out to be a working place. With so much to be done, culture was scorned as effete. And thus developed a nation of great egalitarian vigor, crudeness, impulsiveness, hard work, and ambition. Even today and even among the young, criticisms directed against materialism come up against a stronger demand for goods and services, a stronger need for jobs. [36, p. 90]

But the dominance of materialism in the American lexicon of values has proven something of a mixed blessing. The very fact that the economic system which evolved around the goal of materialism has worked so well is both its virtue and its vice. The success of the economic system in diffusing a high and (almost) steadily rising standard of living within society mitigates against its continued dominance. As material wealth becomes more general, the impetus for economic production and distribution weakens and the organizational apparatus designed to fulfill the economic function loses disciples. Further amplification in the urgency of alternative social and environmental priorities and purposes further undermines the production and distribution functions, and the system begins to feed upon itself. If the economic function is to retain its significance and society its continuity of structure, the impetus for economic production and distribution — the consumption function — must be somehow stimulated. As long as material scarcity was the rule, consumption presented little or no problem. Production *per se* led to consumption. With material affluence, the reverse has largely become true. Consumption, not production, constrains the economic function and thus threatens the foundation upon which the structure of American society was built. This is where marketing comes in. One historically vital role of marketing has been to stimulate demand and hence fuel the economy's continued growth. In a time of recession, inflation, unemployment, pollution, resource scarcity, and ecological imbalance, serious questions are being raised about the price required to maintain a production and distribution oriented economy and the extent to which such a society as presently conceived can remain viable.

Production & consumption

Consumption constrains growth

Demand stimulation

Morality

Morality relates to an ethical orientation in the total constellation of values which forms the underpinning of American culture. Americans see the world, the behavior of institutions, organizations, groups and individuals in terms of black and white, right and wrong. Morality provides a halo — a rationale — for the other values which comprise the American constellation. Where reality and morality diverge, Americans engage in an intricate array of ritualized behaviors to reconcile the two, or rationalize

Halo

the difference. In an effort to reduce morality to practical reality or live with the discrepancy, individuals resort to hypocrisy, cynicism, schizophrenia, and sometimes missionary zeal. The latter has historically justified smuggling the particular brand of American values and virtues into other cultures, under the guise of humanitarian motives. *The principal role of morality in contemporary society is to provide an umbrella protecting and perpetuating a way of life and a system of values.* Behavioral expectations are circumscribed by cultural boundaries. What's right for America isn't necessarily right for . . .

Smuggling values

> Historically, what has united a people has been a ruler, a doctrine, or a destiny — sometimes, in the great periods of a people, a fusion of the three. In the U.S., what gave purpose to the republic at its founding was a sense of destiny — the idea, expressed by Jefferson, that on this virgin continent God's design would be unfolded. On a virgin continent, men could be free, prodigally free, to pursue their individual ends and celebrate their achievements. The doctrine was shaped by a Protestantism that emphasized sobriety and work, which resisted the temptations of the flesh.
>
> Over the years, this quiet sense of destiny and harsh creed of personal conduct were often replaced by a virulent "Americanism," a manifest destiny that took us overseas, and a materialist hedonism that provided the incentives to work. Today that manifest destiny is shattered, the Americanism has worn thin, and only the hedonism remains. It is a poor recipe for national unity and purpose. [8, p. 185]

Is it really this black? Who really knows? Nonetheless, this constitutes the fundamental constellation of values in American culture. It is critical to note that these value systems do not operate independently, but are a constantly shifting mosaic of interdependency. All institutions in American society mirror in varying degree these value systems. Institutional conflict is largely the consequence of conflicting expectations associated with different roles performed by the individual in accordance with the values prescribed by different social institutions.

Institutional conflict

INSTITUTIONAL INTERRELATIONSHIPS

We have noted the various social institutions which comprise the fabric of American culture: familial, educational, political/governmental, economic, religious and stratification. It is essential to recognize that institutions are systems. As such, social institutions exhibit multiple interrelationships and interdependencies. However, some institutions preserve a partial immunity from influence from other social institutions, somewhat segregated, self-contained, and outwardly resistant. And most importantly, the dominant or leading social institution(s) will vary from society to society, and from one era to another within a given society.

Institutional dominance

Clearly the economic system constitutes the most conspicuous and dominant institution in American society. Conversely, the political system forms the dominant institution in Soviet society. Historically, the church dominated Italian society. But the intensified interdependencies among social institutions in all societies make it increasingly difficult to isolate a single institution as dominant in shaping patterns of behavior in a given culture. Institutional *interdependency* is a characteristic feature of technologically advanced countries.

Social institutions are facts of culture and of individual personality, not distinct social structures within society. That is, social institutions constitute patterns of expectations or norms toward which the behavior of all members of society is oriented. Therefore, *interrelationships among social institutions occur through individual performance of the role requirements of different social institutions* (see Figure 4.3). Thus institutional interactions or conflicts may occur at an *intrapersonal, interpersonal,* or *interorganizational* level. In the performance of his various roles the individual functions in accordance with ideals, beliefs, values, and norms which define or circumscribe expected patterns of behavior appropriate to the different social institutions in which he participates. The individual's total pattern of behavior, then, often requires the resolution or reconciliation of the sometimes conflicting norms or expectations associated with the roles he performs in different institutions. Thus the individual frequently must don a different set of behavioral expectations as he moves

Figure 4.3

Institutional Interrelationships through Individual Roles

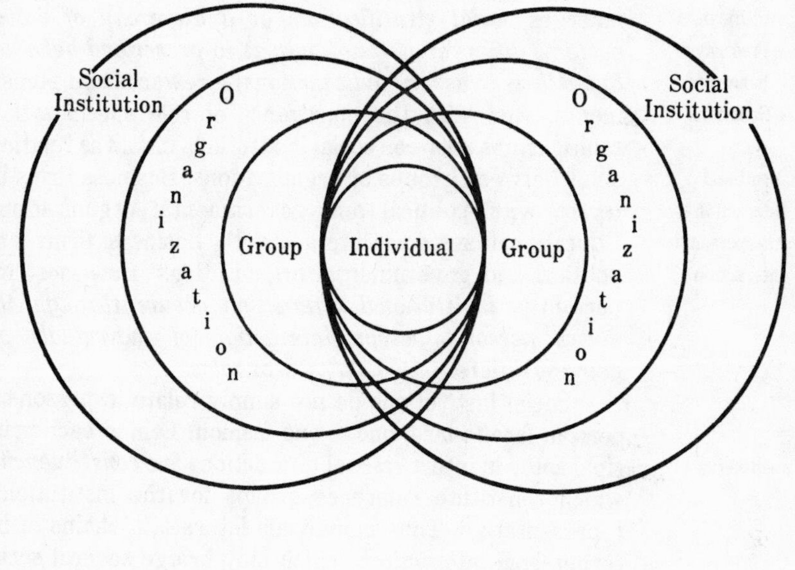

Role conflict

from role to role. In this sense, we all gain ever greater sophistication in responding to the expectations associated with the increasingly diversified roles we must perform, constantly seeking to minimize the conflicts arising out of colliding role requirements. When these conflicts cannot be negotiated, minimized, or out-maneuvered, someone is unhappy, frustrated, or torn, either us or those with whom we interact in different institutional contexts. The result is sometimes neurosis or more severe psychological disorders at a personal level, or loss of job, loss of faith, loss of freedom or incarceration, divorce or alienation at an interpersonal level.

Specialization of roles

In a highly complex technological society like the United States behavioral prescriptions or expectations become highly specialized with respect to specific roles, such as business executive, foreman, or laborer, politician, minister, teacher, doctor, lawyer, or Indian chief. With role specialization and specification of role expectations emerges *social stratification*, or *a hierarchy of status systems differentiated not only as to prescribed behavior but also as to associated sanctions* – rewards and punishments. And with the emergence of role specialization, relationships between social institutions unfold as relationships between groups or organizations. Business firms interact with political and governmental organizations. Educational systems interact with business firms and political and governmental organizations. But, most importantly, *institutional interaction occurs through the direct person-to-person interaction of individuals occupying differentiated statuses or roles*.

Social stratification
- **Prescribed behavior**
- **Sanctions**

Institutional interaction = interpersonal interaction

Constituents

Social institutions do not simply relate in person-to-person, face-to-face, one-to-one fashion. Behind each principal actor in interpersonal interactions are *constituencies* which constitute reference groups for the institutional representative. Thus individuals interact in chains of interpersonal interactions which may bridge several social institutions. Hence a judge may intercede on behalf of a paroled offender in locating employment, whereupon a businessman may seek to relocate the individual's family in a residential neighborhood close to work and local schools, and the offender himself may seek spiritual or psychological counseling. The chains are as intricate as they are varied. But out of these elaborate institutional interrelationships arise highly complex institutional structures. Thus, the Supreme Court evolved within our political system as a complex mediating agency which intervenes in problems involving practically every major social institution. [98, pp. 551-554]

Institutional segregation

A particularly striking feature of American society is the extraordinarily sharp and increasing separation of social institutions at the social level. Each institution tends to be segregated from others within the social system, each having its distinctive statuses requiring role specialization. As evidence for this proposition, consider that we commonly equate education with the school, religion with the church, politics with government, and provision for material needs with the business firm. As a consequence of institutional differentiation and segregation all individuals must conform to the behavioral requirements of multiple statuses in multiple institutional contexts: a juggling act.

Juggling act

Our interpretation is that *social institutions are the principal structural components of social systems*. Social systems are themselves most appropriately viewed as a network of *flows* or *exchanges* among social institutions (see Figure 4.4). Institutions comprise the units or constituent elements of the system, determine the nature of flows or exchanges or the channels of influence, and delineate the rules of exchange or interaction. The units among which flows or exchanges occur include individuals, households, business firms, labor unions, churches, schools, governmental agencies, voluntary associations, clubs, gangs, and others. Flows are three:

Social systems
- **Flows**
- **Exchanges**

- *Resources*, including goods and services
- *Personnel*
- *Information*

Units are in a state of constant interaction through these various flows.

As institutional interaction is translated through the interaction of specific organizations — such as business firms, churches, governmental agencies, or schools — the organization may itself develop considerable autonomy from other organizations with respect to the values, norms, and expectations shaping individual behavior. With growth in the complexity and size of technologically developed societies, these specific organizational structures have grown increasingly large and intricate with control highly centralized. An apparently inescapable result of organizational growth in power is a form of *institutional imperialism* as one organization encroaches on

Organizational autonomy

Institutional imperialism

Figure 4.4

Institutional Flows and Transactions

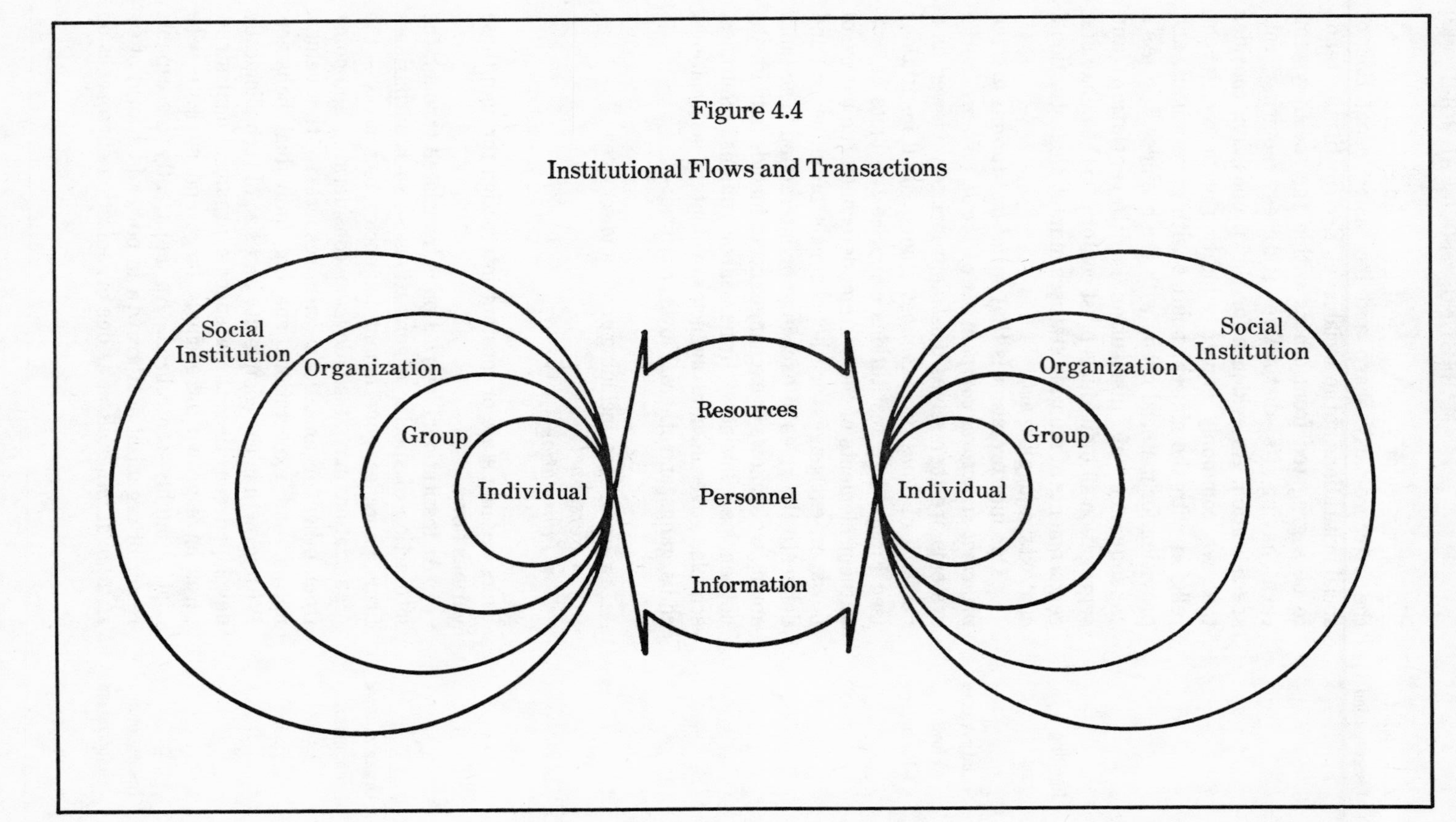

others within the social system. Historically this has been especially characteristic of the United States where the business firm has been propelled into a position of centrality within the institutional framework of society, orchestrating the patterns of interaction among virtually all institutions which comprise American culture. Terms coined to label the particular brand of American social organization – carrying an aura of coercive collusion between government and business – are *technocracy* and *military-industrial complex*.

Technocracy

Fractures, fissures, or collisions in the interrelationships of social institutions are traceable to one of two causes:

- Interpersonal and intrapersonal conflicts resulting from incompatible roles and statuses
- Organizational conflict within and between social institutions, for example, the traditional conflict of business and governmental interpretations of how the game of competition is to be played, or between business firms

Conflict =
- **inefficiency**
- **waste**

These sources of conflict create strains in the functioning of society resulting in waste and inefficiency. It is regrettable that the economic system has shown increasing, rather than decreasing divergence from the priority structure of behavioral expectations of much of American society. The result has been a looming challenge to the continued legitimacy of the business firm and the economic system.

SOCIAL INTEGRATION

Synchronized adaptation

Social integration is a dynamic process of continual synchronized adaptation among social institutions along specific value orientations. Central to an understanding of the notion of social integration is the specification of what is shared, by whom, to what extent, how, and why. At the level of cultural analysis, to speak of social integration is to refer to the consensus of values, knowledge, norms, beliefs, interests, and symbols. At the level of societal or group analysis, social integration refers to efficiency of interaction among groups, associations, organizations, firms, communities, and other interpersonal networks, or

Consensus

Efficiency of interaction

their members. Thus cultural integration is related to but not identical to the integration of society or a group.

It is not uncommon to find groups engaging in regular, orderly, and even efficient interaction although characterized by conflicting values and beliefs. The relationship between management and labor unions is one example. However, essential to the approximation of social integration is a widely accepted set of roles or statuses and associated behavioral expectations: who is to do what, when, where, how, and why. The duties, obligations, privileges, immunities, privacies associated with particular roles or statuses within social institutions must be specified and widely accepted for social integration to exist.

Consensus of role expectations

Social stability or instability, stagnation or growth, maintenance or change are the result of the continuous and numerous transactions or exchanges among individuals, groups, organizations, and institutions within the social system. Thus any behavior is triggered by one or a combination of resource, personnel, or information flows. However, behavior is not random, but is instead prescribed by the expectations surrounding the various roles which comprise the institutional structure of society. These role prescriptions embedded in the institutional structure of the social system tend to channel or direct the process of social change as well as maintain or restore preexisting social states. Thus the conversion of a peacetime economy into a wartime economy and the reversion to a peacetime economy are prescribed within the existing institutional structure of society. *Social integration is therefore as much a dynamic process as is social change.*

Transactions

Roles prescribe social change

A vast amount of coordination of human effort can be explained from the convergence or interdependence of interests in the allocation or use of scarce resources or divisible values. For example, coordination and integration of effort are required in the production and distribution of goods and services among divergent consumer interests. However, the level and type of coordination of individual effort cannot be explained without explicit recognition of common cultural goals, shared aspirations, or values. *In the United States a common denominator or rationale underlying a vast amount of organizational coordination, bridging the full spectrum of social institutions, is the value accorded to material possessions.* In fact, the charge to the American economic

Convergence in allocation of scarce resources

Materialism

system has long been to achieve peak efficiency in the production and distribution of goods and services in conformance with the structure of consumer demand.

The development of society along the high priority vector of materialism has had reverberating consequences in the organization of society, the reordering of social roles, the revaluing of social priorities, and relationships among social institutions (see Figure 4.5). Division and specialization of labor, and the formalization of role prescriptions, have multiplied the number of individual, group, organizational, and institutional interrelationships and interdependencies. However, increased role specialization has tended to thrust interactions beyond the realm of prescribed patterns of behavior, prompting rapid adaptation and accelerating mobility, but along with it fragmentation in values, beliefs, and lifestyles.

Role specialization
↓
- **interdependence**
- **adaptation**
- **fragmentation of values**

Flows of goods or services, personnel, or information constitute the real and potential influences on individual and organizational behavior. Growth in complexity makes the whole social system increasingly dependent upon high level *coordination* and *integration* of roles ranging across institutional boundaries. Extreme interdependence of roles means that even localized disruptions or inefficiencies can cripple the entire system. Witness the enormously disruptive reverberations of the economic recession of the mid-1970's. And the interruptions in educational and business operations in the midst of student protests at the height of the VietNam War.

Coordination & integration

Reverberating disruptions

Advanced societies are wholly dependent upon *procedural agreement*, for efficiency of social interaction and operaton is highly vulnerable to the concerted action of relatively small groups with relatively strong convictions and relatively zealous leadership. Strikes, revolutionary activity, and organized criminal activity are vivid testimony to this premise. In the absence of consensus on requisite behavior and procedures for resolving conflict, disruptions tend to increase and resolution of conflict necessitates the intervention of some higher authority. Intensifying incidence of social disruption invariably carries the prospect of a repressive, centrally sanctioned solution. In the economic sector, of course, this implies increased governmental intervention in all phases of business operations — a last resort solution to the problem of economic or social disruptions in the view of many businessmen.

Procedural agreement

Governmental intervention

Figure 4.5

Social Integration Along the Materialistic Value Vector

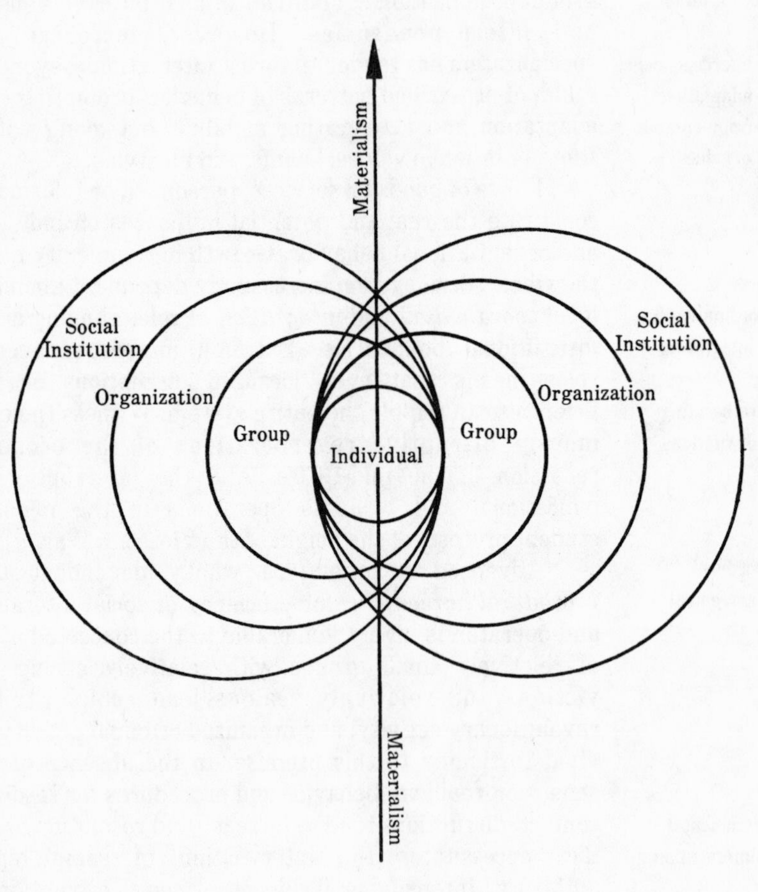

Maintenance of social integration is essential to the continued viability of a social system. Continued *integration requires*:

- *Resistance to external conquest*
- *Sustained commitment to cultural goals*
- *Effectiveness in the attainment of social goals*
- *Resolution of internal conflict*
- *Responsiveness to shifts in cultural goals*
- *Progressive adaptive capacities*

Failure in the latter three arenas — conflict, responsiveness, and adaptive capacity — has been a major cause underlying the challenge to legitimacy business currently confronts. Yet, channeling preventive effort into one or another of these potential causes of social disruption may cause disruptions in another sector, or consume resources required to quell disruptions in another sector. For example, the contemporary concern with maintaining commitment to the goal of social equality and preventing internal conflict has resulted in radically altered employent practices and educational standards and thus compromised short-term progress on scientific, technological educational, and economic fronts.

In the United States interdependence of interest provided the glue that held American society together. But consensus of interests, objectives or values is not sufficient by itself to explain the degree of integration or cohesion in America. Implicit in the collaboration of effort in pursuit of common purposes is some consensus of values. A materialistic orientation has been sufficient to accommodate diversities of all types in the interests of a steadily rising material standard of living. The intensity of this American preoccupation with materialism largely explains:

Consensus of values

Materialism

- The level of social organization
- The degree of labor specialization and coordination
- The extent of social participation in the process and outputs from economic activity

A social system that appeals for allegiance exclusively on the basis of its ability to deliver material goods and services to the individual is on precarious ground indeed. At a minimum, the legitimacy of any social institution, organization or group requires something else. It is especially crucial in a complex social system that differential rewards, scarce resources or values be apportioned according to:

Legitimacy
- **Standards of legitimacy**
- **Distribution of power**

- Common standards of legitimacy
- An equitable distribution of social power or command over scarce resources

That is, unless there is agreement concerning the requirements for legitimacy for any group, organization, or institution, internal conflict will mushroom beyond manageable proportions. Unless there is a distribution of power within the social system which permits a distribution of rewards, scarce resources and values that is at least minimally acceptable to the members of the social system, conflict is inevitable and the system will eventually self-destruct. Thus the civil rights movement of the 1950's and 1960's, and the institutionalization of the goal of equality in employment practices and educational standards in the 1970's, brought about a reordering of numerous groups and organizations within the social system. Examination of the consensual goal of rising standards of material welfare and the distribution of income within society inevitably forces us back to the common denominator of the values which underlie the structure of American society. The process of social integration is dependent upon some measure of consensus of values.

The factors that result in the emergence of social systems are not necessarily sufficient to maintain them. Thus the factors that combine to determine the level of sustained social integration are:

Sustained integration

- Consensus of interests and interdependency of social structures — groups, organizations, institutions — in the pursuit of common objectives
- Some means for resolving or submerging conflict of interests
- Agreement concerning the requisite procedures for pursuing common objectives
- An efficient means for communication and, hence, adaptation to changing environmental conditions

Thus the continued orderly functioning of the economic system in allocating scarce resources among divergent consumption interests is contingent upon:

Continued operation of the economic system

- Continued adherence to the goal of rising standards of material welfare
- Some mechanism for reconciling materialism with conflicting goals, such as environmental conservation
- Adherence to rules of conduct by business firms, labor unions, governmental regulatory agencies, and other social systems which influence economic activity
- Effective communication among all these institutional sectors — particularly between firms and consumers

The mechanisms for resolving conflict among institutional sectors include legal and judicial processes, mediation, arbitration, delegated negotiation or collective bargaining, appeals to common values or third parties, cooptation or dissent, and other procedures. All, of course, involve different forms of communication. *And the importance of communication in facilitating social integration cannot be overestimated. Without communication there can be no society.* The fact that the United States has had a single dominant language as the principal medium for interpersonal interaction, and multiple parallel and reinforcive systems of mass communication, has resulted in a sustained high level of social integration.

Communication

Mechanisms of social integration operate throughout all levels of interaction within the social system: individual, group, organizational, institutional. Group participation provides the individual with behavioral expectations which impose order and organization on the individual's personality. Thus the degree of individual personality integration is largely a function of the integration of groups, organizations, and institutions in which he participates. Without the organizing impact of regular group interaction, the individual suffers personality disintegration, alienation, neurosis, or psychosis. Conversely, disintegration of interaction has disruptive consequences throughout the social structure. For example, Watergate brought about strains in interaction patterns that left their mark not only in government, but in business, in education, in formal and informal groups of all types, and among individuals who found their faith in government severely shaken.

SOCIAL CHANGE

The patterns of change in American society seem to have brought us to a timely period of reevaluation in the last quarter of the Twentieth Century.

> We live at the beginning of the end of a long period in which many social changes cumulatively moved in a similar direction, a direction of increased scale, increasing specialization, increasing complexity of social structure, increasing inequalities, increasing energy-levels based on using up minerals, increasing anomie, decreased kinship ties, increasing secularization, sharpening of distinctions between work and leisure and between "private" and "public" arenas of life. [98, p. 625]

- **Interdependence**
- **Centralization**
- **Formality**
- **Impersonality**

Failure at synchronization

Many of these trends seem to have leveled off, even reversed. But the historical antecedents of these trends seem to have culminated in ever increasing interdependence, centralization, formality, and impersonality. *The fact that ever higher levels of coordination are required to sustain orderly operations within the social system implies that failures in synchronization are not absorbed locally but are transmitted to even remote sectors of the system through a web of interpersonal interactions.* Thus one artifact of change in America is a high degree of structural interdependence and hence vulnerability to disruption. The oil embargo of the mid-1970's is evidence in support of this premise, as is Watergate.

Future shock

Much has been made of the chaotic change occuring in American society. In his immensely influential book *Future Shock*, Alvin Toffler warned of a growing epidemic. Future shock, "the dizzying disorientation brought on by the premature arrival of the future," is essentially

> culture shock in one's own society. But its impact is far worse . . . For most travelers have the comforting

> knowledge that the culture they left behind will be there to return to. The victim of future shock does not. [90, p. 11]
>
> . . . Millions sense the pathology that pervades the air, but fail to understand its roots. These roots lie not in this or that political doctrine, still less in some mystical core of despair or isolation presumed to inhere in the "human condition." Nor do they lie in science, technology, or legitimate demands for social change. They are traceable, instead, to the uncontrolled, nonselective nature of our lunge into the future. They lie in our failure to direct, consciously and imaginatively, the advance toward super-industrialism. [90, p. 314]

Future shock, Toffler contends, "may well be the most important disease of tomorrow." [90, p. 11] Much of the confusion and apparent change that clouds the future of American society, however, is more illusory than real.

Causes of Illusory Change

• Variance between organization and norms

• Relative rate of change

There are two basic reasons for the illusion of change in the United States:

- The *variance* between social organization and norms
- The relative *rate of change* vis à vis other societies

First, actual behavior does not conform absolutely to norms or expectations. Even where norms are relatively stable, a considerable degree of variability in behavior can be observed. Variability in behavior does not necessarily mean the displacement of old norms by new ones. Variability in behavior is the rule, not the exception, particularly in behavior where such idiosyncratic factors as socialization and genetics exercise considerable influence. *Variance in observed behavior, however, does not necessarily mean that norms and values have changed.*

Second, change seems dizzyingly fast in the United States because of the relative speed with which real changes are occuring in contrast to the rate of change in other societies. This does not mean that real changes are taking place rapidly in some absolute sense. Real change at a rate faster than intergenerational change is highly unlikely for a number of reasons.

The rate of real change, then, tends to be lower than it appears because American society is evolving at a rate in excess of that of many other societies. [67, p. 1] Nevertheless, real change is occurring and for relatively clear reasons.

Causes of Real Change

By real change is meant fundamental alteration in the structure of society — new values and norms, or, at least, altered institutions. These real changes can be distinguished from apparent changes in that real changes have causes. Something has happened — some environmental shift has taken place — that requires alteration of the old way of life. An understanding of real change thus involves an understanding of highly complex interactive relations, not the easiest of tasks. Fortunately, it is somewhat simplified by first examining social institutions and then the value system which has dominated American society.

As we noted above, institutions evolve to meet recurring situations or needs with which the society must deal. Clearly, some sorts of situations are highly unlikely to fundamentally change. For example, because of his biological nature, man must go through a maturing process which leads eventually to death. These constants lend a degree of permanence or stability to the institutions designed to deal with the life and death cycle. Such institutions are unlikely to cause fundamental change themselves. They are much more likely to change in response to changes in other institutions. There are other institutions which, while not limited by man's biological nature, are not subject to objective validation. They are, instead, a matter of faith and are, at least in the United States, more apt to be affected by change than provide the impetus to change. Religion is an example. A final group of institutions — political, educational and economic — is relatively more dynamic. It is within this group that most real change originates.

Life & death

Faith

Fundamentally, every society must allocate its energies among four competing demands: [98, p. 630]

• Adaptive capacities: Technology

• First, society must develop some generalized *adaptive capacities*. It must control nature to such an extent that, at least, the society is able to survive. The general term for these capacities is *technology*

• Goals

• Second, societies have particularized *goals*, which require energy. Examples might be settling a frontier or becoming a world power

• Integration

• Third, some societal energy must be devoted to social *integration*, to keeping all the elements of the social system together

• Stability

• Finally, there is a demand for *stability*, for maintaining cultural patterns. This is the antidote to future shock

High priority objectives

Historically the patterns of change in America have been directed principally toward the accumulation of material wealth, knowledge, skill and power, the "instrumental capacities," so-called because they are *all instrumental in controlling aspects of the environment or the attainment of other goals*. These high priority objectives have been localized in the economic and political systems, have resulted in a massive technology and have consumed massive amounts of energy and other resources. Social integration and maintenance of cultural patterns have been traditionally relegated low priority, and have recently been reasserted in the slow reordering of social priorities.

Low priority objectives

Technological determinism

The result of this allocation of energies and resources in the United States is essentially *technological determinism*. Technological and economic innovations, readily accepted because of instrumental effectiveness in achieving high priority social goals, bring in their wake complex reverberating effects upon other parts of the social system. *Technology*, then, is the one fundamental causal factor that has triggered most real change in the American social structure.

Technology ⟶ cause of real change

There are, however, finite limits to the magnitude of change that technology can cause. As long as internal order and social solidarity were not threatened, the capacity for dealing with the physical enironment was intact, and external relationships with other societies were unimpaired, technological and economic development could forge ahead unimpeded. This is exactly what happened in the United States during the past century. The result was unparalleled material wealth and, of course, real change in the value structure.

However, the high energy and other resource commitments required to sustain an intense orientation toward environmental control or adaptation have produced severe unintended consequences in both society and the environment: pollution in mushrooming proportions, congestion, urban sprawl, ghetto blight, resource shortages, economic and social dislocation. *These unintended and undesirable artifacts of purposeful social organization and technology result when segments of society are free to engage in activities with high short-run payoffs but which result in accumulated conditions which diminish the quality of life for society-at-large.* This can continue only so long as the negative consequences of purposeful social organization do not so undermine the quality of life as to require curtailment of activities which lead to undesirable conditions in the first place. For example, Americans blindly ignore the very real energy crisis in favor of maintaining a shortsighted but engaging lifestyle that makes it easy to forget that the energy crisis will inevitably result in an alteration in life patterns in the long run. We are infatuated with style, rather than function or substance, and sacrifice endless energy and other resources to the triumph of style over substance. None of this is bad in itself, but only insofar as it creates negative reverberating effects upon the future quality of life.

- **Positive short-run payoffs**
- **Negative long-term consequences**

The triumph of style over substance

A society so preoccupied with developing instrumental capacities for controlling the physical or social environment will likely exhibit a rapid rate of change. But change is likely to be fitful and somewhat chaotic as different social organizations demand a claim on increasingly scarce resources in pursuit of divergent instrumental purposes. Thus firms compete for resources not simply with other firms seeking to serve the same customers and other firms seeking to serve other customers, but also with other social organizations with other instrumental purposes altogether.

As a consequence of this intense preoccupation with the development of instrumental capacities society has moved to successively higher levels of differentiation and specialization at both the individual and the organizational levels. And with specialization come differentiated abilities and rewards, and divergent interests. These factors combine to channel patterns of interpersonal interaction which produce a scatter pattern of values and beliefs, localized in individuals linked together because of the demands of specialization. Hence integration will inevitably be incomplete in a technologically advanced society, and tension, conflict, instability and ambivalence are built in. Thus social change is itself intermittently chaotic, unfolding in frequently divergent patterns of instrumental activity, but in general *revolving around the major values which underlie American culture*. Although the pace of change in American society is relentless it unfolds along largely predictable paths delineated by the fundamental value structure of the culture. Hence the underlying coherence of American society can be found in its value system.

Integration inevitably incomplete

Change revolves around values

Shifting Value Orientations

The impact of the unimpeded burst of technological and economic development on the value system is difficult to precisely estimate. Essentially, the values remain the same, only more so; they have matured in several directions.

Production ↓ Consumption

Instrumental toward Consummatory. One main direction is toward consummatory and away from instrumental values, or *toward consumption and away from production*. The principal cause of this shift was affluence. The emphasis has shifted from production to consumption for the simple reason that it is now consumption (demand) that threatens to limit continued development along the path of materialism. Indeed, visionaries predict societies of consumption in which the principal function of each member of the society is to consume. [35] The increased importance of marketing derives from the need to spur consumption.

Achievement toward Expressionism. A second direction is from achievement toward expressionism. Again, affluence, the result of technological and economic development, seems to be the underlying cause. As material wealth became increasingly abundant, the Protestant Ethic achievement orientation became more and more difficult to sustain. Fantastic wealth, by any previous standard, became easier to acquire. The result has been a tendency toward expressionism. Again, evidence is abundant. Recognizing increasingly divergent patterns of consumption behavior, Tom Wolfe, the social satirist noted:

> ... Individual climbers are busy moving into separate little preserves that once made up the happy monolith of "the upper class" – such as charities and *Yes!* Culture – and I offer the golden example of Bob and Spike Scull [America's foremost collectors of pop and other avant-garde art] for those who want to make it *Now*, without having to wait three generations, as old-fashioned sorts, such as the Kennedy family, had to do. Of course, with so many statuspheres now in operation, and so many short cuts available, there is a chronic chaos in Society. People are now reaching the top without quite knowing what on earth they have reached the top of. They don't know whether they have reached *The* Top or whether they have just had a wonderful fast ride up the service elevator. But as Bob Scull himself says: "Enjoy!
>
> What struck me throughout America and England was that so many people have found such novel ways of doing just that, *enjoying*, extending their egos way out on the best terms available, namely their own. [99, pp. 8-9]

Competitive Individualism toward Cooperation. A final direction of value change is from competitive individualism to cooperation and individual dignity. The cause here is not affluence *per se*, but the means by which affluence was produced. Specialization and division of labor eventually produced a workman far removed from the product of his labor and highly dependent on others to complete the productive process. Competitive individualism in today's plants is not only unimportant, it is disruptive. Cooperation is the key virtue, and, as any bureaucrat knows, the real rewards are not derived from output, but from the increased status of another worker under his control.

Technological and economic development underlay the value shifts during the past fifty years. The obvious question which remains is whether technology will determine the shape of future value shifts. If not technology, then what?

And the Future?

Three questions are important in trying to anticipate future value shifts:

- Is there a weakening commitment to traditional values?
- Is there a weakening consensus about traditional values?
- What alternative value orientations, if any, are likely?

Commitment and Consensus. The answer to the first question may not be as obvious as it might appear. We have indicated above how affluence has weakened the very values that enable affluence: production, achievement, and competitive individualism. However, a case must be made for the stability of values. The basis of stability lies in the socialization process, particularly in the important influence of the family. Values inculcated by the family provide considerable intergenerational continuity. One factor to consider, then, is the rather stable transmission of values from one generation to the next.

Socialization

Even given the erosion of existing values caused by affluence, the old values are far from extinct. In fact, the traditional reaction of Western man to affluence has been to "create" need. Tom Wolfe has stated the point succinctly:

Create need

> Intellectuals and politicians currently exhibit a vast gummy nostalgia for the old restraints, the old limits, of the ancient ego-crusher: *Calamity.* Historically, calamity has been the one serious concern of serious people. War, Pestilence — Apocalypse? I was impressed by the profound relief with which intellectuals and politicians discovered poverty in America in 1963, courtesy of Michael Harrington's book *The Other America.* And, as I say, it was *discovered.* Eureka! We have found it again! We thought we had lost it. That was the spirit of the enterprise. When the race riots erupted — and when the war in Vietnam grew into a good-sized hell — intellectuals welcomed all that with a ghastly embrace, too. War! Poverty! Insurrection! Alienation! O Four Horsemen, you have not deserted us entirely. The game can go on. [90, p. 9]

A further element of support for the old values comes from those who have been largely excluded from the technological-economic system in the past. As Eldridge Cleaver notes, "The struggle of [a Black's] life is for the emancipation of his mind, to receive recognition for the products of his mind, and official recognition of the fact that he has a mind." [16, p. 186] In summary, one should not underestimate the commitment to traditional values; they will be powerful influences in society for a long time to come.

As to consensus about traditional values, there has been and should continue to be *a weakening of consensus about traditional values*, given that American society remains basically affluent. The break probably will not be sharp or sudden, just a continued drifting or maturing of the old values, particularly toward expressionism.

Drifting values

Alternative Value Orientations. The answers to the first two questions, then, are probably some weakening of commitment, but to a rather limited extent and on a highly selective basis. There will probably be a lessening of consensus about the values — more from drift or maturation.

Alternative value system

If, however, no restraints are applied to the technological-economic development orientation, two results are likely. One is an *alternative value system*. The technological-economic development orientation would fail to devote the necessary energy to social integration and to maintenance of cultural norms and would be cast aside for a value system which placed greater emphasis on these needs. This result seems unlikely because of the strength and pervasiveness of the technological-economic orientation.

Retreatism

The second result is *retreatism*. The continued emphasis on material productivity finally outruns demand completely, or energy and other resources dry up, ending the unending growth to which Americans have become so accustomed. Faced with a stagnating economy, America retreats to a strict interpretation of the old values — achievement and competitive individualism. This result seems the likelier of the two because of the strong faith in the technological-economic development orientation. Problems are apt to be interpreted as the result of a falling away from these values; the solution would be to return to conventional value orientations even more fervently than before.

From much detailed analysis, then, emerges the conclusion that American society has no single identifiable future, deterministically circumscribed by the fundamental social processes and structures currently operating.

No single identifiable future

> It is not inevitably predestined to become a monolithic industrial military order; nor a pluralistic, egalitarian democracy; nor a chaotic, alienated mass society; nor a rigid centralized security society. [98, p. 638]

What American society will become depends to a large extent upon the economic system which is under heavy attack today.

THE AMERICAN ECONOMIC SYSTEM

The dominant and most conspicuous institution in American society is its economic system. Its influence in orchestrating all other institutions which combine to form the structure of American society, although often overstated, is pervasive and persistent. Our purpose here is threefold: To outline:

- The major features of the American economic system
- The role of marketing within the economic system
- The multiple impacts of other social institutions on economic and marketing activity

The fact that human wants and needs are unlimited and that resources available to satisfy these needs are limited is essential in understanding the nature of economic activity. Some allocative mechanism is required to reconcile the two.

Values and Economic Organization

This inescapable resource allocation problem may be solved in any of an infinite variety of ways. But the essential fact is that the particular system of resource allocation which emerges in any society is a reflection of the basic value structure of the culture. We have noted the principal constellations of values which lie behind the institutional structure of American society. *For the most part the system of economic organization which evolved in*

American society mirrors the priority associated with the fundamental values of individualism, activity and work, achievement-success, and materialism.

Capitalism

Capitalism is American society's unique solution to the resource allocation problem, a solution which mirrors the fundamental value structure of American culture.

Socialism

Socialism is the Soviet Union's solution to the resource allocation problem and reflects the fundamental value structure of Soviet society. American society was founded by individuals seeking freedom from religious and political oppression on the fundamental premise that the needs of

Individual needs

the *individual* take precedence over those of the groups or society of which he is a member, within broad constraints established by the necessity of performing certain essential functions in order that society may itself survive. Hence, in the United States the satisfaction of individual consumer material wants and needs has historically assumed priority over the satisfaction of the material needs of society-at-large.

Societal needs

Socialist societies, by contrast, have evolved around the premise that the needs or demands of *society-at-large* take precedence over those of the individuals who comprise society. Hence, the Soviet Union, Communist China, and other socialist systems of social organization have historically placed satisfaction of the material needs of society-at-large above those of individual consumers.

The relative priority associated with individual material wants and needs, as opposed to those of society-at-large, is mirrored not merely in contrasting systems of economic organization between different cultures, but also in contrasting systems of government, education, religion and in all other social institutions. Both capitalist and socialist systems of economic organization, however, are designed to accomplish the same fundamental purpose: to achieve an efficient allocation of society's scarce material resources among the unlimited wants and needs of the consumers who comprise society, in conformance with the basic value structure of the culture.

Cultural Norms and Economic Activity

A second key feature of the American system of economic organization is that it works only so long as the norms and expectations surrounding economic activity and resource allocation are observed. Implicit in the value structure of the culture are behavioral prescriptions outlining proper and improper conduct by participants in the economic process. Social sanctions are levied for misconduct, only some of which are under the auspices of regulatory agencies of the government and the courts. *Thus the marketplace through which economic activity unfolds is a cultural fact mirroring the value structure of the culture and subject to social control.* The cold competitiveness of conventional interpretations of the operation of the economic system misses this vital fact. Economic behavior, like any behavior, is subject to norms, social pressure, sanctions. *There is no "free play of economic forces." Social behavior is regulated by social expectations, not by the "invisible hand."*

Expectations

Principal Structural Features

The main structural features of the American economic system can be outlined rather succinctly. The economy is intensely mass production oriented, with minute specialization and division of labor. Industrial processes and products are highly standardized, although with accelerating affluence has come increased personalization of products. The corporation is the dominant business organization, perhaps not in numbers but certainly in size and power. Corporate ownership is widely diffused but production and control are highly concentrated. Thus ownership and management have been separated. Large scale organization necessitates high degrees of internal coordination in identifying and satisfying consumer demand. But large scale organization also leads to corporate coordination, which in turn leads to price-fixing, heavy lobbying by particular industries, and consumer exploitation. Large labor unions play an important role in the system but unionization seems to have stabilized or declined in many industries. In times of economic recession this trend reverses itself. Likewise, the government plays a large and increasing role in economic activity through a multitude of avenues ranging from purchasing practices to legislation to moral suasion.

Ownership ↕ Management

Several ideological shifts also seem evident. Property or ownership rights are evolving rapidly, with ownership frequently far removed from the management process. Thus the American corporation has assumed a separate identity, distinct from the locus of ownership. Also, wages for work are now no longer enough. Even though compensation has been expanded to include safety, health, medical benefits, and retirement benefits, there is an increasing emphasis on "social security," and much debate on three points:

- What does the firm owe its *owners*?
- What does the firm owe its *employees*?
- What does the firm owe *society*?

It is clear that the firm owes society more than mere products, its employees more than mere wages, and its owners more than mere profits. But what else? The following chapter provides partial answers to these questions. For the present, however, it is sufficient to note that since products, profits, and wages can be readily quantified, firms have shown an historical aversion to seeking other criteria for gauging corporate performance. The consequences of this preoccupation with products, profits, and wages have frequently been disastrous.

Innovation

Finally, the entire economy is continually altered by development and innovation. Innovation and change enter the economic system from a variety of sources, from inventions to politics, but the role of the government in this process is large indeed. From auto safety to space technology, the government through policies and expenditures has increased the flow of innovations.

But this is simply a broad brush outline of the major features of the American economic system. What about the role of marketing within the economy?

THE ROLE OF MARKETING

The responsibility of the economic system in allocating scarce resources is interpreted and facilitated by a set of roles or functions operating within the market mechanism. *Marketing is the process of managerial decision making which performs the resource allocation function.* Decisions made with respect to which resources will be channeled toward the production and distribution of which products and services at the firm level collectively determine how the economic system performs at the societal level, and vice versa.

Reciprocal dependency

The dependency relationship is a two-way street. Marketing managers, indeed all business managers, make strategic and tactical decisions aimed at improving the firm's competitive position relative to firms seeking to serve the same markets or firms tapping the same sources of resources. In the process of jockeying for competitive advantage and simultaneously confirming the legitimacy of the firm, marketing management performs the roles delineated and required by the economic system, ultimately facilitating the allocation of goods and services across society.

Cumulatively, individual decisions by marketing managers have major consequences for the efficient functioning of the economic system. The marketer's conceptualization of his role and responsibilities within the economic system determines, among other things, the efficiency of resource allocation and, therefore, of the economic system. Currently marketers perceive their role as largely one of identifying and satisfying consumers' desires.

Although the *marketing concept* is a compelling view of how the marketer should enact marketing decisions, it is not without serious faults. By narrowly focusing on the consumer, other arenas in the firm's environment vital to the firm's legitimacy have often been obscured or ignored. The consumer is but one element of many whose demands must be met if the firm is to establish sustained positions of legitimacy and power.

INTERRELATIONSHIPS, INTEGRATION, AND CHANGE: SOME ILLUSTRATIONS

We have spent some time developing an understanding of the notions of institutional interrelationships, integration and change. How do these concepts relate to the economic system, and to marketing in particular? [98, pp. 556-578]

Economic and Political/Governmental Institutions

Undoubtedly the most obvious institutional interface affecting marketing activity is that between the economic and political/governmental institutions. With growth in the size and complexity of social and economic organization, the role of government in economic activity has steadily expanded. The higher the degree of specialization in economic activity, the greater the degree of economic and governmental interdependence. And the more massive, specialized and technologically complex the organization of economic production and exchange, the more critical the interdependence of economic and political institutions for the integration of society as a whole.

Economic activity, like virtually all interpersonal interaction in all institutional contexts, *is shaped and channeled by the norms surrounding expected patterns of behavior oriented around the prevailing value structure of the culture*. The interrelationship of business and government is intricate beyond belief, but we can isolate several key areas of interdependency. *First, governmental organizations and agencies operate to facilitate or implement economic activities*. Among the lengthy list of

Facilitating activities

facilitating activities are regulation of stock and commodity exchanges, support for research and dissemination of findings, economic incentives like subsidies and tax breaks, provision for standard currency, provision for limited liability and extended life for business corporations, regulation and support of banking, and others.

The government also regulates business activity. While much regulation is interpreted as a constraint or limit on business activity, and hence detrimental to competitive efforts, the explicit purpose of much governmental regulation is to preserve or protect competition. An intricate array of laws and regulatory agencies has evolved to structure the impact of government on business, affecting every facet of the marketing manager's domain of responsibility: product, pricing, distribution, and communication decisions (see Figure 4.6). We will argue later that much governmental intervention in business activity is misguided because of major misassumptions about how the economic system operates.

Possibly the central fact of governmental-business interrelationships is the movement from a *competitive* basis for economic regulation with minimal governmental in-

Administered competition

tervention toward *administered competition* with heavy governmental involvement and massive organization in business, labor, and government. Large corporations, trade associations, unions, governmental regulatory agencies all testify to this premise. The new fact of life for the marketing manager is that the destiny of the firm has been slowly lifted out of his direct control and is increasingly negotiated in the process of formally and

Figure 4.6

Federal Legislation Regulating the Game of Competition

FEDERAL LEGISLATION	MAJOR PROVISIONS	STRATEGIC MARKETING DECISIONS			
		PRODUCT	PRICING	DISTRIBUTION	COMMUNICATION
Sherman Antitrust Act (1890)	Prohibits monopolies or attempts to monopolize	Prohibits attempts to monopolize product markets	Prohibits vertical and horizontal price-fixing	Prohibits attempts to monopolize distribution	
Clayton Act (1914)	Specified monopolistic practices	Prohibits tying contracts	Prohibits price discrimination Regulates discounts	Regulates exclusive dealings	
Federal Trade Commission Act (1914)	Established FTC to regulate competition		Prohibits basing-point pricing where tendency toward monopoly	Regulates reciprocity	Prohibits unfair methods and deceptive advertising
Robinson-Patman Act (1936)	Prevent injury to any person and to competition		Regulates price discrimination Prohibits predatory pricing	Regulates brokerage allowances	Prohibits discriminatory allowances
Miller-Tydings Act (1937)	Legalized state fair trade laws		Legalizes resale price maintenance	Established non-signers clause	
Wheeler-Lea Act (1938)	Gave FTC jurisdiction over false advertising				Prohibits deceptive advertising
Celler-Kefauver Act (Antimerger Act) (1950)	Prohibits asset acquisition which tends toward monopoly	Regulates product line expansion by merger		Regulates distribution expansion by merger	
McGuire-Keogh Act (Fair Trade Enabling Act) (1952)	Reaffirmed non-signers clause in fair trade		Allows resale price setting for branded products		

tediously reconciling the frequently divergent interests of government, labor and business.

Economic, Educational and Scientific Institutions

Developments in science, education and economic activity have had far-reaching reciprocal impacts. Indeed, the technological developments which fueled the Industrial Revolution were not so much the result of deliberate scientific inquiry or pursuit of knowledge as the consequence of *ad hoc* solutions to practical problems of production. The Industrial Revolution in turn fueled the formalization of the process of scientific inquiry and education to accelerate social progress measured principally in terms of increasing materialism. The institutions of science and education have today emerged as major sources of social and cultural change affecting all other social institutions.

***Ad hoc* solutions**

Like all social institutions, science and education are oriented toward norms and expectations, guided by goals and sanctions, and inseparable from interpersonal processes. Scientific values, symbols, procedures, and philosophies – and their effects – have spread to all other social institutions, including not only the economic system, but also religion and the family. In effect, science and education have emerged as a point of intersection between the other major social institutions, particularly the economic, political, and kinship systems. The examples are endless: joint governmental and private development of military hardware, revisions in theories of the origins of man, methods of management and organization, new product research and development – even business schools.

Point of intersection

Kinship, Stratification and Economic Institutions

In general the greater the importance of kinship in social structure, the more rigid and static will be social strata within the social system. Thus strong extended kinship relationships constitute a barrier to the free mobility of labor and resources among geographic regions and productive applications. Moreover, strong kinship ties are reflected in intense traditionalism not only in patterns of interpersonal interaction, but also in government, education, and religion. Thus strong kinship ties imply resistance to social change.

Barrier to mobility

Resistance to change

Accelerating change

Conversely, it appears that the invasion of the kinship system by other social institutions has paralleled the accelerating rate of social change. Other social institutions have limited the autonomy of the kinship system in determining its own behavioral standards and expectations. The kinship system increasingly plays a dependency role in relation to other social institutions, especially in relation to the economic and political institutions.

Occupational and social mobility

Historically, the family has been the primary source of one's social status. Its primary orientation is to who you are rather than what you can do. Alternatively, the occupational structure of society is oriented around abilities, achievements and capacities, rather than kinship affiliation as the basis of social status. With the rise of an occupational basis of personal status we have seen a decline in the role of kinship, largely the result of competitive occupational placement which strains family solidarity. With occupational and status mobility comes diminished kinship affiliation. Also, the fact that the home or family is no longer the locus of productive economic activity has reduced intrafamily interaction oriented around common purposes, requiring common understandings, expectations, and sanctions. Conversely, however, unemployment seems to intensify latent family structure: solid family structures tend to remain together, unstable family structures disintegrate. Radical economic fluctuations thus have radical reverberating impacts on family structure.

Economic motives

Since the Industrial Revolution, economic and occupational values in America have assumed increasing priority over family values in shaping personal goals and patterns of interpersonal interaction and, hence, in aligning social priorities. Thus materialism has been propelled into a position of dominance in the American lexicon of values. Moreover, the family unit has increasingly assumed the role of articulating and instilling economic motives. Conventional economic theories "that found the key to economic incentive in some sort of egoistic self-interest are quite inadequate: men, in our society as well as in others, typically work not merely for themselves but for an actual or potential family group." [98, p. 560] The job alone does not provide motivation for work. And, of course, different family structures manifest different patterns of purchasing and consumption. This point becomes especially evident when we consider the woman's liberation movement and the associated implications for family structure, occupational role definition, systems of social stratification, lifestyles and patterns of consumption.

CONCLUSIONS

We have argued in this chapter that the concepts of institutions, values, interrelationships, integration and change are essential to understanding the role of the economic system and marketing in society. Like all social institutions, the economic system is American society's solution to a recurring social need and performs an essential resource allocation function, mirroring the fundamental value structure of the culture. Marketing is the process of managerial decision making which performs the resource allocation function. Decisions with respect to which resources will be channeled toward the production and distribution of which products or services at the level of the individual firm collectively determine how efficiently the economic system responds to the structure of consumer demand at the societal level, and vice versa.

The firm and the economic system are inseparable. And the economic system is inseparably interrelated with the other social systems which constitute the institutional structure of American society. With growth in the complexity of social structure the level of institutional interdependence increases. Thus the degree of efficiency achieved in realizing highly valued social objectives or goals is contingent upon the degree of institutional integration or synchronized adaptation among social institutions along specific value orientations. Among the most highly valued orientations of the past has been a steady increase in material welfare.

Integration and conflict among social institutions, or among groups or organizations, is the result of patterns of individual interaction. Individuals perform roles in conformance with the behavioral expectations associated with the various social institutions of which they are a member. Conflict arises when the behavioral expectations of different roles are at cross purposes. While role conflict, and hence institutional conflict is inevitable, the manner in which the conflict of colliding role expectations is resolved determines the degree of social integration. The degree of social integration in turn determines the efficiency with which social goals are realized.

A basic understanding of these five key concepts — institutions, values, interrelationships, integration and change — is essential to understanding the role of marketing in promoting or impeding the achievement of social objectives or goals. For as the fractured goal structure of American society further complicates and confounds the problem of institutional anticipation, adaptation, and integration in their achievement, marketing management must become increasingly aware of the manner in which the process occurs and the facilitating role of marketing in their achievement.

In the following chapter we will examine in detail some major myths or misconceptions about the nature of economic activity and the role of marketing in the economy and society which have had increasingly negative consequences in the achievement of social goals. These myths have become increasingly detrimental in the context of fundamental shifts in the priorities, purposes and goals of American society.

CHAPTER 4: REVIEW QUESTIONS

1. Societies exhibit structure. What does this mean? What is *culture*? How do the concepts of *orientation*, *goals*, *means*, and *perspective* relate to the concept of culture?

2. What are *social institutions*? What are the principal social institutions in American society? How do the various institutions in American society conceive of the individual? How do they encourage conformance to these conceptions?

3. How does the economic system conceive of the individual? Why has the economic system been under such severe attack historically, in contrast with other social institutions? What is the function of the economic system?

4. What are the principal values in the American constellation of values? What is the relationship between values and social institutions?

5. How do social institutions interrelate? What is the cause of institutional conflict? What is the relevance of the concept of "constituency" in the context of institutional interrelationships? What are the principal *flows* between social institutions?

6. What is meant by the concept of *integration* among social institutions? How does social integration relate to resource allocation? What is the relationship between values and integration? What are the requirements for maintenance of social integration?

7. What are the principal causes of illusory social change? What are the causes underlying real social change? Where do most real changes originate? What are the four competing demands any society must respond to? Which of these have absorbed most attention in American society?

8. What is the relationship between values and social change? What are the principal transformations in American values?

9. What are the dominant values in the American economic system? What are the principal structural features of the American economic system? What is the role of marketing in the economic system and in society?

10. How do the concepts of interrelationships, integration, and change relate to the interaction of economic and political/governmental institutions? Economic, educational and scientific institutions? The economic institution, kinship, and social stratification?

MARKETING: A MANAGERIAL PHILOSOPHY

SOCIAL GOALS AND ECONOMIC INSTITUTIONS
PRODUCTIVITY: THE KEY TO ECONOMIC GROWTH
TECHNOLOGY AND CHANGING SOCIAL GOALS
OBSOLESCENT GOALS AND METHODS
THE MARKET MENTALITY
THE MYTHOLOGY OF CAPITALISM
- The Market
- Profitability and Productivity
- Structure and Performance
- Fact and Fiction
- The Role of Marketing

THE REALITY OF CAPITALISM
- Social Mechanisms Regulating Market Conduct
  - The Market
  - Cultural Norms
  - Social Goals
  - Administrative Coordination
- Fact and Fiction
- Satisficing
- Regulation

VALUES AND THE AMERICAN ECONOMIC SYSTEM

FOUR CHRONIC PROBLEMS

- Public Goods
- Distribution to the Disadvantaged
- Demand
- Supply

EXPLODING THE MYTHOLOGY OF CAPITALISM

THE NEW PHILOSOPHY OF MARKETING MANAGEMENT

- Keeping Score
- Structure versus Performance

HIERARCHY OF BUSINESS PURPOSE

IMPLEMENTING THE NEW PHILOSOPHY OF MARKETING MANAGEMENT

Marketing: A Managerial Philosophy

In the preceding chapters we concluded that marketing has typically been viewed from a narrow *managerial* or functional perspective. Much effort has been channeled into analyzing the specific managerial tasks or functions involved in identifying and satisfying consumer wants and needs, but little to examining the role of marketing in society and the managerial philosophy which guides both the operation of the business firm and the American economic system. Without examining the role of marketing in society and marketing as a philosophy of management, against the backdrop of major shifts in society's priorities and goals, the marketer is merely a technician performing functions which may compromise not simply the survival of the firm, but also the continued viability of the economic system and hence society itself.

At risk is the prospect that marketing may be displaced by default. For with continued evolution in the priorities and goals of society, marketers must respond with increased sensitivity and awareness and a reevaluation of the role of marketing in society, or risk obsolescence.

Obsolescence

The exclusive focus on marketing as a managerial process continues to dominate the contemporary marketing literature. In arguing for an "expanded" role for marketing, analysts have emphasized the application of conventional marketing techniques to nonconventional noneconomic problems, including the marketing of political candidates, universities, hospitals, the United States Postal Service, churches, police departments, social action groups such as Nader's Raiders, and charitable organizations. The broader social context within which marketing activity unfolds, and the severe social, economic and environmental consequences of a strict functional or managerial orientation on the part of marketers over time, have been largely neglected. [45, 50, 89] Equally obscured in the myopic focus on marketing functions is the philosophy which guides decision making on the part of marketing management and, hence, shapes the nature of economic development, the level of individual consumer and social welfare, and environmental quality.

Our purpose in the present chapter is to analyze marketing as a philosophy of management in the framework of fundamental changes which are occurring in the priorities, purposes, and structure of American society. In the course of our discussion we will explode a number of long-standing myths concerning the operation and objectives of the American economic system, and the role of marketing in perpetuating its objectives and fueling its operation. Curiously, although the insufficiency of the *mythology of capitalism* to resolve major social and economic problems will become more evident in our discussion, the myths continue to dominate if not the thinking then certainly the behavior of marketers, governmental officials charged with regulating the game of business competition, legislators, and consumers.

Mythology of Capitalism

SOCIAL GOALS AND ECONOMIC INSTITUTIONS

Until relatively recently in human history, nature, not man, dictated the terms of life. Man was largely at the mercy of his environment. And man could only adapt to ever changing environmental conditions, or perish. On one hand, mysticism, philosophy and religion provided ready rationales and partial indemnification or compensation for the victimized condition of human existence. On the other, organization and technology afforded the promise of increased control over the forces of nature, the essence of their enduring and nearly universal appeal. The emergence and evolution of human society, with ever more extensive application of division and specialization of labor, can be explained largely as a consequence of the compelling nature of man's will to survive. The concentration, specialization, and coordination of human effort, and its extension and elaboration through technology, broadened man's control over his environment, increasing the prospects for survival and sealing the course for social development.

As we noted in the preceding chapter, all societies must deal with the problem of economic want. At a minimum all societies must provide food and shelter in sufficient quantities for the survival of their members. More generally, all societies face the continuing problem of determining how to allocate scarce, and frequently dwindling material resources among unlimited, increasingly divergent consumer wants and needs.

Resource allocation

As we have seen, the solution to the perennial resource allocation problem which evolves in any society mirrors the fundamental value structure of the culture. Systems of economic organization are culture bound. Thus differences between the economic systems of different countries exist because of differences in their value structures.

Value structure

PRODUCTIVITY: THE KEY TO ECONOMIC GROWTH

It was not until little more than 150 years ago that Western society unlocked a mystery which had eluded all pre-existing societies. Until the beginning of the Nineteenth Century one group of consumers could only increase its material wealth at the expense of another group of losers: One consumer's gain was another consumer's loss. The term *caveat emptor*, or *let the buyer beware*, was coined to describe this fundamental feature of trade in the pre-industrial era.

Where nearly all previous societies had sought wealth through war, plunder, expropriation, tax-farming or some other means of extortion, Western society mastered the secret of realizing increases in material wealth and standard of living through peaceful means. The secret mastered by modern Western society was

Productivity

productivity, the ability to gain a greater than proportional output of material goods from a given expenditure of physical or financial capital, or a given exertion of labor. The ability to produce more material goods with less effort and less cost meant that there were no necessary losers in the game of increasing material welfare. Everyone could be a winner. [7, p. 9]

Machine

In popular mythology, the development of the machine was the key which unlocked the secret to productivity. The machine is seen as both the architect and the artifact of the drive for economic productivity. More precisely, however, productivity emerged with the conception of a system of organization which determined the

Corporate organization

optimally efficient placement and interrelationship of men and machines: the corporate form of business enterprise. Specialization and division of labor emerged as natural consequences of the drive toward productivity. And, of more enduring consequence, *economic productivity slowly emerged as the unifying focus for all of society. The goal of material wealth and productivity, the means for achieving material welfare, were entrusted to the market mechanism and institutionalized in a renewable, self-perpetuating system of organization, the corporation.* [7, pp. 10-11] The United States became the land of mass production, the assembly line its symbol to the world. [98, p. 166]

Marketing: matching supply with demand

Marketing materialized as the mechanism for matching the fruits of productivity with the structure of consumer demand, wedding production with distribution in resolving the resource allocation problem. Marketing was essentially synonymous with distribution, channeling ever increasing productive output to apparently insatiable consumer demand. Thus marketing in no small measure contributed to the myopic focus on ever higher levels of productive efficiency to achieve ever higher levels of material welfare.

TECHNOLOGY AND CHANGING SOCIAL GOALS

Technological development

Rapidly expanding productive capacity in the wake of the Industrial Revolution inaugurated the era of mass production and scientific management in the early decades of the Twentieth Century in response to a nearly inexhaustible consumer demand for manufactured output. However, with rapid industrialization and an intense preoccupation with productivity and distributive efficiency came deepening disregard for the psychological, social, cultural, aesthetic, economic and environmental consequences of technological development. [69] Indeed, the reverberating, and in some ways irretrievable, consequences of rampant industrialization are only now dawning for all of us. Pollution, inflation, localized poverty, unemployment, energy and material resource scarcity are the harsh realities of a malfunctioning economy.

Affluence

It was not until the decade immediately following World War II that accelerating technology propelled society into the era of economic abundance. For the first time a significant proportion of American society escaped the inevitability of relentlessly having to produce in order to survive. At no previous time in history had any society successfully mastered the key to survival without the constant preoccupation with producing material goods for consumption. Not only had the American economic system found the key to affluence in productive efficiency, but material affluence had become the characteristic feature of significant portions of American society. The real capability to escape from want, or the necessity of producing in order to survive, had existed for some time. Yet, the treadmill of materialism had become a firmly established habit, reinforced by the receding shadow of the Great Depression of the 1930's. The lives of most Americans were still dominated and shaped by the work ethic. Productivity, the means, had supplanted the goal of material welfare. [55] The social goal of survival had been displaced by the method for its achievement.

Productivity & materialism

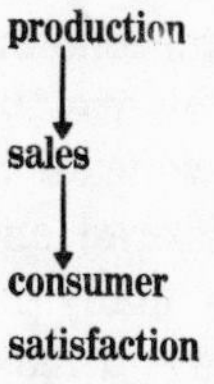

As we have seen, accelerating productivity implied that supply of material goods overtook and, in many industries, significantly exceeded growth in consumer demand, resulting in a shift in managerial orientation from solving problems of productive efficiency to increasing sales of manufactured output. Still more recently, managerial responsibility has been reinterpreted as identifying and satisfying consumer wants and needs. Paralleling the evolution of managerial responsibility, marketing was transformed from distribution into selling, and in recent years into a process of adaptation to consumer needs. The managerial orientation toward the goal of consumer satisfaction is the essence of the philosophy embodied in the *marketing concept*.

Marketing concept

A quarter-century of affluence has produced a legion of modern-day nomads for whom the traditional goal of material wealth no longer suffices and for whom the practiced methods of production and distribution which remain, refined and elaborated to ever higher levels of efficiency, are growing rapidly obsolete. Individuals find it increasingly difficult to serve the single god of material welfare and keep pace on the treadmill of productivity and distributive efficiency.

Modern-day nomads

OBSOLESCENT GOALS AND METHODS

In the past the necessity of producing in order to survive had its virtues. The overriding social goal of material welfare drew few dissenters or conscientious objectors. Economic productivity provided an organizing and integrative framework as all of society was mobilized to deal with the problem of material necessity. [96] A significant portion of working America was occupied in the process of matching supply with consumer demand through performance of distributive functions. Retailing and wholesaling establishments and other marketing intermediaries multiplied at an exponential rate with accelerating growth in manufacturing capacity. Marketing grew increasingly important within the firm and the economic system.

Today, in the era of high technocracy, there is little doubt that a virtually limitless variety of material goods could be produced. As a consequence of this highly developed productive technology the necessity of material production no longer intrudes directly in all socioeconomic strata. Although pockets of poverty linger, they are the result of *distributive* inefficiencies, not deficiencies in production. Even in the face of dwindling material and energy resources which limit productivity in many industries, affluence remains the dominant feature of most

Distributive inefficiencies

of American society. Deteriorating supplies of material and energy resources may eventually restrict production of a vast variety of products, or will prompt technological innovation to produce substitute products or energy sources. Yet, now and in the foreseeable future the majority of American society has eluded the constraints of necessity — the treadmill of production in order to survive.

We are not suggesting that the existing mass production and distribution technocracy is doomed, or that the economic structure is on the verge of collapse. Far from it. For it is the continued existence of an efficient means for eliminating economic necessity, or satisfying survival needs, that is an essential precondition for the continuity and cohesion of social structure. We are simply suggesting that the goal of material production alone can no longer harness the energies and motivations of the entire society. Moreover, as Alvin Toffler notes in his widely-circulated book *Future Shock*,

> It is not simply that we do not know which goals to pursue. The trouble lies deeper. For accelerating change has made obsolete the methods by which we arrive at social goals. The technocrats do not yet understand this, and, reacting to the goals crisis in knee-jerk fashion, they reach for the tried and true methods of the past. [90, p. 404]

These no longer work. Thus the goal of material welfare, and productivity, the method for its achievement, are increasingly insufficient to inspire the unquestioning acceptance and unswerving dedication to the work ethic that characterized American society throughout its history.

With accelerating growth in technology, the methods of mass production should become increasingly efficient. Likewise, scientific marketing promises ever higher levels of distributive efficiency. The continued relentless erosion of the work ethic and increasing disorientation from production- and distribution-oriented institutions and values will leave man detached, alienated, and goal-less. Technocracy can no longer provide unifying objectives and methods for society-at-large. American society must find something else to believe in.

Society seems to have reacted to the splintering of its monolithic goal of material welfare, and the obsolescence of its logic of organization for productivity and distribution in varied, often seemingly contradictory ways. Fluctuations in economic activity, intermittent environmental and energy crises, changes in the political climate, and threats to domestic security combine to produce a periodic reassertion of allegiance to the cause of productivity and serve to keep the productive machinery intact and maintain the labor force in harness. But *the list of social priorities has been extended, elaborated, reordered and politicized and the result is increasing diversity and contrast in lifestyles and goals*. Two obvious manifestations of multiplying social priorities are philanthropy and humanitarianism at home and abroad. These, of course, contradict the competitive prototype of the American culture and economic system.

Continued erosion of the traditional goal of rising standards of material welfare portends major adjustments in existing social institutions oriented toward its achievement. Moreover, marketing methods, practices, and policies, the mechanism for matching material productivity with consumer demand, are undergoing radical redefinition in response to the fractured goal structure of American society. The next sections present the most important of the existing definitions of economic activity and the nature of the pressure for change.

THE MARKET MENTALITY

The market

The emergence of American society into the industrial age involved a massive reorganization of society that derived its name from its central institution, the market. The American economic system is frequently referred to as the market economy. The market mechanism is the arena wherein productive technology is reconciled with the structure of consumer demand. The market provides the solution to the resource allocation problem.

Materialism versus Idealistic

The reorganization of American society around the market mechanism implied two novel notions. The first was that man's motives can be dichotomized as either *materialistic* or *idealistic* and that incentives in everyday life stem largely from materialistic motives. Indeed, throughout American history much of one's sense of self-worth has been defined in terms of the work ethic, production for its own sake. Not until after World War II, however, was it possible for a majority of American society to keep score in terms of the accumulation of material goods. The second novel notion was that a society's economic system determines its institutions. That is, the economic system stands at the center of the constellation of institutions which constitute the structure of society. [7, p. 110]

Economic system & social structure

Americans have long been conditioned to distinguish between things *economic* or *rational*, and things *noneconomic* or *irrational*. The economic aspects of society – products, business firms, the stock exchanges – have been imbued with an aura of rationality and isolation apart from the noneconomic aspects of society – governmental, educational, familial, social. The theory which underlies this distinction is enshrined in the tenets of classical economics, and is traceable all the way back to the year of American Independence. [84]

Classical economics

Classical economics has provided a number of useful fictions, fictions which promoted a rapid rate of economic development in the United States in the early decades of the Twentieth Century, and a rationale justifying the unrestrained pursuit of self-interest on the part of business firms competing in the marketplace. [7, 75, 98] These fictions, however, have had increasingly ominous consequences in many areas of social concern – diminishing material and energy resources, environmental pollution, localized poverty and social dislocation – because marketers, governmental officials, marketing analysts and consumers alike perpetuate a fundamental misconception concerning the manner in which the economic system operates. As a consequence, efforts to overhaul major malfunctions of the economic system are often misguided or misdirected.

In the following sections we will examine the myths which have guided the operation of the American economic system since its inception. We will then evaluate the reality of capitalism in America, and four chronic problems arising from the discrepancy between capitalistic fact and fiction. Along the way we will examine the role of marketing in perpetuating the mythology of capitalism and suggest needed changes in marketing philosophy. Our discussion will reveal in graphic outline the crisis of ideology looming in the American economic system.

THE MYTHOLOGY OF CAPITALISM

The basic tenets of capitalism are drawn from the works of classical economists of the late Eighteenth and early Nineteenth Centuries.

> They postulated an abstract system in which the rational activity of men in the marketplace produced a mechanism for the production and distribution of material wealth that was completely self-contained and self-adjusting. [98, p. 168]

Means & Ends

This elegant, intricate system was intended by its founders as a rationality of *means*, a way of best satisfying a given *end*. [7, p. 10] The priorities toward which human life was organized were never stated. The ends were viewed as being as varied as the members of society themselves who were totally free to choose ends conforming to their own goals or lifestyles. That the individual would pursue self-interest was taken as axiomatic. The economic system provided the mechanism for efficiently allocating scarce resources among these unlimited, highly diversified ends, simultaneously maximizing individual material welfare and the welfare of society-at-large.

Self-interest

Rationality of means

Multiplicity of ends

The significance of the distinction between a "rationality" of means, elaborated to ever higher levels of sophistication in economic doctrine, and the "plurality" or multiplicity of ends cannot be overemphasized. American society has always had an aversion to collective decision making. Indeed, modern industrial society has never felt the need to define its priorities or goals with any degree of consensus or precision. The unifying goals and purposes which began to slowly transform American society 200 years ago were not the result of conscious social consensus. Yet the goals which emerged with the entrance of American society into the Nineteenth Century were all manifested in rising productivity. The artisan, the craftsman, and all traditional alternative modes of life were sacrificed to the system of social organization developing around the goal of material wealth. Rising output of material goods became society's unifying purpose, and productivity its unifying technique or method. The corporate form of business enterprise brought the means of productivity and the end of material welfare into convergence. [7]

Productivity

Corporate form

production ↓ price mechanism ↑ consumption

In theory, the market coordinated production with consumption through the free play of price-making forces in response to the shifting pattern of supply and demand. Each entrepreneur by pursuing self-interest simultaneously maximized his own profits and contributed to the efficient allocation of economic wealth within society. The price system operating through the impersonal mechanism of the marketplace channeled resources toward areas of demand concentration as though guided by an *invisible hand.* [54, pp. 4-9] In its classical conception, the market system required no marketing as we know it today. For both buyers and sellers operated with complete omniscience or total knowledge concerning consumer tastes and preferences, product alternatives, and alternative sources of products. Hence, marketing was merely an adjunct to production, the process of distributing products, or matching supply with the shifting structure of consumer demand.

Invisible hand

Marketing = distribution

Theoretical economic system

That the economic system was *postulated* or theoretical is important. As a conceptual framework it provided an ideal toward which the economic system *should* strive and, as such, specified the guidelines for capitalism's greatest single myth, "the belief that the greatest economic good of the society would be achieved through the unrestrained play of self-interest." [98, p. 172] The arena within which entrepreneurs were to pursue self-interest was the marketplace. Classical economic theory suggested that by seeking to maximize profits the entrepreneur simultaneously maximizes social welfare by contributing to the efficient allocation of scarce resources to competing uses. This, of course, has provided a rationale justifying virtually every form of competitive activity, including predatory pricing, exclusive dealings, tying contacts, and deceptive advertising. The fact of the matter is that the economic system simply does not work that way.

Profit maximization = Maximization of social welfare

The Market

The central institution in the American economic system is the market or, more precisely, a system of markets (see Figure 5.1). The market is that mechanism peculiar to capitalistic systems of economic organization which allocates scarce resources among the unlimited wants and needs of consumers, matching supply of prod-

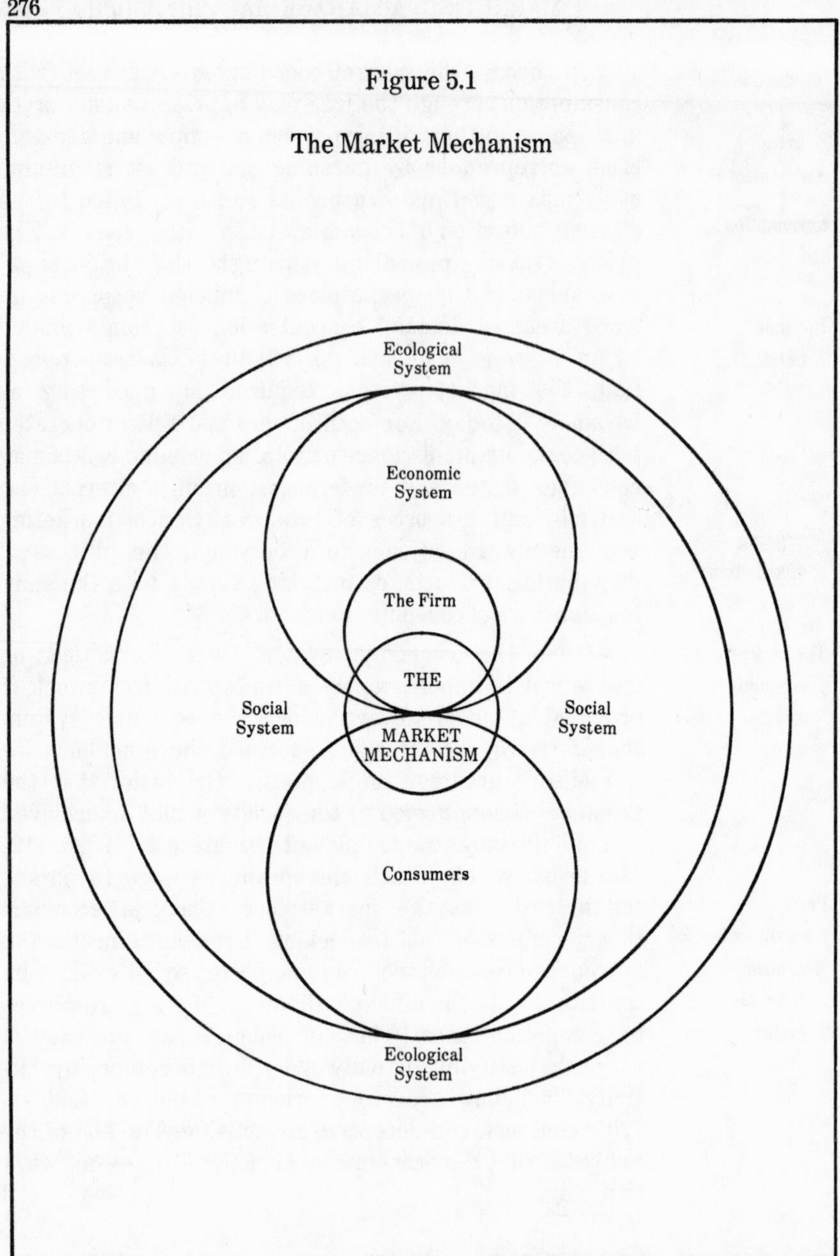

Figure 5.1

The Market Mechanism

ucts with the shifting structure of consumer demand. Theoretically, shifts in demand bring about changes in the structure of prices which in turn initiates a reallocation of resources toward production and distribution of products for which demand is concentrated. But what ultimately

Value structure

provides direction to the economy in resolving the resource allocation problem, as Thorstein Veblen, the maverick sociologist noted nearly 75 years ago, is not the price system but the value structure of the culture in which the economic system is embedded. [93] As noted earlier, the particular form that the market mechanism assumes in American society is a reflection of a consensus of values concerning the relative priority of individual versus societal material needs.

Land & Labor

A critical artificiality of the market is that it permits *labor* and *land* to be marketed as commodities. This, however, is a myth. Land (or nature) cannot be produced. Labor, if it can be produced, is not for sale as it can never be separated from its supplier. Only the products of labor, not labor itself, can be sold. Both land and labor are subject to natural laws and social regulations which are not reflected in the operation of the market mechanism through the hypothetical pure play of economic forces.

> Yet no more thoroughly effective fiction was ever devised. By buying and selling labor and land freely, the mechanism of the market was made to apply to them. There was now supply of labor, and demand for it; there was supply of land, and demand for it. Accordingly, there was a market price for the use of labor power, called wages, and a market price for the use of land, called rent. Labor and land were provided with markets of their own, similar to the commodities proper that were produced with their help. [75, p. 110]

In short, land and labor were arbitrarily handed over to the unrestricted play of self-interest in the marketplace. The myth that land and labor could be marketed as commodities enabled the translation of the work ethic into the market mechanism. All of society became orchestrated to the marketplace. Life assumed an automated, regulated tempo, synchronized to the demands of productive and distributive efficiency. The goal of material welfare provided the focus of motivation for society-at-large, and the requirements of productivity and distribution specified the system of social organization mirrored in the economic system and the occupational structure of the labor force. Land, labor, and products were reduced to a

Marketplace for
- land
- labor
- products

common dollar denominator through the price system, and were exchanged freely within the marketplace. The depth of our cultural binding is reflected in our inability to conceive of alternative mechanisms for incorporating land and labor into the process of production and distribution.

Profitability and Productivity

Survival & Productivity: Hunger & Work

The submission of man and nature to the mechanism of the marketplace established the critical link between the universally motivational goal of survival and the necessity of producing – between hunger and work. The pangs of hunger do not, of themselves, translate into an incentive to produce. Intrinsically, hunger and gain are no more "economic" than other impulses such as hate, prejudice, or pride. But the market as a means of organizing production led Americans to think of hunger and gain as economic. Hunger and gain are linked with production through an income derived from selling goods in the marketplace. All incomes derive from sales, and all sales – directly or indirectly – contribute to production. Production necessarily follows from the need to earn an income. [75]

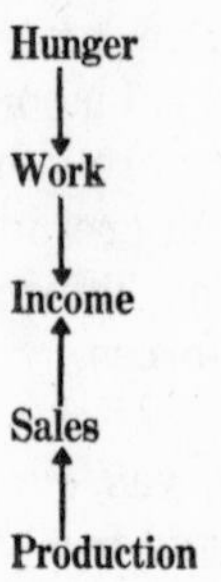

Obviously, the economic system works only so long as individuals have a reason to earn an income. The motives of hunger and gain have provided such a reason historically. How long they can continue to operate is a subject of some conjecture. The fractured goal structure of American society implies a radical reorganization and reorientation of all social institutions including the economic system. For the time being, however, the established connection between hunger and gain – between the goal of survival and the necessity of producing – continues to dominate American economic thinking, especially at the grassroots level: "If you're hungry, get a job."

Invisible hand

Competitive system

The reason for the relationship between hunger and work was clear to the classical economist. It lay in the notion of the invisible hand (see Figure 5.2). The profit maximizing decisions of each enterprise were seen as reverberating among those of all competing firms in such a manner as to create an intricate and dynamic interlocking competitive system which maximized the welfare of society-at-large.

Figure 5.2

The Invisible Hand:
Profitability and Productivity = Consumer Welfare and Social Welfare

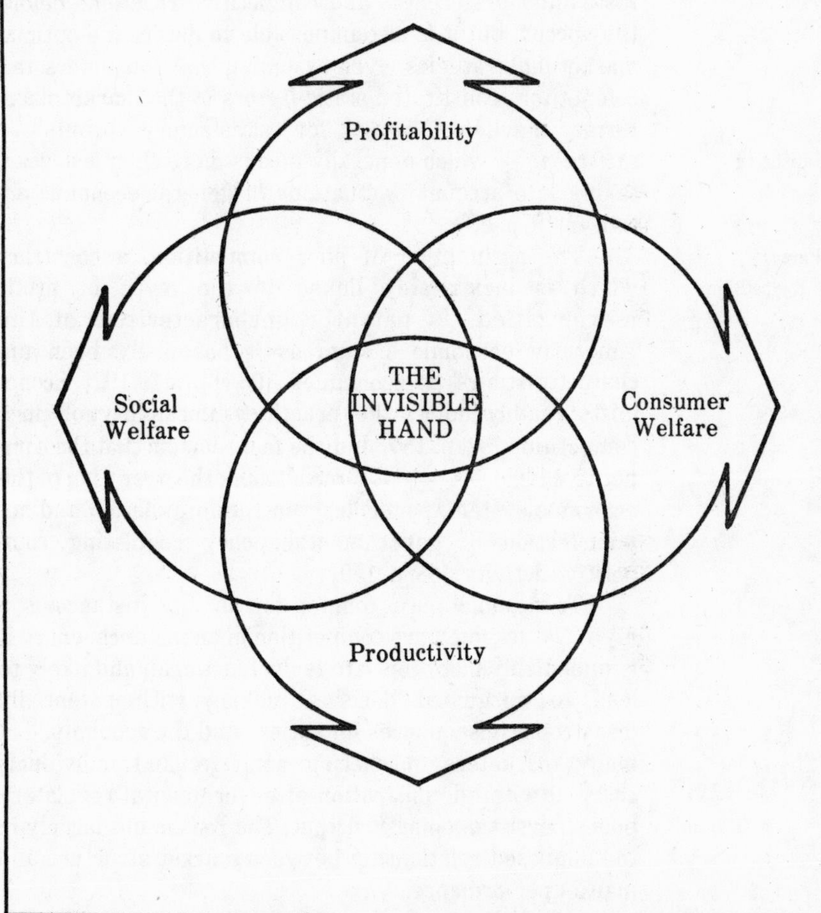

Profit & productivity

Locked into unending competition for scarce resources and customers, profit and productivity provided simplified means for keeping score in the game of competition. The discretionary latitude of any firm was strictly limited by the demands and constraints of the market. Unspecified but implied within this doctrine was a structure of rewards and penalties which promote ever higher levels of enterprise efficiency in the production and marketing of goods and services, the market refereeing the game of enterprise competition.

Rewards & penalties

Profit maximization impossible

Here, as in the market assumption, several myths are evident. As a practical matter, profit maximization is a virtual impossibility. [4, p. 445] Not only is it impossible to precisely gauge and respond to changes in consumer tastes and preferences and competitive reactions before they occur, but it is also impossible to determine optimal marketing strategies, even assuming that consumers and competitors constituted static factors in the marketplace. Firms inevitably settle for satisfactory profits – *satisficing* – which generally means more than last year, taking into account fluctuations in general economic activity. [19, p. 58]

Satisficing

Pure competition

The assumption of pure competition, a construct which is inextricably linked to the myth of profit maximization, is patently uncharacteristic of the American economic system as it has likely been uncharacteristic of all economies. [98, pp. 179-192] Economists readily admit the practical infeasibility of pure competition [82, p. 150], but the fact remains that the competitive ideal is a potent force shaping the operation of the economic system, particularly in the formulation and administration of governmental policy regulating competitive activity. [88, p. 150]

To assume pure competition in any instance is a myth. To assume pure competition in an instance where it is undeniably inappropriate is dysfunctional, and likely to lead to misguided decision making with potentially disastrous consequences for society and the economy. Yet many marketers, marketing analysts, and individuals charged with administration of governmental regulatory policy persist in doing just that. The reason lies largely in the supposed relationship between market structure and market performance.

Structure and Performance

Classical economists assumed that there was a direct relationship between market structure and market performance. One distinguished economist, for example, outlined what he considered the major elements of market structure — industry concentration, differentiation among competitors' products, and barriers to competitive entry into an industry — and then noted:

> The importance of market structure lies in the way it induces firms to behave . . . their market conduct. Conduct links an industry's structure to the quality of its performance [in efficiently allocating scarce resources in conformance with the structure of consumer demand]. [15, p. 37; 5]

This assertion is susceptible to empirical verification or invalidation, but past attempts have frequently been "inconclusive, conflicting, or tenuous." [88, p. 91]

Competitive structure implies efficiency of performance

The basic myth here, based on misassumptions about the functioning of the marketplace and the invisible hand, is that the more competitive the market structure, the better its performance. In an effort to reduce the mythology of capitalism to a practical reality, a barrage of antitrust legislation has been enacted to provide a "more competitive" market structure, presumably because society would be better served by such a structure (see Figure 4.6, Chapter 4).

Anti-trust legislation to promote competitive structure

The existence of a relationship between market structure and market performance is essentially a complex empirical question, given that criteria for gauging market performance can be readily agreed upon. Recent research examining the empirical support for a relationship between market structure and market performance concluded that "as yet little empirical evidence is available which supports the hypothesis that a strong link exists between [market] structure and performance. In fact, the theoretical basis of such a link may be open to some question." [88, p. 150] Nonetheless, the mythology of capitalism contained in the postulates of classical economics is so potent and enduring that a relationship between market structure and market performance is assumed *a priori* in much governmental antitrust policy. This cannot but have a distorting effect at best upon the efficiency with which scarce resources are allocated across society.

Fact and Fiction

These, then are the fundamental fictions on which the American economic system has operated since its inception. It is important to realize that the American economic system has long operated on the basis of fictions which have lost their usefulness in the context of fundamental alterations in the priorities, purposes, and structure of American society. The mythology of capitalism provided perhaps historically useful fictions, but fictions nonetheless. Treating land and labor as commodities for sale in the marketplace and assuming a link between the goal of survival and the necessity of producing – between hunger and work – were surely key elements in America's drive toward material affluence. Myth, however, must not be mistaken for reality. For following the yellow brick road of capitalistic mythology will eventually lead to Oz. It is to the reality of capitalism in America that we must turn. First, however, let us evaluate the role of marketing in the mythology of capitalism.

The Role of Marketing

What was the role of marketing in the mythology of capitalism? Within the classical economists' conception of the market system, there was no need for marketing activity as we know it today. Both consumers and suppliers operated with total market knowledge or perfect information concerning tastes and preferences, product alternatives, and alternative suppliers. Hence marketing was interpreted as merely distribution of products, the matching of supply with demand through a logistic network. The goal of marketing was distributive efficiency, and logistic expertise was the contribution of marketing to the resource allocation problem. As we noted previously, however, the responsibility of marketing within the American economic system has been extended far beyond mere distribution, and is likely to undergo even more radical redefinition.

THE REALITY OF CAPITALISM

As in the case of the mythology of capitalism, the marketplace is of central significance in deciphering the operation of the American economic system. However, it is not the elegant, self-regulating marketplace of classical economics, but the *value system* of the culture in which

Value system

the economy is embedded that provides the key to understanding the reality of capitalism.

The market has never been characterized by the "pure play of economic forces" resulting in an optimal allocation of resources envisioned by classical economists. Rather it has been characterized by a network of social norms and expectations as to how economic action and resource allocation are to take place. [7, 75, 92, 98] That is, within the value structure of American culture are prescriptions outlining proper and improper conduct by businessmen in the marketplace. Social sanctions are associated with misconduct, only some of which are levied by regulatory agencies of the government through the courts.

Norms & expectations

Social Mechanisms Regulating Market Conduct

The pervasive strength of the social norms regulating the game of competition is evident from a moment's reflection about the nature of economic activity. Economic activity by its very nature puts heavy strains on social regulation or control of such socially destructive or disruptive actions as robbery, tribute, bribe, collusion, coercion, fraud, and extortion. Only when the norms of exchange are well established and institutionalized within the market mechanism are these tendencies to take what one wants held in check. In American society, economic norms are perpetuated and protected by several social mechanisms [98, pp. 171-177] which are themselves deeply rooted in the value structure of the culture (see Figure 5.3).

Norms of exchange

The Market. The market itself is one such mechanism of social regulation. The market mechanism constitutes a vast impersonal system of controls over economic behavior. Included in the market are systems of property (ownership) and exchange relationships which, if not the result of the "pure play of economic forces," are also not the result of one specific social authority, as is the case in socialistic systems of economic organization. The market, then, is not an autonomous, self-directing phenomenon but is dependent upon quite specific institutional structures — including retailers, wholesalers, and manufacturers — in sufficient number to insure that the allocative mechanism or economic system is at least minimally responsive to fluctuations in consumer demand. The entities comprising the economic system act in accordance with the norms

Property & exchange relationships

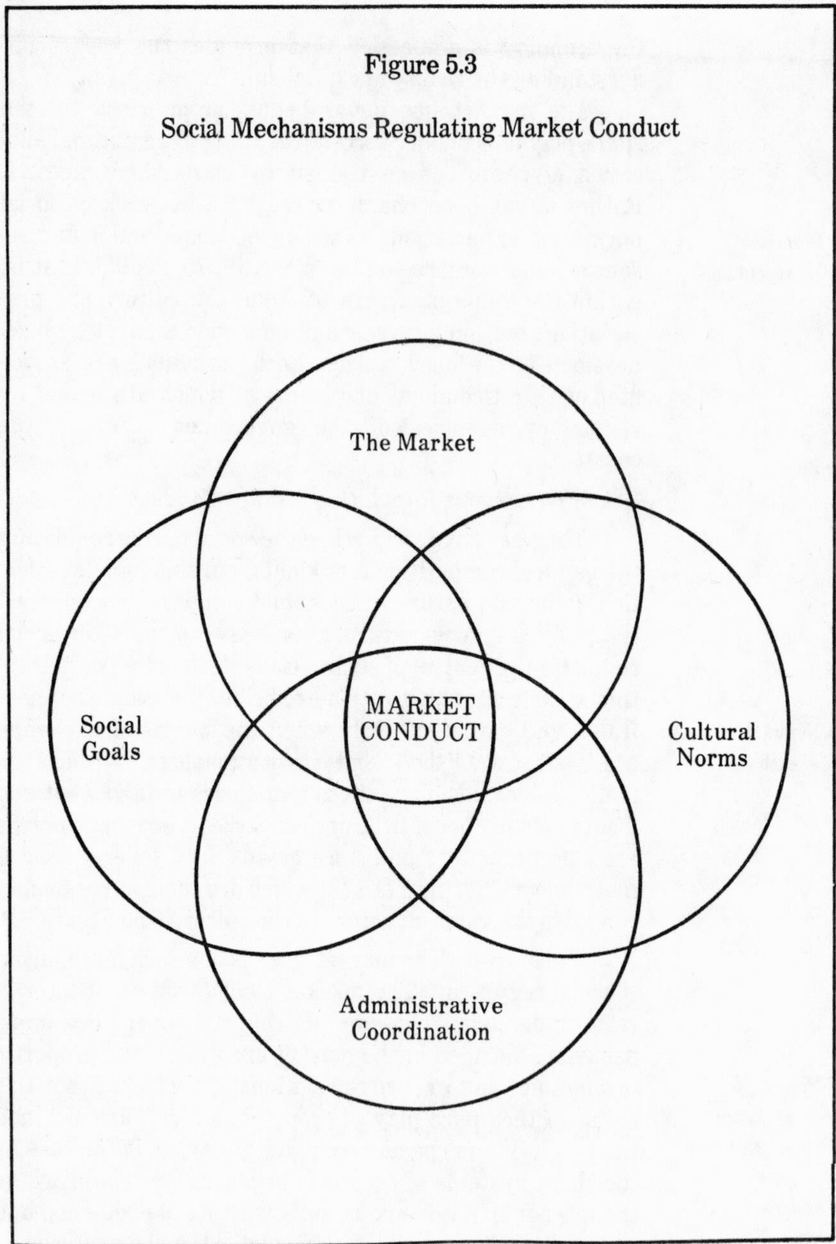

Figure 5.3

Social Mechanisms Regulating Market Conduct

sanctioning market conduct, relying on the expectations that other entities will also adhere to the same norms.

Cultural Norms. The system of cultural norms which have a binding and directing influence upon economic action comprise a second major social mechanism of control. These norms vary widely in object, content, expression, and enforcement but are reflected in laws, governmental regulations and policies, business codes, union rules, customs, trade practices, consumer expectations, and other normative standards. Taken together, these norms shape, guide, and define the boundaries of economic activity in the United States. Examples include the federal laws regulating economic activity, as well as such standards of market conduct as customary channels and prices, ballpark pricing, and implicit rules for competitive bidding and collective bargaining.

Private versus public needs

Social Goals. A third mechanism of social control of economic institutions is the influence of common social goals. The whole pattern of resource allocation is, in large measure, culturally prescribed. The United States, for example, has historically placed almost exclusive emphasis on maximizing material wealth for private consumption, rather than maximizing public goods or allocating resources toward applications which benefit society-at-large, such as interstate highways, parks and recreational facilities, pollution-free air and water, national defense, sound currency.

Profit maximization & the work ethic

The orientation toward maximizing material wealth for private consumption derives from the tenets of capitalistic mythology dealing with individual profit maximization and the work ethic, both potent and enduring cultural values. The goal of maximizing material wealth for private consumption must be brought into balance with the goal of insuring and extending the material welfare of society-at-large. *But it is essential to realize that the priority placed on maximizing individual material welfare at the expense of public welfare is a thread of continuity running through American history.* As recent experience with gas rationing attests, a shift away from historical precedent is unlikely to win widespread acquiescence. Self-interest is deeply embedded in the mind of the American consumer.

Administrative Coordination. A fourth regulatory mechanism consists of organizational or administrative coordination, enforced by a specific, identifiable social organization — corporation, trade association, labor union, or governmental bureau. Organizational coordination tends to be "localized, specific, and susceptible to interpretation in terms of personal or group 'responsibility'." [98, p. 174] In contemporary large scale industry a single enterprise may control a large number of subsidiaries through an elaborate administrative network. While the enterprise is itself subject to the test of consumer acceptance or satisfaction in the marketplace, which will be reflected in profits and losses, the intrafirm allocation of resources among subsidiary units is not susceptible to external market sanctions. Control of behavior, and of economic decision making, is an essentially social phenomenon within the large industrial enterprise and is effected through formalized patterns of authority and responsibility within a bureaucratic hierarchy, not through the impersonal market mechanism.

Immunity from market sanctions

Social sanctions

Moreover, intricate systems of interlocking firms have emerged through the formation of trade associations, conglomerates, cartels, mutual sources of financing, or common interest groups, which have even more fully exploded the myth of an economy of individualistic production and competition for consumer satisfaction. Even among entrepreneurs who are not so formally linked, common background, friends, "old school ties," and shared aspirations and ideals combine to produce a substantial amount of implicit organizational or administrative coordination or "conscious parallelism." Man is a social animal. The cold competitiveness of the economic model of entrepreneurial behavior misses this vital point.

Fact and Fiction

The marketplace is in reality a dramatic departure from the clinical market mechanism of the classical economic model for two reasons:

Market
- **Mirrors value structure**
- **Seldom approaches competitive ideal**

- The market is a vital cultural fact, mirroring the value structure of society and subject to social control
- The market seldom approaches the competitive prototype specified by the model

Products might be distributed on the basis of power rather than exchange. Production might be sustained using slave labor or labor under the control of a particular social authority, or through contributed effort from blood

Perpetuated by norms and expectations

relatives or communal groups. But the system does not operate that way. It is instead protected and perpetuated by social norms and expectations.

Our above discussion sheds light on the second of these factors. To elaborate, the classical economic assumptions are virtually unattainable. Moreover, the American economic system is in reality a dual economy. The bulk of the wealth is controlled by a relatively small number of large corporations. [9] These large scale industrial firms have tremendous power and operate under a quite different set of rules than those which circumscribe the field of competition for smaller firms which have less power and hence are less able to exercise any appreciable measure of control over their environment. Small and intermediate size firms are still by and large subject to the rigorous test of the marketplace, but these firms exercise an ever narrower sphere of influence in economic activity. Increasingly, large firms dominate the economic landscape. For the large scale industrial firm the classical economic model is wildly inappropriate. For the small enterprise it is only inappropriate.

Satisficing

As for the guiding principle of profit maximization, firms apparently seldom attempt to maximize profits, at least in any systematic way. Indeed, as we noted earlier, as a practical matter, profit maximization is a virtual impossibility. [4, p. 445] *Instead, profit maximization is an institutional objective. It is an orientation which lies not within the mind of each entrepreneur, but within the capitalistic system of economic organization.* The difference is critical. "The 'profit motive' is not a *motive* at all but an institutional goal; it is not a psychological state but a social condition." [98, p. 209]

Institutional goal

The profit motive simply does not govern day-to-day decision making by businessmen. This fact is only now being recognized by economists in such concepts as *satisficing*, [19, 58] earning a *satisfactory* level of profit (whatever that means), and is still years away from being acknowledged by the bulk of the business community which still adheres, at least verbally, to the market mentality. [66]

Satisfactory profits

Behaviorally, of course, marketers have been engaged in nothing approximating "profit maximizing" decision making. The real danger lies in the fact that those unfamiliar with the real behavior of real marketers assume that profit maximization is the guiding principle of marketing decision making. And this misassumption is translated into economic theories and antitrust legislation shaping governmental regulation of the game of business competition which are simply hopelessly naive in this key respect. As a result, much governmental regulation of marketing activity is misguided, and yields sometimes severely distorted consequences for competition and for consumers.

Regulation

Failure of risk of failure

Too, risk of failure, the traditional fate of the inefficient in the intensely competitive game of survival, has been radically modified. Many firms have grown so massive and so critical to the continuity and structure of the economy that the system can no longer afford their failure. The impact of such a large scale crash would be too disruptive. Hence, in recent years we have seen such unprecedented developments as government secured loans to Douglas Aircraft and Lockheed, and governmentally sanctioned across-the-board price increases in the steel and petroleum industries, price increases which more than recover increased costs. Moreover, competition among transportation firms on the sea, the land, and in the skies is regulated and, in many cases, subsidized. Financial institutions are so cossetted in regulations that near superhuman effort or misfortune is required to go bust. Shaky brokerage firms are tightly tethered by legal safety nets. The nation's radio and television airwaves are strictly restricted. Public utilities enjoy monopoly status with virtually guaranteed profits. The examples are as varied as they are endless.

Market regulated by social sanctions

Thus, the market is, in reality, a cultural fact governed essentially by social forces. The profit motive has become merely one of many organizational objectives. Entrepreneurial risk taking has been sharply mitigated. A de-emphasis on entrepreneurial risk implies a de-emphasis on profit or return for risk taking. The real driving force behind the economic system, then, is unlikely to lie within the strictures of classical economics. The mythology of capitalism has lost its usefulness in the context of fundamental alterations in the priorities, purposes and struc-

Market mirrors the value structure

ture of American society. The impetus propelling the operation of the economic system is likely to lie at the heart of the culture itself, within the value system in which the economy is embedded.

VALUES AND THE AMERICAN ECONOMIC SYSTEM

Value constellation
- **Individualism**
- **Equality**
- **Activity & work**
- **Materialism**
- **Achievement-success**
- **Morality**

As we noted in Chapter 4, the constellation of values which is of essential importance in evaluating the American economic system includes six: individualism, equality, activity and work, materialism, achievement-success, and morality (see Figure 5.4). Americans have historically placed tremendous importance on activity, "doing something." [17] Activity and work are closely linked to individual achievement-success, the achievement motive providing the impetus for productive effort or work. The particular end or objective toward which the work-achievement value complex has historically been oriented is material comfort. Hard work and clean living have long been thought to be the keys to heaven. This value constellation constitutes the underpinning for the economic system and its artifact, material affluence.

These values have been implemented, protected and perpetuated through fervent application of the principles of classical economics. This continues even today. The reason lies in the fact that the bulk of society continues its adherence to the mythology of capitalism, expounded and evangelized most forcefully and convincingly by business executives who occupy the best position to be exposed to the realities of capitalism in America and who should therefore know better. As one analyst put it, "The ideology of 'free enterprise' is still widely expressed by corporation executives who are not in fact engaged in anything approaching free enterprise in the traditional sense." [66]

Governmental intervention into economic activity itself remains largely inspired by the mythology of capitalism.[88, Ch. 3] The point is that much of society still advocates a set of myths which has never been an unmitigated blessing and which is unlikely to solve or even develop meaningful responses to any of the looming social, economic, or environmental problems facing America

Figure 5.4

A Constellation of American Values

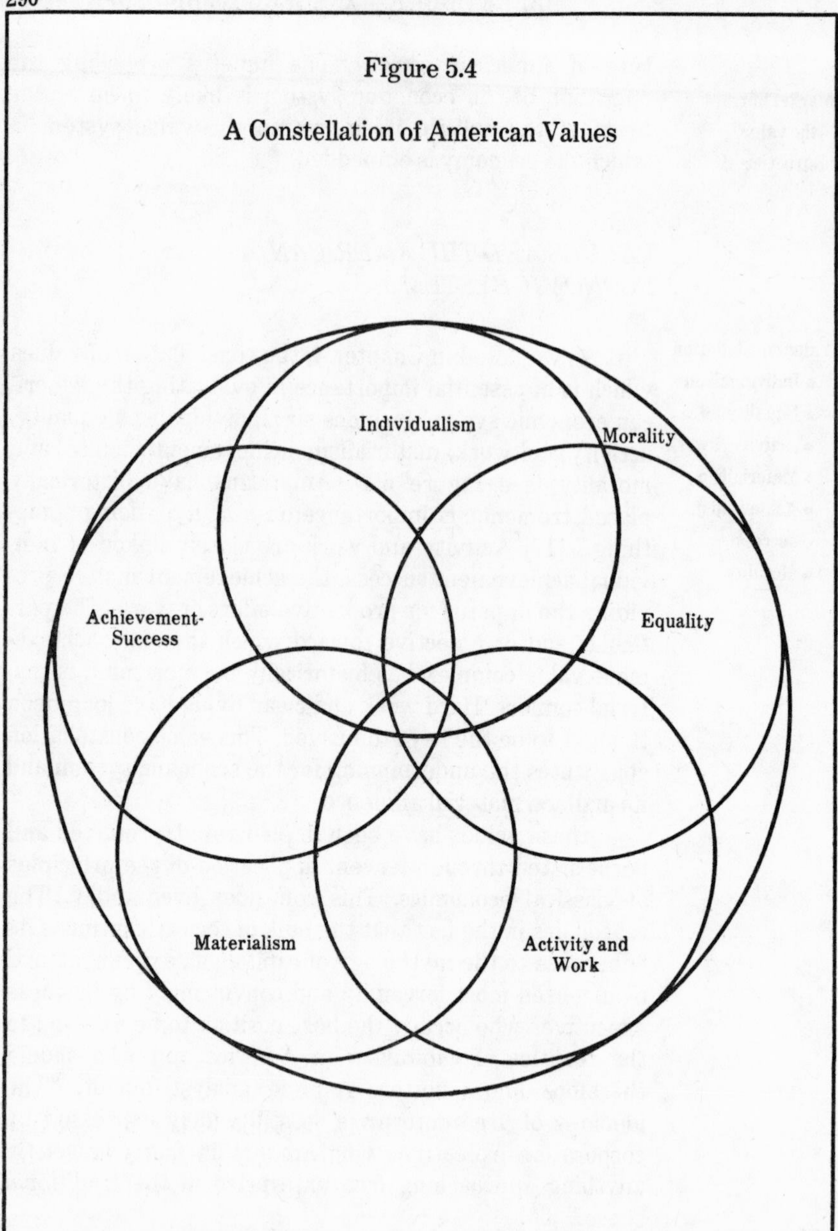

today. In fact, the exercise of protecting and perpetuating the mythology of capitalism masks the key problem, the ideology itself. To illustrate, let us examine a number of critical problems directly traceable to the pervasive influence of the mythology of capitalism.

FOUR CHRONIC PROBLEMS

Blind adherence to the mythology of capitalism has produced especially distorted results in four critical areas: public goods, distribution to the disadvantaged, demand and supply (see Figure 5.5). In each, the myth of a self-regulating marketplace has led to ominous, potentially disastrous consequences.

Public Goods

The most obvious point of departure from the elegant self-directing system described in classical economics lies in the indivisibility of public goods. Western society, particularly American society, has historically placed almost exclusive emphasis on maximizing material goods for individual or private consumption. The whole system of economic organization mirrors the priority associated with satisfaction of individual material wants and needs, rather than the material needs of society-at-large. [7, pp. 8-14] What is rather remarkable is that the emphasis on individual material comfort does not appreciably diminish in times of general affluence, even though widespread prosperity permits certain personal resources to be painlessly channeled into social welfare or public goods.

Public versus private goods

> The family which takes its mauve and cerise, air-conditioned, power-steered and power-braked automobile out for a tour passes through cities that are badly paved, made hideous by litter, blighted buildings, billboards and posts for wires that should long since have been put underground. They pass on into a countryside that has been rendered largely invisible by commercial art. They picnic on exquisitely packaged food from a portable icebox by a polluted stream and go on to spend the night at a park which is a menace to public health and morals. Just before dozing off on an air mattress, beneath a nylon tent, amid the stench of decaying refuse, they may reflect vaguely on the curious unevenness of their blessings. Is this, indeed, the American genius? [32, p. 223]

Public goods indivisible

Public goods, like interstate highway systems, national defense, sound currency, are not readily divisible

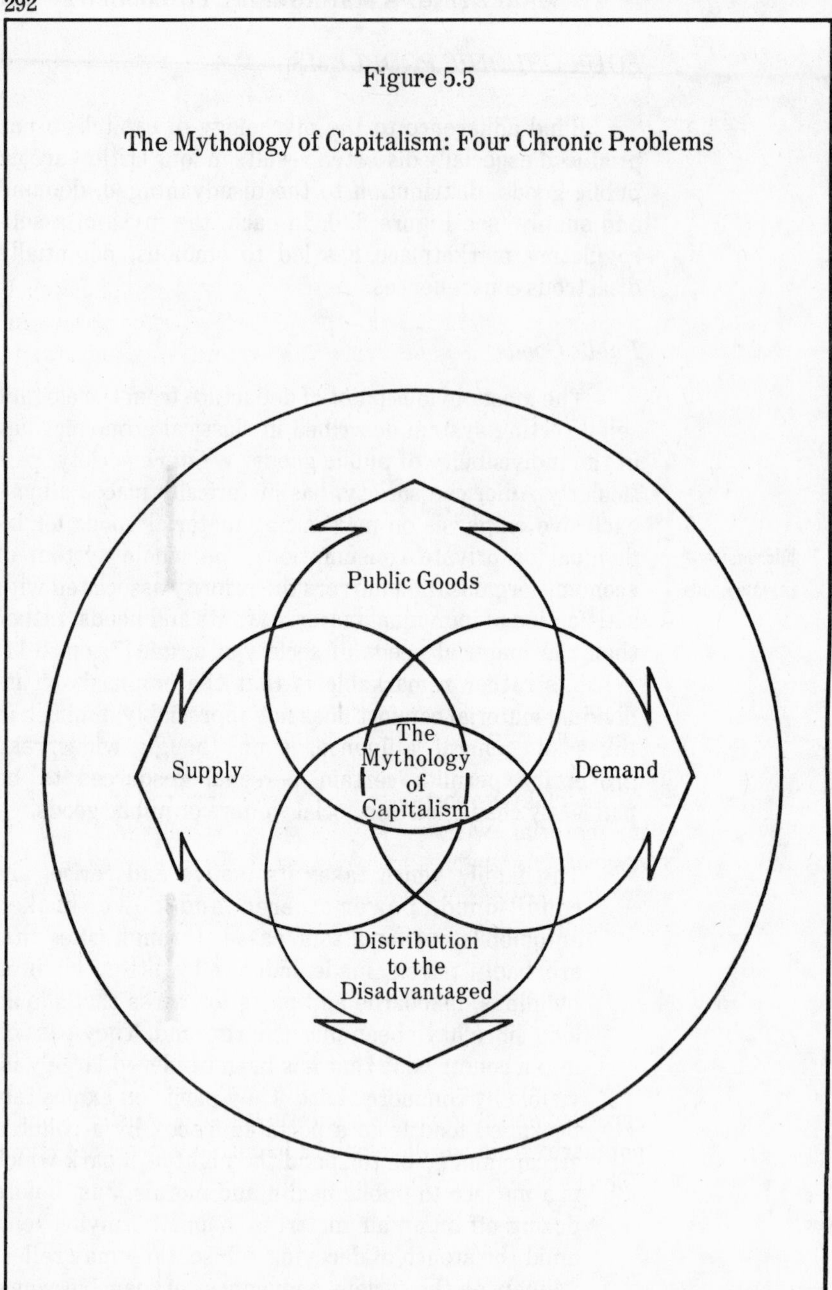

among the members of society and, hence, cannot be effectively handled by the market mechanism. The government handles the allocation of public goods and consumes a vast and rising amount of America's material output

Dual economy

each year. Thus what America really has is a dual system: A modified market system for allocating private goods and an administered, governmentally controlled system for allocating public goods. The government, of course, intervenes in the modified market system to an increasing extent.

> Reliance on government has become commonplace as the government has occupied ever larger spaces in the economy. Through streams of legislation, spreading and minutely detailed regulations, frequent application of moral suasion, and various other means, the government is now present — either in person or . . . in disturbing spirit — at every major business meeting. [37, p. 104]

Intervention is seldom aimed at restoring purely competitive market conditions, typically its avowed purpose. Governmental intervention is instead aimed at perpetuating "viable competition," which translates into protecting competitors from the predatory practices of one another, often at the expense of consumer or societal welfare.

Equally importantly, the orientation toward growth in material welfare implies that social progress is measured only in terms of the production of economic goods. Clearly, however, 'free goods," such as clean air, unpolluted water, unspoiled scenery, to say nothing of occupational satisfaction, camaraderie, friendship, contribute significantly to the quality of life and, hence, our total welfare. Under present accounting schemes such

Free goods

"free goods" add nothing to conventional measures of society's wealth. Nor as they grow less abundant are they recorded as subtractions from wealth. E. J. Mishan's once popular refrain has developed a haunting, discordant ring: "The best things in life are [no longer] free."

A third glaring deficiency of the present system of economic organization is that economic growth tends to generate more and major "spillovers" which are translated into costs which must be borne directly by other private parties or absorbed by society-at-large. "Externalities" or external costs, are unintended or unanticipated consequences or "fallout" resulting from the production of economic goods for private consumption.

- **Externalities**
- **Spillovers**
- **Fallout**

The result, of course, is a social cost (for example, air pollution or scarcity of physical and energy resources) or, infrequently, a social benefit (employment, security, technology, education, innovation) which is not reflected in the common measures of economic welfare.

Taxes

A fourth problem with American society's orientation toward economic growth is taxes. As conventional wisdom has it, taxes are not interpreted as necessary allocations of funds toward the needs of society-at-large, but as money taken from *me* by *them*. Thus, to the individual consumer, taxes are interpreted as subtractions, rather than additions to wealth.

Society is today confronted with mushrooming social, economic, and environmental problems, the result of overreliance on the market mechanism. In a free society, an optimal distribution of resources and goods is achieved where the market price of an item is equivalent to its true economic cost. But as one prominent economist noted, "where private costs and social costs diverge . . . the allocation of goods becomes skewed" and society comes out the loser. [7, pp. 8-9] *Social costs* are costs to society-at-large associated with continued emphasis on serving the material needs of individual consumers. *Private costs* are costs to individual consumers associated with reorienting the economy toward serving the needs of society-at-large. The problem confronting contemporary American society is one of balancing social and private costs. The market mechanism cannot by itself equitably balance social and private costs.

Social versus private costs

Kenneth Boulding, a distinguished contemporary economist, summarizes the debate:

> If one had to sum up what economists have to say on [the] matter [of public goods and public bads] in five or six propositions, the first would be that we produce bads (pollution) because bads are jointly produced with goods. The second is that negative commodities (bads) should have negative prices, and the third is that public goods and bads require political organization if we are not to get too little of the first and too much of the second. A fourth proposition is that goods depreciate and bads appreciate, following the generalized and extended Second Law of Practically Everything, that all things slide down toward a middle muddle unless somebody

> does something about it . . . There is a fifth proposition that depreciation and appreciation are not continous functions of use or load, but exhibit threshold or overload phenomena, which is what causes crises . . . A sixth proposition, which I have been stating on and off for years without anybody paying much attention, is that human welfare is a state, condition, or stock . . . What we think of as the environment, therefore is simply part of the capital stock of human welfare . . . When we are evaluating the environment, we are also evaluating man himself as part of a total system. [11, p. 167]

Human welfare =
- **state**
- **condition**
- **stock**

The implication of all this is that it calls into serious question conventional notions of enterprise performance and market performance. The fundamental issue which emerges, then, centers around not simply the behavior of any given firm, but the viability of the whole pattern of economic and social organization, and the orientations, priorities, and purposes of society. The exclusive emphasis upon the satisfaction of individual consumer wants and needs, a key component of the mythology of capitalism, produces an imbalance between private goods oriented toward the satisfaction of individual wants and public goods designed to meet societal needs. As continued technological and economic growth creates more and major *spillovers*, *externalities*, or just plain *bads*, adherence to the mythology of capitalism becomes increasingly dangerous.

Economic bads

Constructing viable alternatives is tough. Governmentally run businesses and public-minded and non-profit organizations, the expressed purpose of which is to serve the interests of society-at-large, have been less than successful in responding to public needs without simultaneously contributing their fair share to environmental spillovers and economic bads, not to mention poor management. Direct and indirect governmental controls on business too have been largely ineffectual in curtailing or controlling externalities resulting from business operations. What we are advocating, therefore, is not the abandonment of the capitalistic system of economic organization, but simply expanded awareness on the part of marketing management of the negative economic, social, and environmental consequences of business activity resulting from continued adherence to the mythology of capitalism. A moral and social obligation to bear the costs of social *bads* or dysfunctional outputs is implicit in this argument.

Distribution to the Disadvantaged

A second key problem resulting from the mythology of capitalism lies in the area of distribution to the disadvantaged. The market mechanism provides a highly refined capability for delivering a profusion of color television sets while millions lack adequate food, housing, and medical care. As the noted economist Robert Heilbroner observed, "The market is an assiduous servant of the wealthy consumer, but an indifferent servant of the poor one." [39, p. 229] Command over material goods and services is directly proportional to one's command over financial resources. Virtually ignored in the allocation of material resources within society are dollarless consumers.

Market segmentation

"Haves" and "have nots"

As the market approaches *laissez faire*, or the unrestrained competition prescribed in the mythology of capitalism, it fails to meet basic standards of justice. Marketing, as an essential ingredient in the continued functioning of the economic system, fuels this failure through the technique of market segmentation. The rationale underlying segmentation strategy promotes ever more efficient service for the *haves* within society but extremely poor service for the *have nots*. As firms move toward higher degrees of specialization in response to intensifying competition, honed to the product preferences of precisely delineated market segments, they lose the flexibility as well as the inclination to enter the market of money-less consumers. Indeed, the concept of money-less markets is an anachronism. Profit-oriented firms will invariably focus their marketing efforts on monied consumer segments. Most entrepreneurs would concur that only fools and do-gooders would orient marketing efforts to consumers who have no money. This constitutes sound *economic* decision making, but the consequences for society-at-large over time are depressing, sometimes deadly.

Demand

Perhaps the most critical area where allegiance to the mythology of capitalism yields convoluted results is in demand. Theoretically, the self-regulating market mechanism equates supply with demand via the addition or subtraction of producers in response to demand migration patterns. As consumers' preferences shift from one product to another, and finally away from a given product altogether, producers must follow if they hope to survive. In reality such adjustment occurs slowly if at all. The result is a demand crisis. Moreover, belated shifts in industrial output in response to shifting consumer tastes and preferences and changing environmental conditions frequently occur in ratchet fashion resulting in severe economic disruptions. The automobile, oil, and rail transportation industries are notable cases in point.

Labor specialization and technological sophistication have largely eliminated supply of goods as a constraint on economic growth. As we noted earlier, accelerating technology has propelled American society into the era of material affluence, and there is little doubt that a virtually limitless variety of products could be produced. The major constraint on economic development in the United States is demand, and the reason that demand is the limiting factor is affluence.

Demand — constraint on economic growth

The emergence of demand as the critical constraint on economic growth is acknowledged in a number of disciplines. In economics, for example, the economic growth theorists focus their concern on "the question whether and under what conditions a modern economy might generate sufficient aggregate demand to permit continued growth." [1, p. 534] This orientation reflects a far different perspective from that which characterized classical economics, when one prominent economist posited that "supply creates its own demand."

Modern marketing is a child of affluence. The emergence of the marketing concept in the late 1950's and 1960's, with its emphasis upon anticipation and enlargement of demand through an ever more precise refinement of products to consumer specifications, supplanted earlier views of marketing as simply a necessary adjunct to production. Properly applied, marketing matches supply with demand.

We have argued repeatedly throughout the text that the economy is most appropriately viewed as a system. Consumers must work to obtain income to support consumption. This is the linkage between the necessity of producing and the goal of survival — between hunger and work — outlined above. The problem lies in the fact that the economic system needs fewer workers and more consumers if rising standards of material welfare are to remain the priority objective of society. More precisely, consumption must grow at a rate equal to or in excess of the rate of growth in production if society is to benefit from constantly rising standards of material wealth. Capitalism cannot provide constantly expanding consumption to counter-balance constantly expanding production because the self-adjusting and self-regulating marketplace is a myth.

The crisis of insufficient demand is one of the fundamental problems facing America today. Society, by and large, retains its achievement-success, work, and material comfort orientations. Ironically, the means for expressing or satisfying these values lies largely within the mythology of capitalism. Yet, instead of recognizing that the mythology of capitalism is insufficient to solve the demand crisis, many executives fall back to the pat answers of the past: spiraling levels of productive and distributive efficiency. Admittedly the efficiency of the marketplace in allocating resources also depends upon the ability of suppliers to make product responses to alterations in the structure of consumer demand. Because of the imbalance toward productivity, however, adhering to the conventions of capitalistic fiction can only deepen the demand crisis. Only a pragmatic appraisal of the consequences of continued adherence to the mythology of capitalism is likely to solve, or provide meaningful responses to, the demand crunch.

Supply

Recently we have seen the emergence of serious resource shortages which have ominous long-term consequences for not only the quality of day-to-day life, but which also may significantly limit the ability of the economic system to continue to respond to consumer material wants and needs. Dwindling energy and material resources will have inevitable reverberating effects upon the lifestyles of virtually all Americans, the manifestations of which are only beginning to surface.

> The newest dent in the American dream of affluence comes from the discovery that our resources (and the world's) are more finite than we thought. This challenges that delicious American freedom, the right to be prodigal and uncaring – that open, generous, spontaneous attitude sometimes so envied, sometimes so deplored, by more parsimonious and tradition-confined foreigners. Americans have always believed that "there's plenty more where that came from"; you don't divide the wealth, you multiply it. And thus every man's ambitions – to make, to sell, to buy – somehow can be felt to serve the common good.
>
> If rapid growth is no longer the easy answer to our problems, the alternatives to it are difficult for a nation with an economy so attuned to growth. Adding this to so many other matters they worry about, many Americans have lost confidence in what they once regarded as their natural ally, the future. [36, p. 88]

A radical redefinition and reordering of social priorities and consequent reallocation of material resources looms in the future. However, now and in the more immediate future, American society clings to the goal of materialism, perpetuating a system of economic organization which promotes ever higher levels of productive and distributive efficiency. Reconciling the pervasive goal of rising standards of material welfare with the reality of deteriorating material resources looms as a deepening dilemma posing perhaps marketing management's most troublesome obstacle.

Materialism versus deteriorating resources

Implied in the inherent conflict in reconciling materialism and the need for resource conservation is the fact that the process of marketing management will require more and more value judgments among social priorities. Marketing analysts have argued for years that subjective assessments of social priority should be absent from the marketing decision-making process. Sensitivity to social priorities, in their view, simply does not yield a high rate of return in any conventional economic sense, or falls more properly within the domain of governmental or

Value judgments

regulatory responsibility. Exemplary among these is Milton Friedman, the eminent economist, who maintains:

> . . . The doctrine of [executive] "social responsibility" . . . [is] fundamentally subversive." . . . Businessmen [who] speak . . . about the "social responsibilities of business in a free-enterprise system" . . . are unwitting puppets of the intellectual forces that have been undermining the basis of a free society these past decades . . . There is one social responsibility of business – to use its resources and engage in activities designed to increase its profits so long as it . . . engages in open and free competition without deception or fraud. [29, pp. 32-33]

Others, however, argue that with further amplification in the demands for social and environmental responsibility, either in response to spreading social consciousness or perceived or real social or environmental crises, like the energy crisis, the cost to the firm of ignoring the societal and environmental context in which it operates may not be merely profit. The cost may well be survival.

> The Friedman view is okay in the short pull. "But in the long pull, nobody can expect to make profits – or have any meaningful use for profits – if the whole fabric of society is being ripped to shreds." [20, p. 152]

Enterprise versus social welfare

Today there are no ready rationales for the firm which requires economic vindication or financial justification for incorporating social priorities into marketing decision making. However, the marketer who can divorce enterprise from social welfare is duplicitous or two-faced if not schizophrenic. It is a rare executive indeed who can distinguish the environment for business from reality. And as reality registers more directly in the operation of the firm, through deteriorating energy and material resources, executives can ill afford to operate as if it does not exist. Thus,

Social responsibility

> When one uses the phrase "social responsibility" of the corporation, one is not indulging in rhetoric

> (though many corporate officials are), or thinking of *noblesse oblige* (which fewer corporate officials do), or assuming that some subversive doctrine is being smuggled into society (as some *laissez faire* economists suggest), but simply accepting a cardinal socio-psychological fact about human attachments. [7, p. 23]

Sensitivitv to the social, economic, and environmental context in which the firm operates is simply good business and certainly prerequisite to the lasting legitimacy of the firm. To argue otherwise is self-delusion to the marketing analyst and suicide to the marketing practitioner.

EXPLODING THE MYTHOLOGY OF CAPITALISM

The purpose of the preceding analysis was to illustrate the vast gulf between capitalistic fact and fiction. While our dissection of the mythology of capitalism in America might have grown infinitely more intricate and tedious, the implications are clear: The mythology of capitalism, derived essentially from the tenets of classical economics, is at best inappropriate as a guide for the operation of the American economic system. The model has simply left too many gaping areas of social concern neglected too long.

The most regrettable consequence of the gulf between capitalistic fact and fiction is that many business executives, governmental officials, marketing analysts and consumers continue to behave as though the mythology of capitalism works in reality. As a result, decisions are frequently made on the basis of assumptions and assumed relationships which are either suspect or patently false. As to the ramifications of such decisions, environmental pollution of unfathomable proportions, inflation, economic recession, localized poverty, unemployment, are vibrant testimony to the travesty of continued adherence to the mythology of capitalism (see Figure 5.6).

THE NEW PHILOSOPHY OF MARKETING MANAGEMENT

If the mythology of capitalism is so inappropriate to the efficient and equitable operation of the American

Figure 5.6

Key Issues and Relationships: Marketing and Society

Issues and Relationships	Representative Marketing Action
Economic	
•Consumer sovereignty	•Influence taste and preferences
•Inflation and consumer welfare	•Determine general level of prices
•Welfare, effects of nonprice competition	•Engage in a wide range of competitive activities
•Tradition of growth	•Strain on use of resources
•Poverty and needs of the poor	•Neglected segment based on difficulty of providing service at a profit
Social	
•Social goals	•Priority to traditional economic goals, growth
•Social performance	•Efficiency, short-run profit orientation
•Social and macromarketing	•Lack of attention to social costs of traditional commercial marketing
•Marketing in the inner city	•Operation of a deviant marketing system
•Private wealth and public poverty	•Primary emphasis on private benefits
•Disadvantaged groups	•Neglect of public sector
	•The elderly, children, and others placed at special disadvantage
Technological	
•Spread of innovation	•Introducing new products and methods
•Planned obsolescence	•Eliminating the used even if products are not used up
•The technological imperative	•Assumption that technological change is inevitable and beneficial
•Control of technology	•Little appreciation of the need to control technology
•Redirecting the focus of technological innovation	•The potential of a humanized technology rarely being given serious attention

Environmental	
•Marketing and ecological balance •Allocation of costs of pollution control •Improved environmental quality	•Unintended side effects from product use •Pricing to users at less than the full cost to society •Lack of attention to long-term conservation of resources and amenities
Cultural	
•Use of leisure time •Socialization of youth in the consumption ethic •Quality of life	•Catering to the lowest common denominator of taste •Cultivating youth at impressionable age to adopt consumption ethic •Interpreting quantity and quality of life as material consumption
Political	
•Professional marketers and amateur consumers •Concentration of market power •Inequities in the distribution of power •Controlling the use of power	•Marketers selling for a living •Consumers buying to maintain a standard of living •Major corporations dominating markets and influencing consumer welfare •Resources, specialists, and laws maintaining power advantage for marketers •Vested interest groups influencing public policy decisions
Philosophical, Theoretical	
•Microanalytic bias in traditional marketing •Unadopted marketing concept •Demarketing •Social responsibility •Humanism	•Myopic view of macroaspects of marketing decisions •Avoidance of genuine service of consumer interests through lack of attention to safety, side effects, etc. •Emphasis on encouraging consumption even when resources are threatened •Viewed as "do-goodism" rather than responsible social performance •Overshadowed by commercialism in traditional practice

Burton Marcus *et al. Modern Marketing.* New York: Random House, Inc., 1975, p. 655. Reprinted with permission of publisher.

economic system, what should replace it? The first step toward improving economic performance, and marketing performance, is to acknowledge capitalism as largely a fiction, not a realistic guide to action in the marketplace. While society's orientation toward individualism, work, achievement-success, and material comfort is unlikely to exhibit rapid moderation, at least the means of expressing and realizing these values can be removed from the realm of mythology.

Dispelling the illusion of capitalism

The initial step toward a new philosophy of marketing management is to come to grips with the reality of the economic system, dispelling the misconceptions of capitalistic mythology. Marketers must come face to face with the broader social, environmental, and economic consequences of their decisions. Awareness of the symbiotic relationship which exists between the firm and its surrounding environment is a key to deciphering the *formative* and *adaptive* nature of the processes of legitimacy and power seeking. Consumer satisfaction on an individual level, for example, is not necessarily synonymous with the simultaneous fulfillment of the material needs of society-at-large. "What's good for General Motors is [not necessarily] good for America."

The consumer has emerged as a potent force to be reckoned with in the marketplace. Consumers are paramount in the sense that they must demand the output of the firm in order for the firm to survive. Yet, responding to vacillating consumer tastes and preferences is only one of many prerequisites for legitimacy. Governmental regulatory agencies, competitors, and the average consumer/citizen concerned with the quality of American life must be reckoned with. Yet, the manner in which these demands are exacted or registered upon the firm is not specified in the mythology of capitalism. The quest for legitimacy should be translated into the operations of the firm, including the products and services it offers for sale, the communication package it presents, and the pricing and distribution strategies enacted in the manner detailed in our systems definition outlined in Chapter 2. Lasting legitimacy, or power, is synonymous with the ability of the firm to not only adapt to potentially conflicting environmental pressures as they arise, but anticipate them before they occur. Only a thorough understanding of the tenets of the mythology of capitalism, coupled with a firm grasp of systems thinking, can lead to an enlightened philosophy of marketing management. Precisely what does this mean?

Keeping Score

Fundamental to the mythology of capitalism is a system of rewards and penalties which allegedly promote ever higher levels of enterprise efficiency in the production and marketing of goods and services. In theory, profitability and productivity provide highly simplified means for keeping score in the unforgiving game of competition — a yard marker for assessing field position along the competitive continuum outlined in Chapter 3 (see Figure 3.2).

Profit & productivity

Profit and productivity are held to be sensitive barometers for gauging enterprise performance on two fronts:

- The extent to which the firm is responsive to the material wants and needs of consumers
- The contribution of the firm to an efficient allocation of material resources and hence to the welfare of society-at-large

However, conventional measures of enterprise performance are glaringly deficient in two principal respects:

- Profit and productivity disallow the reconciliation of the requirements of legitimacy with the requirements of power
- They disallow the reconciliaton of enterprise and social priorities

Legitimacy versus power

Corporate coffers and social welfare do not necessarily appreciate and depreciate in parallel. The demands of legitimacy may directly conflict with the requirements of power, or lasting legitimacy. One elementary example is a situation where in order to respond to manifest consumer demands for material goods in the short-run the firm drains its energy and other resource supplies to dangerously low levels, placing the long-term survival of the firm in jeopardy. Such is the ominous prospect in the petroleum industry.

Marketing management must at times subordinate the requirements of legitimacy to the demands of power. The process of reconciling the requirements of short-term legitimacy with the requirements of lasting legitimacy or power involves constant balancing of short- and long-term enterprise objectives and evaluations of contrasting enterprise and social priorities. Soul searching assessments of the relative priority of short- and long-term enterprise objectives and of contrasting social imperatives is a growing domain of managerial responsibility, one which departs radically from management tradition where "the unrestrained pursuit of self-interest" or the invisible hand was an umbrella-like rationale justifying all marketing decisions.

Enterprise versus social priorities

Profit and productivity are generally calculated over some restricted time frame, like a quarter or a fiscal year. Nowhere in conventional measures of enterprise performance are the negative consequences, externalities, or "bads" resulting from production or marketing activity accounted for. Moreover, executive performance is evaluated by the same criteria used to evaluate enterprise performance. Profit maximization is a practical impossibility for the executive or the firm, compounding the problem of performance evaluation. Furthermore, sustained high levels of productivity and the profits which are assumed to result may be negated through further deterioration in availability of energy and other resources. As a consequence of these and other shortcomings, conventional measures of enterprise and executive performance merely deepen managerial myopia and reliance on the mythology of capitalism. Hence, emphasis on profit and productivity may compromise lasting positions of legitimacy and market power, and prove suicidal in the long-run.

Social accounting

Accounting theorists are hard at work to devise *social accounting systems* which permit the reconciliation of enterprise and social priorities. Moreover, advances in forecasting techniques have greatly augmented marketing management's ability to reconcile the sometimes divergent demands of legitimacy and power. Until the day that such techniques result in scientific marketing decisions which equitably balance the inevitable conflicts between short- and long-term enterprise objectives and between social and enterprise objectives, marketing management must rely on expanded awareness concerning the consequences of marketing decisions. There are inherent long-term consequences to short-term strategic marketing decisions, just as there are inherent social consequences to marketing activities undertaken to fulfill enterprise objectives. Greater sensitivity to the consequences of every marketing action taken cannot help but improve the calibre of marketing decision making and at least partially offset or avoid the pitfalls implicit in marketing decisions made under the mythology of capitalism. The alternatives to enlightened capitalism are an ever more severely malfunctioning economy or a rigidly controlled economy. Neither is a particularly inviting prospect.

Today versus tomorrow

Structure versus Performance

Marketing practitioners and analysts and governmental regulatory agents have long operated under the assumption that the more competitive the market structure, the more efficiently it allocates scarce resources in accordance with the shifting structure of consumer demand. Or, more simply, the more competitive the market structure, the better its performance. Indeed, our entire legacy of antitrust legislation originated, and enforcement of the rules of the game of competition continues even today, under the lingering influence of this myth.

The fact of the matter is that there is no necessary relationship between market structure and market performance. Moreover, market performance is a construct that has been greatly elaborated in recent years. It is no longer sufficient that the market mechanism provide for an efficient allocation of scarce resources in accordance with the shifting structure of consumer demand. The marketplace must also provide a mechanism for reconciling individual and societal priorities for resource allocation, and for reconciling short- and long-term social priorities.

Market must reconcile individual & social needs, short & long term priorities

Under the mythology of capitalism the divergent demands upon the market mechanism are assumed into extinction through the blind recanting of the assumed relationship between market structure and market performance. Both marketing management and governmental regulatory agents have been propelled into the role of actor in the process of resource allocation. Hence both the marketer and the market regulator must discard the myth that intensified competition necessarily leads to improved market performance. Far more useful is a forward-looking philosophy incorporating intelligent but subjective evaluations of the trade-offs inherent in the process of reconciling individual and social priorities for allocating material resources, and in reconciling short- and long-term social priorities.

HIERARCHY OF BUSINESS PURPOSE

In Chapter 2 we outlined a hierarchy of business purpose paralleling Abraham Maslow's hierarchy of human motivations. We suggested that managerial perceptions of business purpose are arrayed in a hierarchy of prepotency very much like human needs (see Figure 5.7). Lower purpose levels tend to absorb management attention before higher purpose levels become operational. Hence, a firm operating at the survival level within the hierarchy of business purpose seldom concerns itself with identity purposes or with social or environmental responsibility.

The hierarchy of business purpose partially explains, but fails to justify, marketing management's failure to adopt the new philosophy of marketing management. It is understandable that marketers preoccupied with survival or security seldom contemplate the impact upon the firm's operations of possible conflicts between individual and social priorities for allocating material resources, and between short- and long-term social priorities. But . . . marketing management will inevitably have to reconcile these conflicting priorities. Hence *the hierarchy of business purpose does not in any way justify, but merely serves to explain, marketing management's myopic preoccupation with the mythology of capitalism.*

IMPLEMENTING THE NEW PHILOSOPHY OF MARKETING MANAGEMENT

The new philosophy of marketing management is grounded in an awareness of the fictions on which the

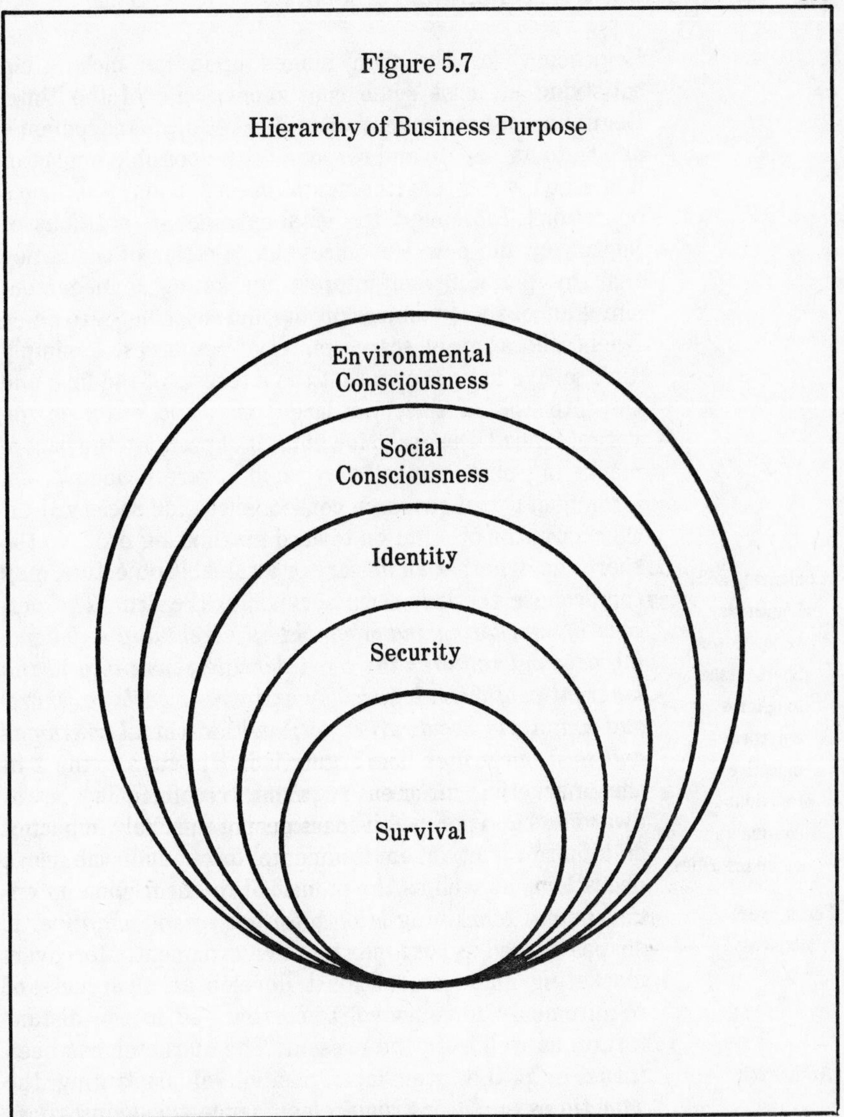

Figure 5.7

Hierarchy of Business Purpose

mythology of capitalism are founded. The key to implementing the new philosophy of marketing management lies in the systems definition of marketing presented in Chapter 2.

Legitimacy

The fundamental purpose of any business firm, indeed any system, is to establish its legitimacy. The quest for legitimacy, however, requires that marketing management discard a number of myths which have guided marketing decision making historically.

Legitimacy for the firm hinges upon far more than satisfying at least some consumers some of the time. Legitimacy is contingent upon marketing management's ability to anticipate and respond to the possible impact of numerous other environmental forces upon the firm's operations. Moreover, the establishment of positions of legitimacy and power requires the rejection of the notion that by pursuing self-interest marketing management simultaneously maximizes profits and contributes to an efficient allocation of scarce material resources. It simply ain't so. We have shown that the interests of the firm and the interests of society-at-large may, and often do, diverge. Indeed, the exclusive pursuit of profit on the part of marketing management may yield severe economic, environmental and resource consequences for society. Furthermore, the orientation toward maximizing profit in the short run, whether an illusory or attainable objective, may compromise the long-term survival of the firm. *The process of marketing management is essentially a balancing act, and requires the most delicate sensitivity to the inherent conflict in legitimacy and power seeking, short- and long-term social priorities, and individual consumer and social priorities* (see Figure 5.8). The management of the marketing process requires a refined sense of awareness and perspective concerning the likely impact of an infinite variety of environmental forces upon the firm's operations, as well as the impact of the firm upon its environment. Marketing is both *formative* and *adaptive*. It shapes as well as responds to its environment. Moreover, marketing management must develop an awareness of requirements for survival tomorrow and in the distant future, as well as in the present. The marketer has been thrust into the unenviable position of arbitrating the sometimes conflicting requirements of today against those of tomorrow, the colliding priorities of individual consumers and society-at-large, and maintaining symmetry with the demands of the surrounding environment. Negotiation is the process by which these conflicting priorities and demands are resolved. But negotiation ultimately reflects marketing management's philosophy concerning the relative importance attached to these conflicting priorities and demands.

A balancing act:
- **Legitimacy versus power**
- **Short versus long term enterprise objectives**
- **Individual consumers versus social priorities**

Formative & adaptive

Arbitration

Negotiation

The tools at marketing management's disposal to effect an efficient negotiation with environmental forces,

Figure 5.8

The Process of Marketing Management: Balancing Conflicting Priorities

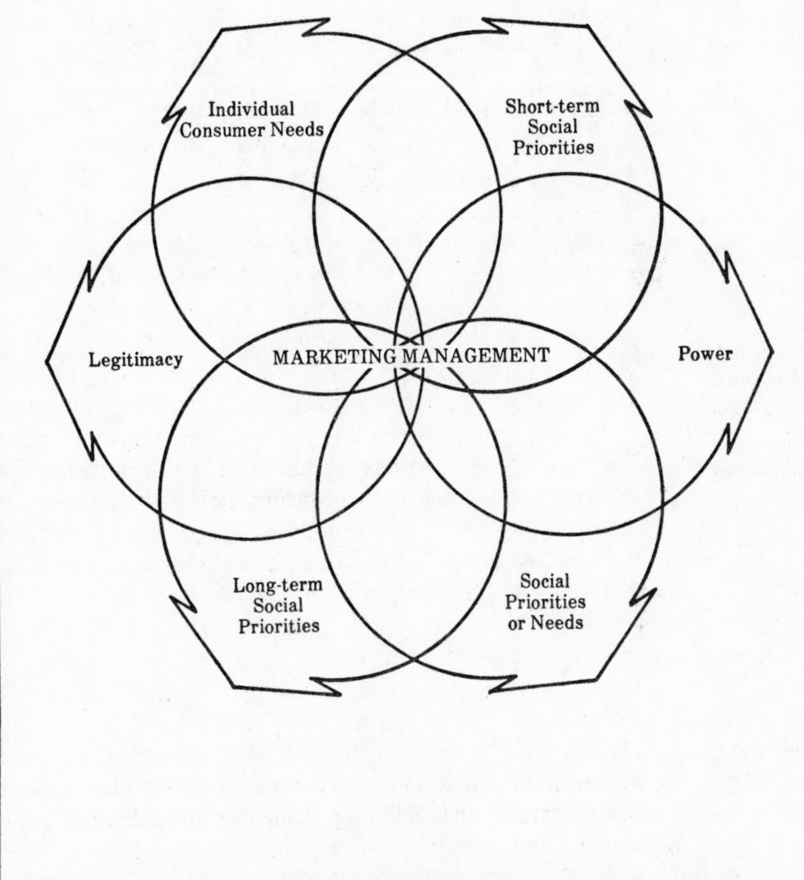

and to balance the requirements of legitimacy and power, and of individual consumer and social priorities, are few and of limited effectiveness. It is noteworthy, however, that the same tools which have been historically misapplied and hence have created the challenge to legitimacy business firms currently confront, provide the means for re-establishing the legitimacy of the firm on a more lasting footing. The philosophy which guides marketing decision making ultimately determines whether marketing tools and techniques are misapplied or not. It is to the new philosophy of marketing management we must now turn.

What if he's right What . . . if . . . he . . . is . . . right W-h-a-t i-f h-e i-s r-i-g-h-t

<table>
<tr><td></td><td></td><td>R</td><td></td></tr>
<tr><td>W</td><td></td><td>I</td><td></td></tr>
<tr><td>H</td><td>IF</td><td>G</td><td>?</td></tr>
<tr><td>A</td><td>HE</td><td>H</td><td></td></tr>
<tr><td>T</td><td>IS</td><td>T</td><td></td></tr>
</table>

— Tom Wolfe
The Pumphouse Gang

CHAPTER 5: REVIEW QUESTIONS

1. What is the principal danger in perpetuating a strict *managerial* perspective in marketing? What are the inherent advantages in assuming *institutional* and *philosophical* perspectives as well?

2. What is the role of *productivity* in economic growth? In social organization? In social change? How does marketing relate to productivity in each of these three arenas?

3. What has been the impact of technology on the organization and goals of American society? How does the concept of *future shock* relate to the accelerating rate of technological progress? What likely lifestyle patterns will emerge in response to further acceleration in the rate of technological evolution?

4. What is "the market mentality?" What are its key features? What is its significance in economic and social development?

5. What are the key features of "the mythology of capitalism?" What is the significance of treating labor and land as commodities? How do these five concepts relate: hunger, work, income, sales, production? What is the significance of *profitability* and *productivity* in the mythology of capitalism? Of *structure* and *performance*?

6. What is the role of marketing in the mythology of capitalism?

7. What are the key features of "the reality of capitalism?" What are the principal social mechanisms regulating market conduct and how do they register their influence? What is *satisficing*?

8. What is the danger of continued adherence to the mythology of capitalism? What chronic problems are traceable to the mythology of capitalism?

9. What are the principal features of "the new philosophy of marketing management?" What are the principal priorities which must be reconciled in implementing the new philosophy of marketing management? How do the hierarchy of business purpose and the concepts of legitimacy and power facilitate implementation of the new philosophy of marketing management?

REFERENCES

1. Ackley, Gardner. *Macroeconomic Theory.* New York: Macmillan, 1961.

2. "Admen Suffer From Overkill," *Time* (October 17, 1970), pp. 132, 137.

3. Alderson, Wroe. *Marketing Behavior and Executive Action: A Functionalist Approach to Marketing Theory.* Homewood, Illinois: Irwin, 1957.

4. Alpert, Mark I, "Pricing: Decision Areas and Models," in *Managerial Analysis in Marketing*, by Frederick D. Sturdivant, et al., Glenview, Ill.: Scott, Foresman, 1970, pp. 436-497.

5. Bain, J. S. *Industrial Organization.* New York: Wiley, 1968.

6. Beckman, Theodore N. and William R. Davidson. *Marketing.* New York: Ronald Press, 1967.

7. Bell, Daniel, "The Corporation and Society in the 1970's," *The Public Interest* (Summer, 1971), pp. 5-32.

8. Bell, Daniel, "The Revolution of Rising Entitlements," *Fortune* (April, 1975), pp. 98-103 +.

9. Berle, Adolf A., Jr. *The American Economic Republic.* New York: Harcourt, Brace and World, 1965.

10. Berlo, David K. *The Process of Communication.* New York: Holt, Rinehart and Winston, 1960.

11. Boulding, Kenneth E., "Discussion," *The American Economic Review* (May, 1971), pp. 167-169.

12. Bucklin, Louis P. (ed.). *Vertical Marketing Systems.* Glenview, Illinois: Scott, Foresman, 1970.

13. Burck, Charles G., "The Intricate 'Politics' of the Corporation," *Fortune* (April, 1975), pp. 109-112 +.

14. Cassell, Frank H., "The Social Cost of Doing Business," *MSU Business Topics* (Autumn, 1974), pp. 19-26.

15. Caves, Richard E. *American Industry: Structure, Conduct, and Performance*. Englewood Cliffs, New Jersey: Prentice-Hall, 1967.

16. Cleaver, Eldridge. *Soul on Ice*. New York: Dell, 1968.

17. Commager, Henry Steele. *The American Mind*. New Haven: Yale University Press, 1950.

18. Cundiff, Edward W. and Richard R. Still. *Basic Marketing: Concepts, Decisions, and Strategies*. Englewood Cliffs, New Jersey: Prentice-Hall, 1971.

19. Cyert, Richard M. and James G. March. *A Behavioral Theory of the Firm*. Englewood Cliffs, New Jersey: Prentice-Hall, 1965.

20. Davenport, John, "Bank of America is Not for Burning," *Fortune* (January, 1971), pp. 90-93 + .

21. Davis, Kingsley. *Human Society*. New York: Macmillan, 1948.

22. Drucker, Peter F. *The Practice of Management*. New York: Harper & Row, 1954.

23. Engel, James F., David T. Kollat and Roger D. Blackwell. *Consumer Behavior*. New York: Holt, Rinehart and Winston, 1973.

24. Engel, James F., Hugh G. Wales and Martin R. Warshaw. *Promotional Strategy*. Homewood, Illinois: Irwin, 1971.

25. Enis, Ben M. *Marketing Principles: The Management Process*. Pacific Palisades, California: Goodyear, 1974.

26. Festinger, Leon. *A Theory of Cognitive Dissonance*. Stanford University Press, 1957.

27. Fisk, George. *Marketing Systems: An Introductory Analysis*. New York: Harper and Row, 1967.

28. Foote, Nelson N., "The Image of the Consumer in the Year 2000," *Proceedings*. Thirty-Fifth Annual Boston Conference on Distribution, 1963, pp. 13-18.

29. Friedman, Milton, "The Social Responsibility of Business is to Increase Its Profits," *The New York Times Magazine* (September 13, 1970), pp. 32-33, 123.

30. Frye, Robert W. *Introduction to the Marketing System*. San Francisco: Canfield, 1973.

31. Furuhashi, Y. Hugh and E. Jerome McCarthy. *Social Issues of Marketing in the American Economy*. Columbus, Ohio: Grid, 1971.

32. Galbraith, John Kenneth. *The Affluent Society*. Boston: Houghton Mifflin, 1971.

33. Galbraith, John Kenneth. *The New Industrial State*. Boston: Houghton Mifflin, 1969.

34. Gist, Ronald R. *Marketing and Society*. Hinsdale, Illinois: Dryden, 1974.

35. Goodman, Paul and Percival. *Communitas*. Chicago: University of Chicago Press, 1947.

36. Griffith, Thomas, "Reshaping the American Dream," *Fortune* (April, 1975), pp. 88-91 + .

37. Guzzardi, Walter Jr., "Putting the Cuffs on Capitalism," *Fortune* (April, 1975), pp. 104-107 + .

38. Hawkins, Edward R., "Price Policies and Theory," *Journal of Marketing* (January, 1954), pp. 233-240.

39. Heilbroner, Robert L. *The Making of Economic Society*. Englewood Cliffs, New Jersey: Prentice-Hall, 1962.

40. Hollander, Stanley C., "The Wheel of Retailing," *Journal of Marketing* (July, 1960), pp. 37-42.

41. Holloway, Robert J. and Robert S. Hancock. *Marketing in a Changing Environment*. New York: Wiley, 1973.

42. Keith, Robert J., "The Marketing Revolution," *Journal of Marketing* (January, 1960), pp. 35-38.

43. Kelley, Eugene J., "Discussion," *Proceedings*, Winter Conference. Chicago: American Marketing Association, 1963, pp. 64-71.

44. Kerr, John R. and James E. Littlefield. *Marketing: An Environmental Approach*. Englewood Cliffs, New Jersey: Prentice-Hall, 1974.

45. Kolko, Gabriel. *Wealth and Power in America.* New York: Praeger, 1963.

46. Kollat, David T., Roger D. Blackwell and James F. Robeson. *Strategic Marketing.* New York: Holt, Rinehart and Winston, 1972.

47. Kotler, Philip, "Diagnosing the Marketing Takeover," *Harvard Business Review* (November-December, 1965), pp. 70-72.

48. Kotler, Philip, "Marketing During Periods of Shortages," *Journal of Marketing* (July, 1974), pp. 21-29.

49. Kotler, Philip. *Marketing Management: Analysis, Planning, and Control.* Englewood Cliffs, New Jersey: Prentice-Hall, 1972.

50. Kotler, Philip and Sidney J. Levy, "Broadening the Concept of Marketing," *Journal of Marketing* (January, 1969), pp. 2-9.

51. Kotler, Philip and Sidney J. Levy, "A New Form of Marketing Myopia: Rejoinder to Professor Luck," *Journal of Marketing* (July, 1969), pp. 55-57.

52. Kotler, Philip and Gerald Zaltman, "Social Marketing: An Approach to Planned Social Change," *Journal of Marketing* (July, 1971), pp. 3-12.

53. Lasswell, Harold D. *Power and Personality.* New York: Norton, 1948.

54. Leftwich, Richard. *The Price System and Resource Allocation.* New York: Holt, Rinehart and Winston, 1960.

55. Levi-Strauss, Claude. *Tristes Tropiques.* New York: Atheneum, 1969.

56. Levitt, Theodore, "Marketing Myopia," *Harvard Business Review* (July-August, 1960), pp. 45-56.

57. Luck, David J., "Broadening the Concept of Marketing – Too Far," *Journal of Marketing* (July, 1969), pp. 53-54.

58. March, James G. and Herbert A. Simon. *Organizations.* New York: Wiley, 1965.

59. Marcus, Burton, et al. *Modern Marketing.* New York: Random House, 1975.

60. Marketing Staff of The Ohio State University, "Statement of the Marketing Philosophy of the Marketing Faculty of The Ohio State University," *Journal of Marketing* (January, 1965), pp. 43-44.

61. Maslow, Abraham H. *Motivation and Personality*. New York: Harper & Row, 1954.

62. McCammon, Bert C., Jr., "Perspectives for Distribution Programming," in *Vertical Marketing Systems* by Louis P. Bucklin (ed.), Glenview, Illinois: Scott, Foresman, 1970, pp. 32-51.

63. McCarthy, E. Jerome. *Basic Marketing: A Managerial Approach*. Homewood, Illinois: Irwin, 1971.

64. McGinniss, Joe. *The Selling of the President 1968*. New York: Trident, 1969.

65. Merton, Robert K. *Social Theory and Social Structure*. New York: Free Press, 1957.

66. Moore, Wilbert E., "The Emergence of the New Property Conception in America," *Journal of Legal and Political Sociology* (April, 1943), pp. 34-35.

67. Moore, Wilbert E. *Social Change*. Englewood Cliffs, New Jersey: Prentice-Hall, 1963.

68. Moore, Wilbert E., "Social Structure and Behavior," in *The Handbook of Social Psychology*, Vol. IV, by E. Aronson and G. Lindzey (eds.), Boston: Addison-Wesley, 1968.

69. Mumford, Lewis. *Technics and Civilization*. New York: Harcourt, Brace and World, 1954.

70. Myers, James H. and William H. Reynolds. *Consumer Behavior and Marketing Management*. Boston: Houghton Mifflin, 1967.

71. Myrdal, Gunnar. *Asian Drama*. New York: Twentieth Century Fund, 1968.

72. Packard, Vance. *The Hidden Persuaders*. New York: David McKay, 1957.

73. Packard, Vance. *The Waste Makers*. New York: David McKay, 1960.

74. Perrow, Charles. *Organizational Analysis: A Sociological View*. Belmont, Calif.: Wadsworth, 1970.

75. Polanyi, Karl, "Our Obsolete Market Mentality," *Commentary* (February, 1947), pp. 109-117.

76. Pollak, Otto, "The Outlook for the American Family," *Journal of Marriage and the Family* (February, 1967), p. 194.

77. Potter, David M. *People of Plenty*. Chicago: The University of Chicago Press, 1954.

78. Robertson, Thomas S. *Innovative Behavior and Communication*. New York: Holt, Rinehart and Winston, 1971.

79. Rogers, Everett M. *Diffusion of Innovations*. New York: Free Press, 1962.

80. Rogers, Everett M. and F. Floyd Shoemaker. *Communication of Innovations*. New York: Free Press, 1971.

81. Rostow, Eugene V., "To Whom and For What Ends is Corporate Management Responsible?" in *The Corporation in Modern Society* by Edward S. Mason (ed.), Cambridge, Mass.: Harvard University Press, 1960, pp. 46-71.

82. Samuelson, Paul A. *Economics*. New York: McGraw-Hill, 1967.

83. Schramm, Wilbur. *The Process and Effects of Mass Communication*. Urbana, Illinois: University of Illinois Press, 1965.

84. Smith, Adam. *The Wealth of Nations*. New York: Random House, 1957.

85. *Society Today*. Second Edition. Del Mar, California: CRM Books, 1973.

86. Stanton, William J. *Fundamentals of Marketing*. New York: McGraw-Hill, 1975.

87. Staudt, Thomas A. and Donald A. Taylor. *A Managerial Introduction to Marketing*. Englewood Cliffs, New Jersey: Prentice-Hall, 1970.

88. Stern, Louis W. and John R. Grabner, "Competition: Its Meaning and Measurement" and "Competition: Market Characteristics and Public Policy," in *Managerial Analysis in Marketing* by Frederick D. Sturdivant, *et al.*, Glenview, Ill.: Scott, Foresman, 1970, pp. 37-155.

89. Sturdivant, Frederick D. "Distribution in American Society: Some Questions of Efficiency and Relevance," in *Vertical Marketing Systems* by Louis P. Bucklin (ed.), Glenview, Ill.: Scott, Foresman, 1971, pp. 94-113.

90. Toffler, Alvin. *Future Shock*. New York: Random House, 1970.

91. Toynbee, Arnold. "Advertising is Moral Mis-Education," *Printers' Ink* (May 11, 1962), pp. 43.

92. Tucker, W. T. *The Social Context of Economic Behavior*. New York: Holt, Rinehart and Winston, 1964.

93. Veblen, Thorstein. *The Theory of the Leisure Class*. New York: Macmillan, 1899.

94. von Hayek, Frederick A. "The *Non Sequitur* of the Dependence Effect," *Southern Economic Journal* (April, 1961), pp. 346-358.

95. Webb, Walter Prescott. *The Great Frontier*. Boston: Houghton Mifflin, 1952.

96. Weber, Max. *The Protestant Ethic and the Spirit of Capitalism*. New York: Charles Scribner's Sons, 1930.

97. Webster, Frederick E. Jr. *Marketing Communication*. New York: Ronald Press, 1971.

98. Williams, Robin M. Jr. *American Society*. New York: Alfred A. Knopf, 1970.

99. Wolfe, Tom. *The Pumphouse Gang*. New York: Bantam Books, 1968.

INDEX

Achievement-success values 224-225
Activity and work 224
Administered competition 254-256
Administrative Coordination 284-285
Adopter categories 122
Adoption or rejection decision 123
Adoption or rejection process 120-121
Alternative value orientations 248-249
American economic system 249-253
  role of marketing in 252-253
  structural features 251-252
Capitalism 53, 250
Change 47, 51, 240-249, 253-258
  anticipation and adaptation 47, 51
  illusory 241-242
  real 242-245
  social 240-249, 253-258
Channel of distribution 153-174
  alternative channel alignments 162-165
  and conflict 159, 160-161
  channel captain 159
  contractual arrangements 162
  defined 154-155
  franchise 162
  functional approach 154-155
  horizontal integration 159-162
  institutional approach 155
  institutional structure 155
  vertical integration 159
  vertical marketing systems 155-162
Classification of goods 118-120
  consumer 119
  convenience 120
  industrial 118
  shopping 120
  specialty 120
Cognitive dissonance 126
Commitment and consensus 247-248
Communication 174-198, 239
  advertising 174-178, 193
  and social integration 239
  dependence effect 174, 176-177
  effectiveness 188-189
  efficiency 190-192
  factors influencing 186-188
  fidelity 189-190
  image of the firm 196-198
  mass media versus interpersonal 191-194
  noise 186
  prerequisites to 187-188
  process 183-185
  purpose (persuade) 188
  role in the firm 178-179
  role in society 175-178
  social influence 194-196
  strategy 174-198
  system 185-187
Competition 92
  pure 279
  viable 292
Competition for differential advantage 69, 92
Conflict 71-72, 159-161, 220, 233
  and the definition of marketing 71-72
  in channels of distribution 159-161
  in society 220
  institutional 233
  resolution of 71-72
Consensus of values 237-239
Constellation of values 219-227
Consumer behavior models 127-129
Consumer decision process and classifications of goods 112-129
  as a transaction 112
  models of 127-129
  stages in 114-129
Consumer products 119-120
  convenience 120
  shopping 120
  specialty 120
Consumer market 117
Consumerism 55
Consumers 8-10, 47, 63, 72-82, 117
  and enterprise goals 47, 72-82
  and the marketing concept 8-10, 63
  industrial 117
  ultimate 117
Consummatory values 245
Consumption and production 295-297
Controllables 19
  and uncontrollables 19
Cooperation 246
Corporation 267, 273
Costs 147, 152-153, 293
  and pricing 147, 152-153
  private 293
  social 293
Cultural goals 215-216
Cultural norms 250-251, 283-284
Culture 215
Death (and religious institutions) 216-217, 242
Delineation 104-132
  and product market 104-105
  and segmentation 104-112
Demand 62-63, 117, 295-297
  derived 117
Differential advantage 69
Differentiating actions 68-69
Diffusion process 122, 144
  and adopter categories 122
  and the product life cycle 144
Distribution 153-174, 295

agent middlemen 165
and classification of goods 162-165
channel structures 165-167, 158
channels of distribution 154-155
efficiency 61
exclusive distribution 162-165
intensity of distribution 162-165
intensive distribution 162-164
management 162
merchant middlemen 165
retailers 165
selective distribution 162-164
to the disadvantaged 295
wholesalers 165
Distribution of power (and political/governmental institution) 253-256, 216-218
Economic bads 26, 293-294
Economic goods 26, 293-294
Economic institution 52-54, 218-219, 249-258
Economic system 53, 218-219, 249-252
American 249-252
function of 218-219
norms and 250-251
Soviet 53, 250
structural features 251-252
values and 249-250
Ecosystem 50
Education (and educational institution) 216-218, 256
Educational institution 216-218, 256
Enterprise goals 10, 15, 101-104
and legitimacy 15
and the marketing concept 10
specification of 101-104
Environment 5-7, 12-15
Environmental consciousness 78-79, 96
Environmental forces (influences) 12-15, 49-50
Environmental responsiveness 50, 79
Equality 223-224
Exchange myopia 72
Expressionism 245-246
Externalities 292-294
Feedback 28, 130
enterprise 28
system 28
Field of competition 92-96
Four P's 92
Free goods 292
Future shock 240-241
Goal and resource specification 98, 100-104
Goal specification 101-102
Goals 15, 139, 215-216
and means 215, 216
cultural 215-216
enterprise 15, 139
system 15
Gross market 105
Hierarchy of business purpose 72-79, 305
Hierarchy of needs, Maslow 73-74
Hunger 277
Idealistic motives 271
Identity 77
Income 277
Individualism 221
Industrial market 117
Industrial products 118
Innovations in retailing 167-174
automated merchandising 167, 172
boutiques 167, 173
chains 167
convenience stores 167, 172
planned shopping centers 167, 169-172
supermarket merchandising 167-169
Innovativeness 121
Inputs 15-18
enterprise 15-18
system 15-18
Instrumental capacities 243
Integrated hierarchy of business purpose 72-79
Institution, social 52, 214-233
Institutional flows 231-233
Institutional imperialism 231-233
Institutional interrelationships 228-233, 253-258
Invisible hand 274, 277
Kinship institution 216, 256-258
Labor 276-277
Laissez-faire 295
Land 276-277
Legitimacy 4-7, 15, 45-46, 69-70, 304, 306-307, 309-311
and legality 6
and the definition of marketing 69-70
confirmation of 5
establishment of 5, 66-69
goals 15
in the marketplace 5, 45-46
requirements of 15
Lifestyle 74
Management control 100
Managerial myopia 10
Market 52, 62, 105-112, 274-277, 282-283, 285-286
and market segmentation 62, 106-112
commonwealth of the market 52
Market delineation (see delineation) 104-132
Market mechanism 52, 54, 274-277
Market mentality 271-272
Market performance 279, 280, 308-311
Market sectors 124-126, 149
Market segment 106

Market segmentation 62, 104-112, 295
  advantages of 109-112
  and delineation 104-112
  segmentation variables 110-111
Market structure 279-280, 308-311
Marketing 59-72, 83, 91, 96-98
  defined 64-72, 83, 91, 96-97
  evolution of concepts 59-64
  the process of 96-98
Marketing and society 51-55, 252-253
Marketing concept 8-10, 32-34, 63
  broadening the 32-34
Marketing controllables 20, 68-69, 98, 132-134, 205
Marketing definitions 64-72, 79, 83, 91, 96-97
  Beckman and Davidson 96-97
  environmental responsiveness 79
  McCarthy 65
  Ohio State 64, 96-97
  systems 66-72, 68, 83, 91
Marketing efficiency 65
Marketing information system 62, 130-132
  and innovation 131
  and marketing research 62, 129-132
  defined 130
Marketing myopia 105, 135
Marketing orientation 58-59
Marketing process 96-100
  functional approach 96-98
  systems approach 98
Marketing research 62, 129-132
  definition 129
  marketing information system 130-132
Marketplace 285-286
Materialism 225-226, 234, 237-239, 298
Materialistic motives 271
Morality 226-227
Motives 271
Mythology of capitalism 40, 273-281, 300
  role of marketing 281
Needs 73-74, 114
  biogenic 74, 114
  defined 114
  hierarchy of 73-74, 114
  prepotency 74
  psychogenic 74, 114
Negotiating ability 70-71
Negotiation 70-71
New philosophy of marketing management 300-305
New product adoption 142-145
  and adopter categories 142-144
  and product characteristics 144-145
  and product life cycle 144
  level of 144
  rate of 144
Norms 214, 220, 250-251
Open system 11
Opinion leaders 194-196
Outputs 20-28
  dysfunctional 26
  enterprise 20-28
  functional 26
  system 20-28
Perceived need 114-116
Performance 279, 280, 308-311
Political/governmental institution 216-218, 253-256
Post-decision evaluation 126-129
Power 70, 304, 309-311
Pre-decision activity 116-123
Price 147-152
Price system 274-276
Prices 147-148, 152-153
  externally determined 153
  internally determined 152-153
Pricing 147-153
  and governmental regulation 149
  and industrial or consumer product classification 148-149
  and market sector 149
  and market structure 149, 152
  and stage in the product life cycle 148
  and total costs 147-148
  controllable or uncontrollable 147
Processes 19, 20
  enterprise 19, 20
  system 19, 20
Product 118-146
  and company objectives 139-140
  and image 134
  and the marketing concept 134-136
  defined 134, 136
  iceberg principle 139
  item 136
  line 136
  mix 137-140, 146
  product classifications 118, 119-120
  product life cycle 140-145
  product-market strategies 139-140
  proliferation 136
  rate of new product adoption 144-145
  strategy decisions 136-138
Product audit 145-146
Product characteristics and new product adoption 144-145
Product life cycle 140-145, 201
  and adopter categories 144
  and reprogramming 201
  stages in 140-145
Product mix 137-140, 146
  consistency 138
  depth 138
  width 138
Product utility 52

Production orientation 55-56
Productivity 266-269, 273, 277-279, 304-307
Profit 15, 101, 277-279, 285-287, 304-307
  and enterprise goals 15, 278-279, 285-287
  and legitimacy 15, 101
Profit maximization 274, 286
Profitability 15, 101, 277-279
Programming 132-198
  and differentiation 132
  communication 174-198
  distribution 153-174
  marketing mix 134
  pricing 147-153
  product 134-146, 134, 136
Public goods 290-295
Pure competition 279
Quasi-marketing functions 95-97
Ranking (and stratification institution) 216, 256-258
Reality of capitalism 281-288
Regulation 287
Religious institution 216-217, 242
Reproduction (and kinship institution) 216, 256-258
Reprogramming 200-205
  and the product life cycle 201
  anticipation and adaptation 201-204
  automobile crisis 204
  defined 200
Resource allocation 53, 54
Resource specification 100
Role 228-230, 234-235
Sales 31, 101
Sales orientation 57-58
Sanctions 214
Satisficing 279, 286-287
Scrambled merchandising 169
Security 77
Segmentation axes (variables) 107-111
  criteria for evaluating 107-108
  example variables 110-111
Self-interest 272-273
Social auditing 102-104, 307
Social change 240-249, 253-258
  illusory change 241-242
  real change 242-245
Social consciousness 77-78
Social goals 284
Social institutions 52, 214-233
  and norms 216-218, 214
  and sanctions 214, 216
  and values 219-227
  defined 216
  interrelationships 228-233
  flows or exchanges 231-233
Social integration 233-240, 253-258
  defined 233
  requirements 237
  sustained integration 238-239
Social mechanisms regulating market conduct 282-285
  administrative coordination 284-285
  cultural norms 283-284
  market 282-283
  social goals 284
Social structure 272
Socialism 53, 250
Strategic planning (and goal specification) 101-102
Stratification institution (and ranking) 216, 256-258
Structure 18, 19, 155, 158, 165-167, 279-280, 308-311
  and functions 19
  enterprise 18, 19
  channel 165-167, 158
  institutional 155
  system 18-19
Supply 297-300
Survival (and economic institution) 76-77
Systems 10-30, 66-72, 83, 91
  components 12-30
  concept in practice 29-30
  defined 10
  definition of marketing 66-72, 83, 91
  view 10
Target market 104-106
Taxes 293
Transaction phase of the marketing process 127-129, 198-200
  defined 127-129, 198
  exchange of values 127-129, 198
Use behavior 123-126
Utility 124
Value 219-227
Value structure of society 52, 219-227, 249-250, 281-282, 288-289
  and economic organization 218-219, 249-250, 281-282, 288-289
Value vector 236
Values 219-227, 245-249, 281-282, 288-289
  achievement-success 224-225
  activity and work 224
  equality 223-224
  future 246-249
  individualism 221
  materialism 225-226
  morality 226-227
  shifts in 245-249
  system of 219-227, 281-282, 288-289
Vertical marketing system 155-162
  characteristics of 158
  implementation of 157-162
  implications of 156-157
Viable competition 292
Wheel of retailing 168
Work 277